THE
48 LAWS
— OF —
HAPPINESS

SECRETS REVEALED
FOR BECOMING THE HAPPIEST YOU

DR. ROB CARPENTER

RMC Lit
New York, New York

ISBN: 978-1-7366155-0-8 (print)
ISBN: 978-1-7366155-1-5 (eBook)

For information about this title or for bulk orders,
email books@DrRob.TV.

Publisher's Cataloging-In-Publication Data
(Prepared by The Donohue Group, Inc.)

Names: Carpenter, Rob, 1985- author.

Title: The 48 laws of happiness : secrets revealed for becoming the happiest you / Dr. Rob Carpenter.

Description: New York, New York : RMC Lit, [2021] | Includes bibliographical references.

Identifiers: ISBN 9781736615508 (print) | ISBN 9781736615515 (ebook)

Subjects: LCSH: Happiness. | Positive psychology. | Self-acceptance. | Self-actualization (Psychology) | Mind and body.

Classification: LCC BF575.H27 C37 2021 (print) | LCC BF575.H27 (ebook) | DDC 158.1--dc23

PRAISE FOR
THE 48 LAWS OF HAPPINESS

"Open this book if you want to discover the secrets of happiness."

— Andrew Carlberg,
Producer of Academy Award-Winning Film 'SKIN'

"Not only an entertaining and informative page-turner, but this book will truly change—and heal—you from the inside out."

— Bonnie Benjamin-Pharris,
2X Emmy, Grammy, & Peabody Award Winner

"This should seriously be assigned life reading."

— Elizabeth Gracen,
Former Miss America

"This insightful book can help you achieve genuine happiness and comfort with yourself. Dr. Rob teaches how to attain what is truly important, not just the look of happiness created for social media."

— Bruce Finn,
Emmy Award-Winning Director of Photography

"Buy a copy and you will make use of it for life"

— Blinky Rodriguez,
World's #1 Kickboxing Champion

"Dr. Rob combines cutting-edge science and heartfelt soul that will lift your spirit to new heights."

— Dr. Roberta Golinkoff,
New York Times Bestselling Author

"By far the most thorough, comprehensive, and compassionate book on happiness ever written. Every teacher, student, and therapist in America should read this book over and over again."

— Dr. Mia Adler-Ozair,
Educator & Clinical Psychotherapist

"Fabulous read to discover and explore secrets towards your happiness. As always, I am impressed by Dr. Rob, and grateful for this extremely timely and important work."

— Garvey Chiu,
Former Wall Street Executive & Digital Nomad

"If you want to be happy, confident, and as powerful as you can be, read this book—and give it as a gift to everyone you know."

— Michelle Crames,
Harvard Business School Alum, Serial Entrepreneur, and Founder of Pogo.io and Rush.Business

"A perfect roadmap to happiness."

— Dr. Kathy Hirsh-Pasek,
New York Times Bestselling Author

CONTENTS

hap-pi-ness:

The state of liking yourself and being content
with who you are and what you have.

"Happiness consists of living each day as if it were the first day of your honeymoon and the last day of your vacation."

— *Leo Tolstoy*

DEDICATION

This book is dedicated to you—and to anybody who wants to be happy.

Whether you know it or not, you are beautiful. You are amazing. You are strong. You are worthy of love. You have dreams and gifts and talents nobody else has. You have insights and life experiences that are truly valuable. You are a diamond, a pearl, a fine piece of rare gold worth more than all the money in the world. Even if nobody has ever told you this, YOU ARE. You are perfectly and wonderfully made, and I appreciate the fact that you would even pick up this book—I wrote it just for you. So from the bottom of my heart, THANK YOU, and enjoy.

INTRODUCTION

Welcome to your happiness journey!

You picked up this book because you want to be happier—and you will be. Regardless of whether you currently have lots of happiness in your life or little to no happiness, this book will help guide you to becoming the happiest possible version of yourself by revealing the secrets of happiness.

Although part of happiness is genetic—meaning part of your genes determines how much happiness you're born with—most of your happiness is a decision.[1] A choice. A mindset and approach to life that you can learn so that you can experience happiness wherever you go.

But this book is about more than hearing you can just decide to be happy if you want to be. Growing up I would hear this but couldn't stop thinking to myself, "I know I can choose to be happy, but how the heck do I choose it? What do I need to do? What practical steps do I need to take? Can I get some specifics?"

This book provides the specifics I always wanted—and perhaps the specifics you've always wanted too.

While there are other great books out there on happiness that discuss research studies on happiness or people's individual journeys to finding their own happiness, this book is different. This book is a practical roadmap you can use right now—and anytime in your life. It really is the "how to" approach to finding and keeping the happiness you deserve.

When you do get this happiness, here are just a few of the benefits you'll experience according to world-class research:

- Your body will naturally release more happiness hormones into your system (like endorphins, dopamine, and oxytocin that kill pain, increase pleasure, and bring you feelings of love and trust).[2]

- Your body will start limiting stress hormones that make you unhappy (like cortisol).[3]

- Your energy levels will increase, your immune system will strengthen, and you will increase the odds that you will live a longer life.[4]

- Your productivity and creativity will increase and you will likely make more money.[5]

- Your thoughts, emotions, and relationships will become more positive.[6]

- You'll become more resilient and confident in every area of your life.[7]

- And you will appear more attractive, charismatic, and even popular.[8]

The benefits of happiness are clearly tremendous—which is why all of us want to be happier. But unfortunately, most of us have been taught the wrong approaches to try to access these happiness rewards by society, myself included. And as a result, many of us end up living less happy than we otherwise could.

Here are just a few of the things we are (consciously or subconsciously) taught when it comes to how we think we can access happiness:

- That we need more money, power, or status to be happy.
- That we have to be better looking to be happy.
- That we have to "fit in" to be happy.
- That we have to have the perfect spouse or relationships to be happy.
- That the people around us have to behave a certain way for us to be happy.
- That we need our circumstances to be ideal so we can be happy.
- That we have to live for happy hour or the weekend or "experiences" to be happy.
- That we have to achieve all of our goals to be happy.
- That we have to be "successful" to be happy.
- That we have to "chase happiness" to be happy.

In this book, we'll see that the things we've been taught about finding happiness are not only often wrong, but sometimes dangerous. We'll see how the things society has taught us have left us feeling insecure about ourselves and often sad, complacent, disillusioned, and unhappy. We'll see that chasing after these teachings have not only decreased our happiness, they have also increased our levels of frustration, depression, suicide, self-harming, and substance abuse to all-time highs.

But again, this book is not an academic exercise talking about how we haven't achieved happiness as individuals or as a society. It really is meant to reveal the specific traps you and I face in every area of our lives that are obstacles to our happiness and how we can overcome these obstacles with practical tools we can use right now. It really is a book that will help you progress higher on what I call the "Happiness Spectrum" (or the vast range of happiness we are capable of experiencing in life).

The book is meant to be the official start of your happiness journey and, as such, is designed in a straightforward way so you can get what you need to maximize happiness in every area of your life. It is broken into seven sections—on your mind, emotions, relationships, health, work, circumstances, and the world—and the common traps you face in becoming happy within them.

In each section, there are bite-sized chapters of a few pages meant to be read in only five or ten minutes a day. Each chapter features a different trap—and a different "law" or secret for how you overcome that trap—as well as practical advice, science-based solutions, and affirmations you can use.

Each chapter also features a different inspirational story from somebody from around the world who learned to overcome their own happiness traps so that they could be happy. These stories come from literally every continent around the globe and represent all ethnic, gender, religious, income, age, and political groups to show us that happiness truly is universal despite our differences.

Ultimately, I wrote the book to be read one chapter at a time—over forty-eight days—so that you can digest it in your free time.

But I also wrote it this way so that you can have time to think about and reflect on your own happiness without feeling the need to rush through everything. This book is all about you and how you can get from Point A to Point B bit by bit. It's about how you can get to the next (and highest) level on your own Happiness Spectrum by making little amounts of progress every day.

At the end of the book in the appendix, I also include a fun reference section that covers:

- How to naturally increase your body's happiness hormones.
- 15 steps to build happiness into your daily routine.
- The types of clothes to wear to naturally increase your happiness.
- The foods to eat to become happier (hint, chocolate is on this list).
- How to design your home for maximum happiness.
- The songs to listen to that improve your mood.
- 47 "everyday" things that make most people happy.
- A few interesting research studies on happiness.

It is my sincere hope this book benefits you and blesses you. If you like what you're reading, I invite you to check out hundreds of empowering and entertaining resources I have for you on my website, www.DrRob.TV, as well as a free gift I have for you.

I also invite you to check out enrolling in my School of Happiness if you want to explore the principles and solutions in this book further. Please don't hesitate to contact me through my website or social media if you ever need a little extra support as I am your new friend, guide, and coach on this journey and am here to help you and serve you like the special person you are.

Now let's go get your happiness!

PART ONE

MASTERING HAPPINESS IN YOUR MIND

MASTERING HAPPINESS IN YOUR MIND:
Introduction

Our happiness starts in the mind. But the problem is our minds are either our biggest cheerleaders or our worst critics.

On the one hand, our minds have the power to encourage and inspire us, to give us the determination we need to be successful and to accomplish all of our dreams. They have the power to make us feel peaceful and grateful, counting all the many blessings in our lives. In short, our minds have the power to make us feel incredibly important, valued, and happy.

On the other hand, though, our minds also have the power to discourage us, to make us feel unworthy, unappreciated, and unloved. They have the power to make us self-critical, judgmental of others, bitter, egotistical, and highly negative about ourselves, our circumstances, and the world around us. In short, our minds have the power to make us feel deeply unloved, insecure, and unhappy.

In this section, we're going to explore how you can start to take power back over your mind. We're going to look at the eight traps you face in your mind and how you can overcome them. And we're going to empower you so that you can begin to be the master of your own thoughts, not just the servant. Here we go!

CHAPTER 1

HAPPINESS BEGINS THE MOMENT YOU ACCEPT YOURSELF UNCONDITIONALLY

The Law of Acceptance

"What self-acceptance does is open up more possibilities of succeeding because you aren't fighting yourself along the way."

— *Shannon Ables*[1]

You are not an accident.

You were created with exactly the right looks, the right personality, and the right nationality. You were created with the right intelligence, the right emotions, and the right talents. You were created to be the perfect version of yourself. You are not meant to be a carbon copy of anybody else.

The more you accept yourself as the person you were originally designed to be—warts and all—the more relief and satisfaction you will experience in your life. The more you love yourself and realize you do not have to be perfect in all (or any) areas of your life, the more liberated you will become. Simply put, the more you accept your own imperfections, the more happiness you will allow into your life.

No matter who you are or what your background has been, you are worth far more than you realize. Your happiness has nothing to do with your looks, personality, intelligence, possessions, degrees, accomplishments, or experiences. It has everything to do with you being valuable as a human being. Studies show that if you sold all of your body organs on the market they would go for more than $45 million.[2] Morbid yes, but still stunning. You are more than a multimillionaire—you are a BEAUTIFUL MASTERPIECE.

But You May Not Always Feel So Hot About Yourself

Yet I know that you struggle with feelings of insignificance. Maybe not all the time, but more often than you should. You criticize yourself so harshly that you could win the award for being the world's worst self-critic. You feel frustrated with this flaw or that shortcoming. You feel that there are things about yourself that disqualify you from being acceptable to yourself and others.

You think if only you could change this about yourself or if only you could get that, then you could be happy. Or at least happier. You want more things, accomplishments, and experiences because you think they will make you feel less insecure. You think that gaining something that you don't have right now will make you feel like you're good enough.

The Mind Trap Affecting You

The thought that you are not good enough is one of your mind's most deadly traps. Research shows that 85% of people suffer from not feeling good enough.[3] Imagine that: Eighty-five percent of people are unhappy with who they are or what they have. And not only is this stressing them out, but it is making people feel miserable and depressed. Most are walking around with a big sign on their forehead that reads, "UNWORTHY." I know this because I used to walk around with this sign myself.

In my life, because I did not feel good enough, I was deeply insecure. I would accomplish and accomplish but the accomplishments did not seem to matter. Even though I got straight As, skipped grades, went to the most prestigious schools, and worked at the highest profile organizations and with the most famous celebrities in the world, none of this made me feel worthy.

Sure, I had moments of feeling good about myself and was successful, but at my core I was a part of the group of people who felt like something was inherently wrong with them when, in fact, nothing was. I felt unworthy and it was eating me alive.

Perhaps you can identify with this feeling of unworthiness too. It most often shows up in one or more of the following ways when:

We become the moper. We develop feelings of self-pity as Debbie or Donald Downer and feel our lives are terrible or unfair. We start to see the glass as half empty and believe if something can go wrong, it will. Our life seems to be filled with constant storms and we have the voice of our worst enemy stuck inside of our heads: ourselves. We become unhappy and we wear it on our faces and in our attitudes.

We become the pretender. We start to strut like peacocks, trying to show off our accomplishments, possessions, and manufactured social media images because we desperately need validation. We let low self-esteem get the best of us and feel the only way we can ever be good enough is by impressing others, trying desperately to make it and fit in, or by trying to prove we are better (or smarter or richer or more popular) than everybody else. We get caught up in insecurity and a rat-race mentality so that we can shift attention away from our perceived flaws.

We become the escape artist. We escape into excessive binge watching, video games, social media, food or drugs, or mindless activities and busyness to distract our minds so we do not have to confront the feeling of not feeling good enough and other deadly mental traps we might be experiencing. We find our favorite things to escape into, sometimes find other people who will escape with us, and over the long-term never really confront the low self-esteem that might be rotting like mildew inside of us.

Socorro's Story

Here's what Socorro from Los Angeles wrote to me about her experiences with these things, about her experiences of not feeling good enough:

> For much of my twenties, I was at war with self-doubt.
> I was at war with my own insecurities. But here's the

most ironic part about it: I was trained as a therapist and was supposed to know better! I went to some of the most prestigious schools in the world, had the best education and mentors imaginable, and yet I couldn't apply what I had learned to my own life. I understood the inner workings of the mind, but I didn't fully understand the inner workings of my own mind.

Even though I was born with good genes—I am intelligent, tall, athletic, and attractive—I was still struggling with believing whether I was good enough. I'd walk into different rooms and I'd notice the people who I thought were good enough: the smart people, the best dressed or best looking, the people who I thought had arrived. And when I would secretly compare myself to them, I wondered if I would ever arrive myself. I would question why I wasn't "there" yet. Deep down, I wasn't sure if I could ever get "there."

Sometimes, this was a minor struggle but other times it felt like it consumed me. But if you were to look at me from the outside, you would have never known it. I hid insecurities so well you would have thought that I had life all figured out. I wanted others to believe that but for years I didn't believe it myself. I found myself spending countless hours daily dwelling on the things I felt I needed to be complete—and feel complete.

But then one day my mentor said to me that I had to get over my insecurities. She told me I was smart and beautiful and successful, and I actually started to believe her. I started to believe her because she is a bossy a** chick who doesn't lie or say things to just say them. She says things because she means them. And guess what? Now I believe I am bad**s. In fact, I know I am a bad**s. It's like a crown that I have that I wear everywhere I go. And I'm going to say to you what my mentor said to me: Get over the fact that you don't think you're good enough because you are. You are smart, you are beautiful, and you are successful. You are a bad**s. Take that bad**s crown, put it on, and feel damn good wherever you go. Walk into that room, know who you are and what you bring to the table, and completely own it. YOU ARE GOOD ENOUGH.

This is so powerful and healing. I know because like Socorro I had to learn how to get past the mind trap of not feeling good enough myself. You can too if you're currently facing it. Here are a few helpful tips you can use today that might help:

Research-Based Solutions for You

1. Talk about how you're feeling with a trusted and compassionate friend, coach, or therapist. Speaking your feelings in a constructive way is half the battle.[4]

2. Identify any troubling, insecure thoughts about yourself and journal them.[5] Write freely and openly as the experience of just writing about them will be healing. You can write this in your own journal or in the sister workbook I designed just for you.

3. Find ways you can reinterpret any negative thoughts about yourself in a more positive way.[6] Instead of magnifying your perceived shortcomings, for example, choose to see these as things that help make you vulnerable and authentic, not unworthy. After all, everyone who has chosen to be authentic feels so much freer—and happier—than those who are trying to pretend they have it all together.

Review:

Point to Ponder: Happiness Begins the Moment You Accept Yourself Unconditionally

Law to Remember: The Law of Acceptance

Affirmation to Declare: "I have struggled with not feeling good enough. I have struggled with not accepting myself. But you know what, I choose to now accept the good parts of myself. Unconditionally. And in fact, starting today I now accept every single part of myself. Warts. Flaws. And all. I accept all my imperfections unconditionally. I may not be perfect, but I'm still valuable. I may not have it all together, but I'm making progress. I may not always feel like a hot shot, but I deserve happiness and I'm going to give myself permission to be happy by accepting who I actually am. I know I am a BEAUTIFUL MASTERPIECE and this is my declaration of happiness."

For more free resources on this topic, go to www.DrRob.TV/happiness/Chapter1

CHAPTER 2

A HAPPY PERSON REALIZES
THEY DON'T HAVE TO FIT IN

The Law of Realization

*"So you're a little weird? Work it! A little different? OWN it!
Better to be a nerd than one of the herd."*

— Mandy Hale[1]

You are not a big fat phony.

Yet over 70% of people believe that they are.[2] You might even be in this group. I know I was. You might feel a sense of fear that you will be exposed as an imposter or as something you are not. Even if you accept yourself unconditionally, you may feel that you are not good enough for other people. You might believe you are good enough for yourself, but underneath you may feel that this may not be *good enough*.

And this thought of not being good enough for (some) other people is terrifying to you. And robbing you of your happiness.

Depending on who you are, you may have, like me, tried fitting into one of the following groups to prove you are good enough for others:

- Being a perfectionist
- Being a superman/woman
- Being an expert
- Being a unique individualist
- Being the cool kid, the nerd, or the gamer
- Or being some other "type of thing" just to fit in and gain acceptance from others

The fear you and I have of being rejected is real. So we make efforts to blend in as much as possible. We think we have to be this way to be acceptable to our friends and family, coworkers, or society in general. We feel we have to be something other than our most authentic selves.

The craziest part about this thought is that we fear something else even more than not fitting in. We fear that others are going to discover we are not whatever thing(s) we are claiming to be.

So we go through life with a sense that we may one day be exposed as a fake, as a phony, or as an imposter. We hide our true selves from others and, at times, even from ourselves. As the stress builds, we look for ways to escape this trap but can't because we feel we would be revealing too much if we showed "the real us."

Feeling like a phony is especially common in the most successful of people.[3] When they are successful, they feel that somebody is going to uncover their lie—that they are not what they say they are. So they add more accomplishments and more success—or more labels—which causes them to feel like an even bigger phony. They secretly fear they are not good enough and that one day somebody is going to expose it to all the people around them.

Here's what Regina from Madison, Wisconsin said about her fear of being exposed as a fake and the anxiety it was causing her:

Regina's Story

As my classmates introduced themselves at the dinner celebrating the start of our doctoral program, I was a nervous wreck. I listened to people confidently share their names and what they did for a living. There were superintendents, military officers, CEOs, and a host of other impressive positions. What was I doing here? I didn't belong in this group. Who was I after all? What have I done?

When it was my turn, I stood up and with a quiver, stumbled over my very own name. I'm sure they could all see right through me. If they didn't already know, they would know soon enough. I'm an imposter.

Yes, an imposter. A phony. I don't belong. I haven't done anything spectacular, and if I have had success, it's just been luck. This has been my outlook for many, many years. I have always been afraid that people would one day realize that I really wasn't as good as they thought I was. In fact, they would realize I wasn't good at all. And this fear pushed me. I had to be the

MVP of the softball team. I had to get straight As. I had to be the first to work and the last to leave. I had to be the president of the PTA. I had to prove myself. I never celebrated the climb of one mountain; I simply looked for the next, higher one. I'm not really a success. I'm an imposter.

These are very dangerous but not uncommon traits for successful people. I don't know the psychology behind it all, I only know the symptoms. I promise you, it's real. The self-imposed pressure may be a way of masking insecurity. It's a way of seeking external validation.

But there's hope! If you suffer from any of the same imposter symptoms like I did, know that you can find joy. As a recovering imposter, I'd like to share a few tips that have helped me. Recognize and name the syndrome. Try to understand the power the syndrome has on you, and let it go. Then refocus or reframe your outlook. Seek internal validation, not external. Give yourself permission to take a break from work or school without feeling guilty; you'll come back feeling refreshed and probably be more productive. Take a compliment on your success and be proud of yourself. Foster the relationships in your life that bring you joy. Share your thoughts with a trusted associate. Practice these things every day and trim away at the insecurity and anxiety that the imposter syndrome is imposing on your life. I bet you'll find that you are the real deal! Celebrate your successes and find joy in each one!

Steps to Defeating Imposter Syndrome

Regina is so right. We do have to strip away the insecurities and anxieties imposter syndrome—or feeling like fakes and phonies—is causing us. Here's how we can do it:

1. ***Stop pretending to be something we're not.*** If we're currently pursuing labels or goals or groups just to fit in and prove ourselves, we will never be truly happy. We will have to start living to make ourselves happy and not just pretending to be something to make others happy.

2. ***Highlight our authentic selves and imperfections to others.*** If we become more truthful and vulnerable with others, we will be liberated from ever feeling like fakes because we'll have nothing to hide— and this will bring us great relief.

3. ***Stop fearing rejection, but instead start celebrating it.*** If we are rejected for being who we truly are, it's time to party because those who reject us have now disqualified themselves from access to our lives and from keeping us trapped in the fear of not being good enough for them. In other words, we can stop fearing rejection because if people have cut us out, they have rejected themselves from our lives and we should be grateful we don't have to waste any time trying to get their approval.

4. ***Stop attributing our accomplishments to luck.*** If we're feeling our success is accidental, we can instead start to understand that we earned it through hard work or because of our talents.

5. ***Create a compliments journal.*** If a compliment comes our way, we can journal it so that we can go back and review it and the other great things people have ever said about us. Regularly. Doing this will help us be proud of who we are, tear down any walls of feeling like a phony, and bring us happiness anytime we need it or want it.

Review:

Point to Ponder: A Happy Person Realizes They Don't Have to Fit In

Law to Remember: The Law of Realization

Affirmation to Declare: "At times, I have felt like a big old phony. Like a total fake. But starting right now, I'm changing that. I'm changing it because I realize it's not true. Not only do I embrace my imperfections, but I will no longer hide them from others because I'm so desperate to fit in. I will stop fearing other people's potential judgment and rejection because even if I get judged or rejected for being the real me, I will make room for the people who truly belong in my life and genuinely accept me for who I am. And this is totally liberating. This is my declaration of happiness."

For more free resources on this topic, go to www.DrRob.TV/happiness/Chapter2

CHAPTER 3

HAPPY PEOPLE RECOGNIZE THAT THE GRASS IS NOT GREENER ON THE OTHER SIDE

The Law of Comparison

"Learn to…be what you are, and learn to resign with a good grace all that you are not."

— Henri Frederic Amiel[1]

We should humbly embrace the fact that other people are not better than us. Even if we feel some other people have more money, better looks, more popularity, or more accomplishments than we do, the simple fact is they are still not better than us.

Nobody is superior to us. And for that matter, nobody is inferior to us. It may be true that some people are better OFF than us in some ways, but it's also true that some people are WORSE off in other ways.

Much of the stress we feel in our minds when we compare ourselves to others is because we are often focusing on the wrong things. Consciously or subconsciously, we're constantly looking to see how we match up to others in everything from our homes to our cars to our looks and more.

If we feel we don't match up with others on one or more of these things, we start to feel inferior and insecure, perhaps even jealous or dismissive of those who in some way we perceive as having more than us. On the other hand, if we feel we have more or better things than others, arrogance can sneak into our hearts and make us feel like we're superior to them.

Either way, this type of thinking is killing our happiness.

When we're comparing ourselves to and competing with others, we forget that this is not the purpose of life—and definitely not the pathway to happiness. It might bring us some type of social or financial success to compete with others and out do them, but we'll be miserable getting to and holding onto that success. Why?

Because the temporary feeling of happiness we get by feeling better than or impressing others—the rush of the chemical dopamine we get in our brains—quickly fades as we become dissatisfied with what we have.[2] So we want MORE and MORE and MORE social or financial success—thinking that this next success will finally make us happy this time because we have achieved our true standing on the social hierarchy we've built in our minds.

I say this not to criticize us, but to show us that the way society is set up has been causing us to stay on the lower realm of the Happiness Spectrum. Society has been trying to trap us in a mental rat race we cannot win in the long run—because the mental rat race is not designed to produce a happiness winner; it is designed to produce people who can only achieve temporary happiness by getting more of something that will quickly dissatisfy them.

Why Comparisons Hurt Us

When we compare ourselves to others, we choose to live life based on the illusion that getting more than others—or impressing others so that we can be accepted—will make us happy. The reality is that this is just not true. The comparison trap makes us prisoners of our own minds—never able to escape the feeling of inferiority or superiority to others which strips us of being content with just ourselves and what we have (which is the true foundation of happiness).

Here's what Merja from Serbia wrote to me about her experiences with comparing herself to others:

Merja's Story

For most of my life, I've had a feeling that almost everyone else had a better life than me. I thought they were cooler, prettier, richer, funnier, and more popular. I thought they were just better than me in every way.

As a result, I believed that nothing good could happen to me because everybody else had things that I didn't. I thought other people had better jobs and cooler online pics and hotter boyfriends. I thought other people wore cooler clothes and had their lives all figured out. And meanwhile, what did I have?

I just couldn't stop comparing myself to them. And the more I compared myself, the worse I felt.

I just couldn't stop thinking, why were they getting to go to all of the cool parties and I wasn't? Why were they getting all of the likes online and I wasn't? Why were they so popular and accepted and I wasn't? I just couldn't stop thinking why were they such worthwhile winners while I was such a worthless loser?

As I let these thoughts dominate my mind, the more unhappy I became. And the more unhappy I became, the more I believed that happiness was NOT for me. The more I believed that a good job, a good relationship, and a fulfilling life were NOT for me. The more I believed that a good life was simply NOT for me.

But as I grew older, I began to realize that the people I envied weren't so happy—or even as cool or as beautiful or as put together—as I used to think. I realized that even though they seemed to have everything on the outside that it was just a false image they created for themselves because they were feeling insecure and didn't know how to get healthy validation. As I grew older, I started to realize the problem wasn't my own life—or even other people's lives—but was my own point of view. I started to realize that I simply couldn't see realistically. I started to realize I was drawing false conclusions about people—and myself—because I was making false comparisons.

I do believe that we all get handed different cards at the time of our birth. But I now know that we can choose to accept our cards and deal with them. I now know we don't have to compare our cards to other people's. And I now know that we don't have to think that other people are living happier or better lives than us, because they're not.

These are such honest and wise words from Merja. She recognized something that all of us can take heed to—that our happiness is truly not about what we do or don't have compared to others, it is about how we think about what we do or don't have in and of ourselves.

Entering into the comparison trap—the mental rat race of life—keeps us constantly trying to do more or be more and never really allows us to be satisfied with our own lives. The way we can more fully accept Merja's truth to overcome this trap in our lives is by embracing the following couple of things:

1. **Learn to understand that others often present half-truths to us.** Regardless of how perfect others might seem—or how great their life might appear—we should know they are only presenting the abridged version of themselves to us and the world. We shouldn't compare their highlight reel with our behind-the-scenes—and we shouldn't be comparing ourselves to them because it will always undermine our happiness in the long run.

2. **Learn to accept that everyone is different.** People have different looks, different levels of wealth, different social connections, and so on. And this is perfectly ok. When we beat ourselves up for not having what others might have,

we become like a cat beating herself up for not being a dog. Everybody is different and that's what makes life so great. We should embrace others' differences from us and our differences from them. They have their wonderful things and we have our wonderful things.

The reality is we don't need to compare ourselves to or compete with others to make ourselves feel better or validated. We are already perfectly and wonderfully made on our own. We should reject the trap society has forced upon us of comparing ourselves to others, run our own races, and be happy while we do it.

Review:

Point to Ponder: Happy People Recognize That the Grass Is NOT Greener on the Other Side

Law to Remember: The Law of Comparison

Affirmation to Declare: "I've struggled with comparing myself to others. At times I've felt inferior to some people and superior to others based on how well I thought I was doing. But I give this thinking up right now. I give it up and throw it away. Nobody is living as they say, and I'm going to humbly embrace this. My life is my life and I need to focus on me. That's good enough. And I'm good enough, really I am. This is my declaration of happiness."

For more free resources on this topic, go to www.DrRob.TV/happiness/Chapter3

CHAPTER 4

HAPPY PEOPLE STRIKE "I CAN'T" FROM THEIR MINDS

The Law of Abundant Thinking

"Be somebody nobody thought you could be."

- Paula Maier[1]

We should eliminate "I can't" from our thinking.

While we may not be able to do some things, we can do a lot of things. We can think, breathe, see, hear, and laugh. We can pick our friends, the entertainment we consume, and the purchases we make. We can choose our interests, our goals, and the kinds of experiences we have. In short, we can do many, many things—millions and millions and millions of things.

But at times we also might believe we can't do some things. Or we might believe we can't do some things right now. We might even believe we have the capability to do some things but that we don't know how to do them right now, so we don't ever do them.

Whichever we look at it, it is easy for us to fall into an "I can't" mindset. Or an "I can't right now" mindset. Or an "I can't but someday wish I could" kind of mindset.

This "I can't" perspective is giving us a defeatist attitude in some aspects of our lives and causing us to think less of our capabilities. And whatever causes us to THINK LESS of ourselves causes us to BE LESS of ourselves. If we're a lesser version of who we were created to be, we will never be able to reach the top of the Happiness Spectrums in our lives.

For the sake of our own happiness, we must eliminate "I can't" from our thinking.

Now this doesn't mean we can't be practical and realistic about what we're capable of and the most appropriate timing to do things in our lives. But it does mean that we should eliminate all excuses from our lives holding us back from being fully who we are right now. There is not some magical time in the future when we'll arrive; we can be and experience the completeness of who and what we are meant to be in this present moment.

Common Things People Think They Can't Do, Be, or Have

But most people have one or more "I can'ts" present in their life causing them not to be as happy as they could be. They either think 1) they will never be or get what they want; 2) that they can't be or get what they want *right now*; or 3) that they *don't know how* to be or get what they want - right now.

A few common "I can'ts" include:

- I can't have complete happiness—right now.
- I can't have total peace—right now.

- I can't have the money and freedom I want—right now.
- I can't achieve work-life balance—right now.
- I can't have maximum self-confidence and personal fulfillment—right now.
- I can't write a book or achieve my dreams—right now.
- I can't overcome my fears and phobias—right now.
- I can't [insert your issue] —right now.

Many of these "I cant's" are present in either our conscious or subconscious thoughts. But the important thing to realize is that our minds have a negativity bias causing us to focus on what we can't do or be rather than what we can do and become.[2] Our thoughts tell us that we have to wait for perfect circumstances to have or become what we want. And importantly, they tell us we have to have something external to ourselves (a perfect job, home, spouse, or life) to be truly happy. This is simply not true.

But perhaps the worst part about this "I can't" thinking is that others often inflict it upon us (which is why we consciously or subconsciously adopted it in the first place). Through their words and actions, others try to reinforce our deep-seated fears. And it is such a shame. Here's what Russ from Portland, Oregon said about how he grew up feeling he could not do things because of how his family treated him:

Russ's Story

I grew up with two brothers who were more athletic and popular than me. My friends and relatives often talked about how cool they were, but never talked about how cool I was. In fact, they didn't talk about me much at all.

In response, I decided to focus my time on the things that my brothers were not: being well read and having deep conversations with people that didn't focus on me being cool (because I wasn't). Consciously or subconsciously, I started to define myself by being the person my brothers weren't and being in the open spaces they would not go.

This became my regular pattern: to fill the voids they left and recognize what I wasn't or couldn't be. But over time, instead of only letting my brothers tell me what I wasn't or couldn't be I started to let other people determine what I wasn't or couldn't be. I started to let other people define WHO I WAS.

Nowhere was this truer than when people told me that I would never be attractive or a good writer.

As a child, everyone always told me I was the "smart" and "good kid." But the message to me was obvious: You might be smart but you are not good looking. You might be good, but you are fat. I believed this and decided to limit how I saw myself—that I would never be good looking or physically fit, and so I let my weight balloon and let my health grow poor.

The same is true when people told me I would never be a good writer. In my former role as co-founder of Idealist, I achieved massive success but was told that I was a "poor writer." I let this message from others sink in, and it became a part of my identity. For over twenty years, I decided not to write a word (outside of email, of course). I also decided not to speak publicly because I believed I wasn't a good communicator. Others told me so and it was simply the gospel to me.

I was a smart person who believed in limitless potential, yet I was limiting what I thought I could be or do because others labeled me. Because others defined who I was or what I could do, I lived in fear and timidity for DECADES. But one morning I woke up and decided I would take baby steps away from these fears. I started to write—and then write some more—and now more than half a million people have read my articles and tell me I'm a great writer. I started to diet too, and now I have lost weight and others are telling me I'm looking quite handsome. Me believing I couldn't do something was defined by others, but me believing I could do something was defined by me. I wanted to re-write my script and so I did. You can do the same if you simply choose to—it's that easy.

How We Can Eliminate "I Can't" Thinking Through New Habits

Russ is obviously right. We can be who we are and get what we want if only we change our thoughts. And the great news is we don't even consciously have to focus on changing our thoughts to do so. Instead, if we focus on changing our daily habits, we can automatically change our thoughts and re-train our minds.

We can change our "I can'ts" to "I cans" through small behaviors. We can build small, step-by-step achievable habits to reprogram our minds in an almost effortless way. We don't have to meditate deeply (though I encourage that for other reasons), we just have to make small changes to what we're currently doing. A small change on our part can create big impacts in our lives. Here are four simple steps we can take to change our thoughts.

1. **Create micro quotas and macro goals.**[3] A micro quota is the minimum amount we have to do every day to reach our big goal—to reach our "I can" and "I just did" goal. For example, our big goal might be to reach the top of our Happiness Spectrum. To do that, our micro quota would be to set aside 5-10 minutes to read *The 48 Laws of Happiness* every day over forty-eight days and an additional 5-10 minutes to put into practice its strategies (shameless self-promotion but, hey, you're already reading the book!). When we do this over time, we micro train our minds to be happier on a daily basis. (With *The 48 Laws of Happiness*, we will be spending nearly 2 months retraining our minds for happiness—a small investment we can make so the rest of our days are the best of our days.)

2. **Create behavior chains.**[4] A behavior chain is doing one small thing and then adding another small thing to it. And then another small thing. We could, for example, commit to reading *The 48 Laws of Happiness* when we get off of work or school and then commit to watching a funny clip of our favorite comedian online immediately afterward. The next day, we could read the book, watch a funny clip, and then add singing our favorite song to this. It's a simple behavior chain with one behavior leading to another so that we can build momentum through small steps—and turn on happiness in our lives on-demand.

3. **Visualize the process, not the result.**[5] We can visualize the PROCESS of achieving our goals (our "I cans" and "I

just did") rather than the end result of our goals. When we visualize the individual steps to our goals, it will reduce anxiety or pressure in reaching these goals. Instead of visualizing what peak happiness will be for us, for example, we can visualize the specific daily steps we can take to be happier. And in time, we will reach peak happiness—step by simple step.

4. **Identify exact moments we tend to give up on our goals.**[6] In pursuit of our goals, we can identify moments when we are more likely to quit and then study these moments. When we study these moments, we'll see the patterns that not only make us quit but cause us to think we can't reach our goals. We can then take steps to avoid putting ourselves in positions that make it easier to quit. For example, if seeing the image of an ex or listening to a sad song makes us unhappy and causes us to want to give up on love, we can immediately remove these things from our environment so as not to thwart our goal of being at the top of our Happiness Spectrums.

These simple steps will empower us to change our habits. And when our habits start to change, our thinking will start to change too.

If we think we could never lose weight but are now walking for a brief 20 minutes a day, we will start to see the weight come off. If we think we could never have work-life balance but instead wake up an hour earlier so we can devote more time to our family after work, we are seeing more balance. There is some truth to seeing is believing. All we have to do is take small action steps daily to change our "I cant's" to "I can" to "I just did."

Review:

Point to Ponder: Happy People Strike "I Can't" from Their Minds

Law to Remember: The Law of Abundant Thinking

Affirmation to Declare. "I know I've been guilty of thinking I can't do or be certain things right now. I realize this "I can't" thinking has been holding me back from being my best self, which is my completely happy self. I will start to implement small daily practices to change my habits so that I can change my thinking. This is my declaration of happiness."

For more free resources on this topic, go to www.DrRob.TV/happiness/Chapter4

CHAPTER 5

A HAPPY MIND BLOWS UP
ITS TIME MACHINE

The Law of Living in the Moment

"Forever is composed of now."

- Emily Dickinson[1]

We all own imaginary time machines that we should blow up for the sake of our happiness.

But for most people, this seems nearly impossible. Why? Because we have them set to 88 miles per hour and we are determined to live "Back to the Future." We are determined to live everywhere but our present moment. And we are determined to accept everything but the things right in front of us.

Research has shown that most of us spend at least 50% of our time thinking about the past or thinking about the future.[2] While it's important to learn lessons from the past or prepare for the future, doing this in excess is causing us some serious unhappiness.[3] It's also releasing nasty chemicals like cortisol into our bodies making us more stressed and less healthy.[4]

This happened in my own life, but I didn't even realize it. I wasn't in the moment and so it caused me to be severely aloof to so many people around me. It wasn't that I was uncaring about others, it was just that I was off in my own little world. And it was costing me my own happiness.

When you and I think too much about the past, we tend to invoke feelings of guilt, regret, sadness, unforgiveness, and other negative memories.

When we think too much about the future, we invoke feelings of stress, anxiety, fear, and worry.

In other words, when we think too much about the past or the future, we're often thinking about them in very negative ways. It's not that we want to, but it's just that we do.

What this means is that we're spending more than 50% of our time—more than 50% of our lives—thinking negative, unhealthy thoughts, causing us to be less happy than we otherwise could be. Can you imagine? We're racing around in the time machines in our minds missing real life as it passes us by. And what do we have to show for it?

Common Things We Do When We Think Too Much About the Past

When we live life in our time machines racing toward the past, it is usually because:

We are clinging too much to a specific memory. In this state, we are overthinking about a person or situation that either brought us great happiness or great sadness. We keep replaying our memories with these things as a way to stay connected to that person or situation. We've set our time machines on a never-end replay loop.

We feel we may not reach a certain "peak high" again. In this state, we think that we will never be as happy, successful, wealthy, healthy, socially connected, or (insert whatever it is we don't think we'll ever get) again. We want to feel these highs but we don't know how, so we cling to the memory hoping to relive the joy of these moments, hoping we can feel the same dopamine release in our brains just like before.

We're frustrated with where we are currently in life. In this state, we start thinking about the good old days we used to have. These were the days that were the best in our lives and we compare them to where we are now. We believe happiness was something we once had but don't know if we can ever have it again.

We like being sad. In this state, we think about the past as a way to be sad. We have accepted sadness as our identity, and it brings us our significance. We figure if we can't be happy being happy, we'll be happy being sad.

On the other hand, though, sometimes we set our time machines to race toward the future. But this has the same impact as when we are racing toward the past.

Common Things We Do When We Think Too Much About the Future

We become anxious about what will happen over the next few days, weeks, months, and years. In this state, we can't stop thinking about what's next. We have no idea what's going to happen but we need to know. And desperately. We want to control situations to reach our goals and/or prevent our fears from happening to us or those we care about. We worry and worry about what might happen and think our worrying is a sign of maturity instead of what it really is: our insecurities run amok.

We feel frustrated or stuck in life with uncertain plans to move ahead. In this state, we don't know how we will ever make it out of our current position in life. We may have a plan to get out of our uncertain situations but we're not sure if our plan will work. It's like we want to drive our time machines to a different place, but they seem suspended in space or out of gas.

Here's what Becky from Texas wrote to me about her experiences living in her own time machine:

Becky's Story

I couldn't stop thinking about him. After sharing a life for over three decades with my husband, that all came crashing down. All of the love. All of the trips. All of the sweet words. All of the memories. Completely gone.

I wanted to understand—I needed to understand—what had just happened. So I thought. And I thought. And I thought some more. I just couldn't accept that it was over. I just couldn't accept that life I had always known had just ended.

The pain that we had when we were together was fierce, but I realized the pain that I experienced when we were apart was even worse. I wondered why society portrays divorces and breakups in such a lighthearted way? There was absolutely nothing lighthearted about what I was feeling.

But even though I was feeling great pain, I didn't know what I would do with all of the memories we had. So I found myself reliving them over and over. And as I relived them, I wept. I shook. I froze myself in time so that I could hold onto whatever memory I had with him—even if that memory was going to bring me great misery. Even if that memory was going to be the end of me.

After crying too many tears, I knew I needed to stop thinking about him. I knew I needed to stop thinking about my past. So I devised a retraining plan for my mind. I decided that each time a memory would come to my mind, I would simply shove it aside and think of something else. And do you want to know what happened when I did this? I became quite an expert. Almost chillingly so. I had learned to cut off all memories and feelings of my husband and marriage in my conscious mind. I had learned how to become numb.

But the problem with my strategy was that the memories I shoved aside escaped during the day had seeped into my dreams during the night. I would lay my head down and immediately wake up with nightmares. I realized my subconscious mind was still full of (good and bad) memories even if my conscious mind wasn't.

These days, instead of pushing my memories away, I allow myself to remember—but in a healthy, objective way. I give myself permission to recall both the good moments and the bad moments. When appropriate. And in doing so, I allow my dreams to take me anywhere they'd like to go—which, so far, is not back to nightmares.

Ways We Can Set Our Time Machines to the Present

What an incredible story from Becky (that millions of people have gone through). Like her, we can learn how to break free from being frozen in time from whatever things are causing us to be anywhere but in the present. Here's how:

1. **Savor the present moment.**[5] By focusing on the sights, sounds, smells, and feelings of the present we'll begin to savor it more. But we have to be intentional about it. We have to open our eyes, our hearts, and our senses to the beautiful things all around us.

2. **Focus on our breathing.**[6] When we are more conscious of our breathing—of controlling our breathing—we become more aware of our surroundings, more intuitive, and more present.

3. **Get into "flow."**[7] We can learn how to lose track of time on all our tasks (regardless if they are ones we enjoy or not). In fact, we can start with just 5 minutes of flow where we put our total focus and attention on whatever we are doing in the present moment. Once we master five minutes, we can add

five more minutes, then five more, and so on. The great artists get lost in flow and we can emulate their experiences to maximize our happiness.

4. **Accept whatever is bothering us.**[8] Instead of constantly worrying about what is bothering us, we can learn to accept it and set aside a specific time to worry about it. We don't have to like whatever it is that's bringing us stress, but we can learn to move on with our days until we are in the position to fix the thing bothering us. If we can't fix it, we accept it anyway without adding unnecessary stress, suffering, and unhappiness to our lives. What's done is done.

5. **Experience new routines.**[9] While our routines and rituals can be very good things, we've got to shake things up every once in a while. We should drive a different way to work, for example, or make a certain change to our favorite recipe or workout. We should do whatever it takes to adjust our routines regularly, even in small ways, as the new experience will not only break monotony, it will also release positive chemicals in our brains.

6. **Create something.**[10] When we create things - a blog, a poem, a painting, etc - we are more likely to lose ourselves in the creation of that thing and stop overthinking about the past and the future. And the best part is what we create doesn't have to be a masterpiece, professional, or for anybody else's consumption. We can simply create for ourselves. When we create, we make it easy to step outside of our time machines (and begin to blow them up if we want to).

Review:

Point to Ponder: A Happy Mind Blows Up Its Time Machine

Law to Remember: The Law of Living in the Moment

Affirmation to Declare: "I have been overthinking my past and my future. This has been a cause of great stress and regret and has kept me from being as happy as I could be. I'm going to take intentional steps to not travel in my time machine as much as I have been so that I can live more in the moment. I realize the more I live in the moment the more I can awaken to the BEAUTIFUL MASTERPIECE that exists within me and that exists all around me. This is my declaration of happiness."

For more free resources on this topic, go to www.DrRob.TV/happiness/Chapter5

CHAPTER 6

HAPPY PEOPLE REJECT THE LIE THAT NOBODY CARES ABOUT THEM

The Law of Recognition

"At times, some may think that no one cares, but somebody always cares!"

- Thomas Monson[1]

Other people care about you and me.

We are who we are because somebody loved us, cared for us, protected us, and promoted us. We are who we are because other people have paved the way so we could live better lives.

Now, others may not have always done this perfectly. Some may have even abandoned, rejected, or hurt us—just like my biological father did to me.

Not only was my biological father severely negligent to me before my mom left him, but he never once sent a birthday or holiday card or ever called me to ask how I was doing one time in my life. If he is still living and you asked me to point him out in a crowd, I wouldn't even know what he looked like—that's how much he rejected me from his life. I don't say this to make you feel bad for me or because I'm angry at him—I'm not. I say it because I know some of you might have experienced the same thing so, as a friend to you, I feel your pain.

But regardless of who hasn't been there for us, more people have cared about us than we might realize.[2] Even though most of us have thought at one point or another that nobody cares about us, this is simply not true. Many people have cared about us—both those we know and those we don't. Let's explore this point just a little bit further.

Strangers Who Care About You

I care about you. I wrote this book because I hoped that you would read it. I may not know you personally, but I specifically wrote it because I wanted to show you HOW TO BE HAPPY. I believe you were meant to read this book and felt like there were few other books that did what this book does, so I wanted to show you how special you really are because I care about you.

Entrepreneurs and inventors care about you. The stores we shop at and the products we buy were all ideas of entrepreneurs or inventors who thought that they could provide a service that would make your life better. Sure, they might have had a profit motive, but they still cared enough to make something for you. Nobody forced them to put in the crazy hard work to make your and my life a little more convenient.

Social activists care about you. The people who have demanded better rights and conditions for you care about you.

Dr. King and Cesar Chavez and Elizabeth Cady Stanton cared about you. A host of other activists who have wanted to right wrongs care about you. We may not know them personally, but they have cared deeply about you and me.

Soldiers care about you. When a man or woman becomes a member of the armed forces, they are saying that they care about you. They are willing to put their lives on the line for you. What an amazing thought: a stranger who would die for you and me.

Of course, I could list lots of other examples of strangers who care about you and me, but we get the picture. There are people out there who care enough about us so that we can live an easier, better, and happier life. This is a big deal.

But strangers aren't the only ones who care about us. So do people in our everyday life.

People We Know Who Care About Us

Our family cares about us. The reality is, we probably have had a mom or dad who cares about us. They may not have done it perfectly, but they cared enough to raise us in the best way they could given their own limitations, imperfections, and personal demons. If we never had a mom and dad or never had a good relationship with them, we probably had other family members or caretakers who tried to help care for us. When thinking about our family, it is important that we provide them with a lot of grace, understanding, and forgiveness for all of the mistakes they have made with us, especially if we feel nobody in our family has ever cared for us. I guarantee there is somebody in your family who does care whether you know it or not.

Our friends care about us. We choose our friends and our friends choose us. Friendships are extremely important relationships and they can often stick closer than siblings. We have had friends who we have confided in, hung out with socially, and done lots of other fun activities with. But as with family, it's important we use gentle gloves with our friends as they are human and fail too. It's also important to recognize that every friendship we have is not meant for life; some are seasonal, so a friend might care about us for a season and then exit our life. Appreciate the season they cared for us and move on.

Our boss or workplace cares about us. Even if we have a rude or demanding boss or workplace, they care enough about us to let us keep our job. Whatever their motivations, they care that we are there. If they didn't, they would hire somebody else. (Most of them do really have a heart for us, even if it exists deep, deep, deep down.)

Our teachers care about us. Whether we're still in school or not, we had teachers who cared about our minds, our hearts, and our souls. Not every teacher did, but those special ones did. And we know who they are.

Our coaches or extracurricular instructors care about us. The people who taught us sports or special skills like dance or singing cared about us. Some may have had great and loving personalities or others may have been cold and cranky. No matter their packaging, they cared about us.

As we can see, many people care about you and me. An unhappy person often thinks that nobody cares and it's because they forget about all the strangers and people in their personal life who actually do care. In order to grow in happiness, we must continuously think about all of the people who care about us. The more we focus on this fact, the less we will succumb to the mindset that nobody cares when we hit a rough patch in our lives, circumstances, or various relationships.

Here's what Arienne from Alaska said about feeling like nobody cared about her:

Arienne's Story

There has never been a day in the past where I have felt "not alone." That's right, not alone. But what exactly does that mean?

Well, I was raised in a household where my grandparents, mom, aunts, and cousins all surrounded me daily. I participated in many sports and theatre activities all throughout school. In my early twenties, I was very social and went to clubs and other events all the time. Needless to say, I had many, many friends and acquaintances. Yet, strangely—and I know [it] doesn't make sense—I often felt lonely and like nobody cared about me.

I didn't know how to handle this feeling, so I would put on my headphones and dive into music. I would just feel the words and be more emotionally connected to the singers than to what was going on in my life—or to many of the people in my life. As I began to do this more and more, I shifted my attention from music to television shows and movies to fill my emotional voids that I didn't feel people were providing for me.

During these teenage and young adult years, I just wanted to "feel" something—even if that something was sadness or melancholy. But this desire to feel made me want to feel other things, too, and led me down a dark path. I started to experience depression, which made me long for romantic relationships that I thought would help me feel happiness, to help me cover up this emotional void for needing to be cared about. Needless to say, this didn't work; it only made things worse. I started to think that maybe I wasn't good enough for my boyfriends. Maybe I wasn't skinny enough or charming enough or smart enough. I didn't feel that I mattered to them (or others) and therefore believed that others saw me that same way too—that they thought I didn't matter either.

I realized this was a lie but it took a long time to break this lie in my life. In fact, it took over a decade of hard work. I credit my relationship with God for helping me snap out of this. But it wasn't easy. If you're feeling like nobody cares about you, I can assure you that other people do care about you—and that God cares about you. I spent too much unnecessary time being unhappy—listening to the negative voice between my ears—and beating myself up mentally, emotionally, and even physically because I felt nobody cared. I spent too much time believing this lie. I want to spare you of this. Other people really do care about you. You're not alone.

Review:

Point to Ponder: Happy People Reject the Lie That Nobody Cares About Them

Law to Remember: The Law of Recognition

Affirmation to Declare: "Recognizing that many people care about me is refreshing. I'm a truly rich person because of all the people who have helped create some of the good in my life. In my tough moments, I'm going to remember how blessed I am to have so many people around me who care. Even though some people have hurt, rejected, and ignored me, I'm grateful for the solid people in my life who haven't. This is my declaration of happiness."

For more free resources on this topic, go to www.DrRob.TV/happiness/Chapter6

CHAPTER 7

A HAPPY PERSON EVICTS ITS NEGATIVE AND CYNICAL TENETS

The Law of Positive Thinking

"Remember, what you 'feel' and what is 'real' are often very different."

- Eddie Capparucci[1]

Our worst-case scenarios almost never come true.[2]

That's right, thinking the worst about situations is usually an exercise in futility. Social science and statistics show the worst probably won't happen to us, but our minds sometimes believe that they will.[3] This is called "catastrophizing"—or catastrophic thinking—and it's the worst.[4]

Whether we're thinking about our jobs, health, relationships, circumstances, or other areas, the worst-case scenario mindset is a recipe for anxiety.[5] When we escalate situations into the most negative thoughts possible without concrete evidence, it leads to a host of negative byproducts.[6] Our productivity lowers, our creativity becomes greatly limited, our stress rises, and our unhappiness multiplies.[7]

But that's not all. Our worried minds can create actual harmful physical symptoms and go into fight or flight mode.[8] I remember a specific example from my own life. I was directing my first feature film—a fun but crazy experience—and I was worried that it would turn out horribly. I was worried my investors would hate it and that, if I didn't deliver at a high level, I would never work again (in Hollywood at least).

This caused many sleepless nights and high anxiety, to say the least. And when I delivered the first rough cut of the film to my investors, guess what happened? They **DID HATE IT!** But they allowed me to continue to develop and refine it and, by the time I delivered my second and third cuts to them, they called it "a brilliant masterpiece."

I was worried they would remove me as director if the film wasn't good enough—which I thought would have ended my entertainment career—but instead they believed in me, which helped launch me into greater projects.

But my happy ending aside, I'm not saying that you and I shouldn't be prepared for all possible scenarios. We should objectively understand the reality of our situations. But objectively understanding the reality of whatever we're going through is very different from jumping to conclusions and believing that our worst-case scenarios will come true. We should definitely let this sink in.

Although this is easy to understand in theory, it is very difficult in practice. It is difficult because we assume the worst about things often without any evidence for our assumptions. It is difficult because we exaggerate the significance or impact our worse-case scenarios might have on our lives. And it is difficult because we don't give ourselves enough credit in potentially being able to overcome the worst case just in case it does happen.

Let's think about some of these common worst-case scenarios for just a moment and our mental reactions to or interpretations of them.

Scenario 1. We are late on our rent or our mortgage. Do we believe we will be evicted? If we are evicted, do we think the world will be over or that our reputations will be ruined? Do we think we can bounce back on our feet? Are we more afraid of the actual eviction or of letting down loved ones and feeling embarrassed? Do we believe we can overcome this?

Scenario 2. Our boss chews us out. Do we believe we will be fired? If we are fired, will everything be over for us or will we eventually get a new job? Have we thought about the millions of other people who have been fired one day and hired by another organization the next? Have we really put things in perspective?

Scenario 3. Our spouse just sent us a suspicious text. Do we believe they are cheating on us or that they will dump us? If they are or if they do, do we think we will ever recover emotionally? Have we given away so much of our personal power that this person controls our happiness/unhappiness? Is the real issue our spouse acting suspiciously or is the issue us giving away our personal power to them through our own insecurities? What is our suspicion really about?

Scenario 4. Some people are gossiping about us. Do we think we can survive their gossip? Is it too embarrassing to take or overcome? Have we ever overcome gossip or people speaking negatively about us before? Are other people's opinions so strong and life-sucking we feel we just can't take them?

Scenario 5. We have been issued a bad medical report. Do we believe we will become sicker or die? Do we believe we will recover? Do we believe whether we live or die we can still choose to be happy? Are we believing the best or the worst?

After looking at some of these worst-case scenarios, most of us might have identified with experiencing at least one or two of them. But even if you didn't, you and I can still understand that our worst-case thinking is mostly just a matter of our perspective. Whatever happens with our circumstances or to us, for example, we can likely overcome with a little ingenuity—or with a little bit of better thinking. And the better and more positive our thinking is, the happier we will be become.

Here's what Jonique from Jamaica wrote to me about her experience with a worst-case scenario mindset:

Jonique's Story

The older I got, the more I would over-think. I would analyze every detail of things and stress myself out to the max about every potential negative outcome. My worst-case scenario mentality caused me severe anxiety—to the point of panic— and many bouts of unnecessary depression.

For example, I once got news that my dad needed to do a series of bone scans at the hospital. But instead of looking at this objectively as a normal routine, my mind immediately went to the worst-case scenario. I began to imagine what it would be like to lose my father. I began to imagine the pain I would feel knowing that he would never walk me down the aisle. I began to meditate on the thought that my unborn children would never know their grandfather. And so I started to cry. Uncontrollably.

I kept myself up on most nights just so that I could worry.

I stopped eating.

And I hid myself away from everyone— from all of my family and friends—because I couldn't stand the pain that I could potentially lose somebody that I loved dearly.

I behaved this way BEFORE anything had ever happened to my dad— and BEFORE we got back the results of his tests.

While I'm very happy to report that his test results were not bad, I'm sorry to say that I was. I couldn't see past my own dark what-ifs. I couldn't see past my mind's own negativity bias. I couldn't see past the crazy place I now called my mind. I couldn't see past my own worst-case scenarios. And this was my turning point.

I realized that I had adopted a dangerous mindset that would drive me insane—or worse—if I did not take action. So I immersed myself into reading and research about how to overcome it. I started to have many conversations with friends about what I needed to do to be better. And I started to read the scripture and developed the habit of stopping my mind from literally wandering into negative territory whenever it felt like it. Doing these things not only set me free, but made me much happier in the process.

A Few Ways to Overcome Worst-Case Thinking

If you find yourself being sucked into worst-case scenario thinking like Jonique, here are a few things you can do to counter it:

1. Identify when your thoughts slip from realistic anxieties to unusual, unlikely, or worst-case scenarios—or catastrophizing as the pros say.

2. Think of the various choices you have to overcome your potential worst-case scenarios so that you can stop feeling helpless and trapped by them.

3. Do your research and identify possible best-case and worst-case scenarios and see if they are likely outcomes (weigh the evidence and the facts to empower yourself).

Review:

Point to Ponder: A Happy Person Evicts Its Negative and Cynical Tenets

Law to Remember: The Law of Positive Thinking

Affirmation to Declare: "At times I've been guilty of worst-case thinking. But I realize that these thoughts are just that—thoughts! They probably won't come true and even if they do, I am resilient and can overcome them and go on with my life. I will start to think more positively in all areas of my life even if this is hard at times. This is my declaration of happiness."

For more free resources on this topic, go to www.DrRob.TV/happiness/Chapter7

CHAPTER 8

HAPPY PEOPLE EMBRACE
THEIR "FUN" SIDE

The Law of Fun

"The purpose of life is to do good and have fun.
Everything else is secondary"

- Dr. Rob Carpenter[1]

We should all be having more fun.

Yet people are having less fun today than ever before. In fact, statistics show that the average person stops having fun at age forty-five and doesn't have much fun after that.[2]

As a society, we should embrace the fact that life is about more than chores, obstacles, and getting ahead. We should embrace the fact that life is about more than trying to do or become something.

Instead, we should fully embrace that life is about enjoying ourselves. Life is about enjoying the limited time we have on this planet. Compared to the amount of time the earth has been around—4 billion years—our lives will last only half a second (seventy-eight to eighty years—or if you're really fortunate a little more than half a second, or one hundred years).[3]

Now, enjoying ourselves doesn't mean that we should shirk our responsibilities or not get things done. And this also doesn't mean that we should live a life of hedonism or simple pleasure-seeking. Doing this will leave us with broken finances, broken relationships, and in complete unhappiness.[4]

But what it does mean is that we should give ourselves permission to let loose—daily. As the famous Van Wilder (in the movie of the same name) said, "Life is too short, you're never going to get out alive."[5] And this is all too true.

If we're not enjoying ourselves every day, if we're not laughing and smiling every day, what is the point of living? No degree, goal, accomplishment, material item, or money we have in this life can be taken with us into the next. It all stays here.

If we're busting our chops living stressed, frustrated, and not enjoying ourselves because we're trying to get some temporary things we can't take with us when we pass, this seems like a worthless way to live. It doesn't matter if people applaud us or if we are considered successful; all of this is worthless if we are not enjoying life.

We need to be having more fun.[6] We need to laugh more—and we need to laugh more at ourselves.

But even though most of us probably agree with this, it might be hard to put it into practice when dealing with the everyday pressures of life. Here are some obstacles we often face in having more fun.

Obstacles to Having More Fun

- Feeling like we need to defend ourselves constantly
- Getting upset or offended when other people question our beliefs (at home, work, or on social media)
- Becoming angry or defensive about people or situations
- Worrying too much or being constantly stressed out
- Being too harsh on ourselves
- Holding onto grudges from people who hurt us
- Comparing ourselves to other people constantly
- Never laughing at ourselves
- Taking ourselves too seriously
- Thinking we're the center of the universe

Of course, in a crazy and hostile world it's easy to fall into these traps. But that said, even if we have fallen into these traps, we don't have to stay in them. We can get out. We must get out—for our own sake and for the sake of our happiness. Here's what happens when we do escape these traps and start having more fun.

Benefits of Having Fun

- We statistically lengthen our lifespan.[7]
- We decrease the odds of a heart attack or heart disease by 40%.[8]
- Our muscles stay relaxed for up to 45 minutes afterwards.[9]

- Our immune system improves, our blood pressure lowers, and our oxygen and blood circulation improve.[10]

- Our anxieties and tension ease, and our mood improves.[11]

- We have a higher threshold for pain and become more resilient against adversity.[12]

- We lower our stress levels and become more relaxed.[13]

- Our short-term memory is 200% greater than when we don't.[14]

- The quality of our sleep improves by 400%.[15]

- And our relationships with people dramatically improve.[16]

Here's what professional comedian and Hollywood actor Kelly Perine had to say about having fun in life:

Kelly's Story

HOW DARE YOU CALL ME OVERLY SERI-OUS! I don't want to hear crap about studies that say you can't be happy after forty-five. I'm fifty-one, and there was a time at forty-seven where I remember smiling almost every third day. So screw the statistics that says people stop having fun after forty-five.

Yes, I've had obstacles. Yes, I've had trials and tribu-lations. But I've earned my badge of toughness. I've also earned a sweet Sag/Aftra pension because I've worked hard at my career for twenty-six years. And I believe the fact that I get to have fun every day is because I've made my own opportunities and lived life the way I wanted to. But I'm not just talking about Pollyanna nonsense here: I just looked at what I'll be making every month from my pension when I hit fifty-nine and a half. And daaaanggg…I'm going to get PAID.

In my work, I've been serious about being on time, being a professional, showing kindness to everyone on the set, hitting my marks and knowing my lines, but I've also made sure to have fun along the way. If I didn't, I wouldn't be enjoying the sick sundeck I'm going to have added to my house…

As we can see, laughing and having more fun like Kelly mentions can dramatically improve our lives. We should resolve today to live a life of fun—and be a person of fun. We should start a "fun" journal and record all of the fun and funny things we have done or that have ever happened to us—and review it regularly (I promise you it'll bring us great happiness!).

Review:

Point to Ponder: Happy People Embrace Their "Fun" Side

Law to Remember: The Law of Fun

Affirmation to Declare: "Starting today, I'm going to live a life of healthy fun. I'm going to be a fun person, and I'm going to try to squeeze as much joy and fun out of each day as possible. In order for me to be at peak happiness, I need to be having as much fun as I can at home, at work, and in my daily life. Yes, I will get done what I need to, but I'm going to have fun doing it. This is my declaration of happiness."

For more free resources on this topic, go to www.DrRob.TV/happiness/Chapter8

PART TWO

MASTERING HAPPINESS
IN YOUR EMOTIONS

MASTERING HAPPINESS IN YOUR EMOTIONS:
Introduction

Now that we've explored the traps our minds face, let's turn to the traps we face emotionally. Our emotions are wonderful things, but they can also be double-edged swords.

On the one hand, our emotions can add passion to our relationships, meaning to our work, and add excitement to our lives and our futures. They are one of the greatest gifts we have as human beings, and can bring us immense pleasure, joy, and happiness. Our emotions can help us feel like the BEAUTIFUL MASTERPIECES that we truly are.

But emotions can also do the opposite. They can stress us out. They can bring us sadness and depression. They can create fear, anger, and jealousy inside of us. And they can do a litany of other negative things in our lives. In short, our emotions can stir up intense feelings inside of us that sometimes feel inescapable— and sometimes make our lives feel like total wrecks.

Like with our thoughts, the way we allow ourselves to feel about the various issues in our lives is completely up to us. Let's continue our journey so that you can begin to see how you can master your emotions so that you can climb higher on your own Happiness Spectrum.

CHAPTER 9

HAPPY PEOPLE STARE FEAR STRAIGHT IN THE FACE

The Law of Fearlessness

"Everything you've ever wanted is on the other side of fear."

- George Addair[1]

H uman beings are, unfortunately, wired for fear.[2]

The most powerful media organizations know this.[3]
The most dominant corporations know this.[4]
The most cunning politicians know this.[5]
And the most deadly criminals, drug syndicates, and rebel and terror groups know this too.[6]

They know they do not have to appeal to our logic to get us to purchase, believe, watch, or do something. All they have to do is appeal to our fears.

This is one of the reasons so many people are unhappy and living anxiously—it is because fear has become a strategy and commodity in society, and it is everywhere. It is the secret to success for many and it is the secret to control. And no wonder: Research shows that 84% of people are afraid of something, often of one of more of the following:[7]

- Fear of failure
- Fear of rejection
- Fear of being judged
- Fear of embarrassment
- Fear of public speaking
- Fear of abandonment
- Fear of loss
- Fear of the unknown
- Fear of death
- Fear of missing out
- Fear of [insert the blank]

News agencies, television shows and movies, and other creative types have made a fortune off us by exploiting or emphasizing one or more of our fears.[8] Unfortunately, study after study shows exactly how they strategically tap into our phobias.[9]

But regardless of the motives for why this is happening or the means by which it is happening, what is most important is that it *is* happening. I want to help us move beyond the culture of fear we live in, however, so that we can better understand our fears. When we do, we can learn to deal with them so that we do not have to let them control us or cause anymore unhappiness in our lives. After all, empirical research shows that the overwhelming majority of our fears will never come true so why live with all of this baggage in the meantime?[10]

The Fears in Life

The reality is there are some major and minor fears that we have experienced ALL our lives. Some of our fears came as a result of intuition, for example. Some of our fears came from a negative experience (or negative experiences). And some of our fears came because of excessive worry about how something could hurt, ruin, or destroy our lives.

In other words, some of our fears originated naturally, some of our fears originated through experience, and some of our fears originated because we learned them.[11] And understanding how our fears begin is the first step to managing and defeating them—and to improving our happiness.

1. Fear is natural.

Any therapist will tell us that some of our fears are natural and intuitive without any prior causes. And in some cases, this is healthy. We need to intuitively know, for example, when and if we are in danger, and how to take steps to avoid it. We need to recognize the voice telling us not to trust this person or enter into that bad financial deal and the like.

2. Fear is experienced.

We also have fears that result because of an experience (or experiences). We remember the moment we got the bad news we didn't want to hear, for example. We remember experiencing the traumatic events that rocked us physically, mentally, emotionally, and even spiritually. We remember those experiences and we never want them to happen again—and so therefore we fear them.

3. Fear is learned.

And sometimes we fear things because we learn to fear them—even if we have never personally experienced them before. We might have never paid attention to an issue before, for example, and after watching a news segment on it, we might go out and search for every negative piece of information on it and make ourselves afraid. We might call it educating or informing ourselves, but when done in excess we learn to fear things that maybe we shouldn't.

Here's what Joe from Claremont, California told me about his experience with fear:

Joe's Story

I always wanted to be an actor. Even from the time I was a little boy, I knew I wanted to be in front of the camera or on stage. It was just in my bones and I don't know why. I remember one time my parents had guests over who asked me and my brother what we wanted to be when we grew up. I told them proudly that I was going to be an actor. My brother said he was going to be a watermelon.

But despite the laughs, my father—who was a serious professor at a very prestigious university— sat me down and told me how foolish the thought was. How could I ever be an actor? He said. How could I know the first thing about acting? He said. How could I possibly beat out thousands of other people to land gigs? He said.

How could I really out-compete others who were better looking and more talented than me? He said.

I was six.

My father's own fears were so strong that he decided it was better to try to talk me out of my dream early on than to support me—even in grade school—to see if I could really make it in acting.

And year after year, he told me how he had no confidence in my ability to be successful.

But instead of rebelling against him, I started to believe him. Maybe I wasn't good enough, I thought. Maybe I wasn't talented enough. Maybe I wasn't good looking enough. And before I knew it, I had caught his fear like a virus and made it my own.

Even though I still pursued acting, the doubts of my father—and now my own doubts—were weighing on my mind constantly. I even found myself in the middle of auditions not only nervous, but shutting down. I would sweat. I would hyperventilate. And I would get piercing anxiety. There were some auditions where I even experienced full on panic attacks. All because of my fear.

I learned fear from my dad and, in some ways, I was guilty of passing on my fears to others. Not only about acting, but about other things I had learned to be fearful about. Without even knowing it, I thought I was being reasonable or responsible—or keeping it real—but my maturity was just fear wrapped in sophistication.

> I ultimately was able to overcome my fears. But not without a lot of effort. I had to put one foot in front of the other and do the work I felt called in my heart to do to break the grip of fear on my life. You can too, if you take steps to help yourself.

These are great words from Joe that I'm sure many of us can identify with. We must learn to trust ourselves to overcome our fears so that we can become happier. But now the question is how?

Our Minor Fears Can Be Managed and Changed

Regardless of whether our fears are natural, experienced, or learned we can take basic steps to alter how we perceive them. This is important because our fears can only harm or control us if we let them go unchallenged.

Fear can be unlearned.[12] If we learn something, we can unlearn it. Just as we can learn an incorrect way to solve a math problem, we can learn a correct way to solve it. Unlearning fear comes by not giving it a place in our lives. If we fear certain things, for example, we should not watch television shows, listen to music or podcasts, or read about these things that trigger our fears (you'd be surprised at how many people actually do this). The less we focus on fear the less our fear will focus on us—because what we feed our minds grow. If we feed it weeds, it will grow weeds (and fear is weeds). However, if we feed our minds the right nutrients and maintain them, we can have nicely manicured thoughts and emotions that are based on reality, not paranoia.

Fear can be un-experienced. Sometimes the best way to overcome a fear is to experience it ourselves. If we fear flying, for example, we can hop on a plane and see that everything will be just fine. If we fear drowning, we can take a swim class. If we fear dogs, we can go to a local pet store and pet a sweet puppy. Whatever our fear, we can take it head on. This may not always be possible in certain cases (we do not want to overcome sickness by making ourselves sick, for example, or other cases that would bring us harm), but it is possible in many cases. We often fear what hurt us in the past because of one or two negative experiences. However, if we have one or two positive experiences with the things that originally brought us fear we can profoundly change how we perceive them and our fears related to them.

We can educate ourselves about our fears to overcome them. There are some things we have always been afraid of. We may have always been terrified of roller coasters, for example. But the best way to deal with roller coasters is to educate ourselves on their safety and expose ourselves to them. This can be true of so many other issues that we fear too. We fear these issues because we do not understand them and because we have not had any real experience with them. Information and immersion are key for us to dethrone many lifelong fears we might be facing.

One Bonus Tip to Overcome Fear

But in addition to unlearning, un-experiencing, and educating ourselves about our fears, we can also do something else to help us in our journey to greater happiness: we can learn to look at our fears objectively.[12] We can learn to detach ourselves from them. We can learn to become a third-party observer to our fears.

To do this, we should simply imagine writing a letter to somebody else who is experiencing one of our fears. (Imagine, too, that we have already broken this fear in our life and have become an expert for others on how to break this fear.) We should describe the fear they are facing objectively to them, why they may or may not be experiencing that fear, and offer some rational, objective solutions for them to help get over it.

Now, let's do this exercise for ourselves. Let's grab something to write with and write an objective letter to ourselves about our top three fears and how we can start to get over them. Go ahead. We have time.

If you did the exercise, congratulations! You have just done something 99% of people in the world have never done. If you have not, please go back and do it—it will be so helpful to your growth and happiness, and help you understand why much of what you fear is just in your head.

How does looking at your fears objectively make you feel? Does it expose any unhelpful thinking or irrational thoughts you have about your fears? Do you feel more empowered to manage and overcome them now that you see through a third-person's perspective?

I hope so. This exercise helped me tremendously and I hope it brings great comfort to your life

Review:

Point to Ponder: Happy People Stare Fear Straight in the Face

Law to Remember: The Law of Fearlessness

Affirmation to Declare: "In the past, I've had fears that I allowed to exist unchallenged. But today I am choosing to dethrone these fears. Today I am choosing to look at my fears objectively knowing that most of what I fear will never come to pass, and I take great comfort in that. I'm not going to allow my fears to continue to make me unhappy. I'm choosing to be more fearless in my life little by little. This is my declaration of happiness."

For more free resources on this topic, go to www.DrRob.TV/happiness/Chapter9

CHAPTER 10

HAPPY PEOPLE UNDERSTAND WORRYING IS A HUGE TIME SUCK

The Law of Chill

"Worry often gives a small thing a big shadow."

- Swedish Proverb[1]

Worrying is the source of most of our problems.

Worrying is the source of most of our unhappiness.

We worry about money, relationships, and our health. We worry about getting old, feeling attractive, and meeting our goals. And we worry about thousands of other things.

Most of our worries are due to two factors. First, overestimating the likelihood that our fears will happen to us. And second, underestimating our ability to cope or handle a situation if our fears do happen to come true.

The Stress Hormone

When we worry we release the stress hormone called "cortisol."[2] Cortisol not only raises our heart rate and blood pressure, but it also attacks our immune systems, leading to a host of other negative health issues.[3] These health issues range from higher likelihood of catching a cold and having digestion problems, to developing cancer or having a heart attack, to erectile dysfunction and fertility challenges.[4]

Yet despite many of us knowing the risk worrying poses to our health, we continue to worry about many things. As we explored in the last chapter, even though most of our fears will statistically probably never come true we worry about them anyway.

Anxiety and Panic Attacks at an All-Time High

Right now, millions of people are suffering from severe worrying, also known as anxiety.[5] In fact, almost one in five people are— over 68 million people.[6] But the sad reality is that 75% of people have never or are not able to seek proper treatment for it.[7] Left unattended, anxiety can spiral out of control and usually starts manifesting with one of these types of thoughts:

"I'm losing control"…

"I feel like I'm going crazy"…

"I can't breathe"…

This type of anxiety can easily turn into panic attacks (traumatizing emotional nightmares).[8] They leave us feeling a sense of terror and doom, and often repeat in cycles—striking at any time. But they affect not just our emotions. They also affect our bodies. Our heart rate increases; we experience dizziness, heaviness, and chills; our muscles twitch; our palms sweat; and a host of other negative, uncontrollable physical ailments attack our body.[9] Panic attacks are some of the worst things we can ever experience as a human being, and millions of people are having them at this very moment.

But even if we don't experience panic attacks, even normal worry and anxiety can have debilitating effects on us. Here is how Mary Grace from New York handled her penchant for worrying:

Mary Grace's Story

My life was stressing me out. And so were the expectations others were putting on me and that I was putting on myself. You see, as an actress and model, I'm constantly being told by others what I should look like. How I should dress. What roles I am acceptable and unacceptable for. And what my relationships should look like. I'm constantly being told what restaurants I should go to, what makeup and hair styles I should wear, and what my life should be like in order to be cool.

For most of my life, I have felt like I have to live up to some societal idea of beauty and success to be acceptable to others or even to myself. All of this pressure from others—all of this pressure I put on myself—used to stress me out. Major league. In fact, it more than stressed me out. It caused excessive worry at times and even anxiety.

For me, I believed the story that I had to do more to be more, that I had to achieve society's standard of success to be happy. So I juggled having multiple jobs, graduate school, staying fit, and trying to go to every social event I could just because I thought I had to do these things to be successful. To be accept-able. I kept adding balls in the air that I had to jug-gle just to keep up. But the funny thing about this is that the more balls I added, the more likely I was to drop one of the balls. I noticed when one ball would drop, all the other balls would fall down with it!

When I realized this domino effect, I started to set priorities in my life and surrender the results to God. I increased my time in meditation and prayer, cut my hours at work, spent more time with the people I loved, and began the process of healing from the expecta-tions placed on me by others and myself. My health turned around, my bookings increased, and spiritual, relational, and financial abundance began to appear effortlessly in my life. It hasn't always been easy, but realizing that I don't need to juggle all of these balls has helped set me free of worry and anxiety.

There's Good News: We Can Reduce Worry

The good news is, just like Mary Grace, we can overcome our worries. We do not have to accept our fate as being that of a worry wart. We can change how we feel about what stresses us out. We can change our thought patterns, emotional responses, and daily habits to gain control of our worry. Here are a few scientifically proven tips to help show us how.

1. **Journal our worries**. Similar to the writing-our-fears-down exercise in the last chapter, we can journal our worries and look at them objectively.

2. **Identify a "worry-time."** We can pick 30 minutes a day to have a meeting with our worries and how we will solve them, and then move on with our day.[10]

3. **Breathe, meditate, and exercise daily.** Using yogic breathing techniques, meditation, and low- or high-level exercise to get our bodies moving will release the happiness hormone (dopamine) in our body to counter our negative cortisol.[11]

4. **Reduce social media engagement.** Social media increases our stress levels, so we can cut them back in small doses starting right now.[12]

5. **Hug someone daily**. And I mean a real hug—not a butt out, barely touching someone kind of hug. Connecting with somebody else is one of the greatest stress relievers we can regularly experience, so we should hug someone deeply.[13]

These practices will help us reduce the worry in our lives. I encourage you to do the ones that work best for you and to research other techniques most appropriate for your life. The less you worry the happier you will become.

Review:

Point to Ponder: Happy People Understand Worrying Is a Huge Time Suck

Law to Remember: The Law of Chill

Affirmation to Declare: "I admit that I have been a worry wart at times. But I now understand that worrying can negatively affect my health, and so I choose not to worry like I used to. In fact, I choose to just chill. This will be a process for me, but I will get better at managing and reducing my worry. I will stop overestimating my fears and underestimating my ability to handle them. I may not be worry-less, but I choose to worry-LESS. This is my declaration of happiness."

For more free resources on this topic, go to www.DrRob.TV/happiness/Chapter10

CHAPTER 11

TRUE HAPPINESS IS REFINED IN DELAYED GRATIFICATION

The Law of Patience

"Without delayed gratification, there is no power over self."

- Sunday Adelaja[1]

Most of us live with a great sense of urgency. We must hurry up, act faster, and get moving. We feel restless often and are intolerant of delays. Our goals, our schedules, and our instant gratification are incredibly important to us.

It's no wonder that we feel stress if anything thwarts our plans. If something causes a hiccup to our agenda, we think:

- Why is this taking so long?
- Why are they being so slow?
- Can't this just speed up?
- Ugh, this is so frustrating.

The more ambitious we are, the more likely we are to think these thoughts too. We are in a rush because we're fixated on the future or some end goal. We are skipping the present moment so we can live in the future where we think we'll be happy.

Why Impatience Is Hurting Us

But our impatient attitudes have the potential to hurt us.[2] I remember a time from my own life where it almost cost me everything. I was raising money for a project and paid lots of money to an investor (who was on a very popular reality television show) who promised to introduce me to other major investors. I wanted the fast track to other investors so I could launch my project quickly (I wanted things to happen right away).

But after paying this reality TV investor, he went radio silent, to my chagrin. Day after day and week after week went by and still I had not gotten a single introduction from him. I remember praying and asking God why things weren't happening faster? I heard nothing, so I decided to confront this investor (by going to his office unannounced) to see when he was going to make the introductions so I could launch my project. Needless to say, he wasn't happy I did that.

Months went by and still I had not gotten any meaningful introductions. I felt stupid for not only losing the money I paid him but also because I felt like I lost the larger opportunity for my project (as it seemed it was fizzling out). But then something happened.

I opened the *LA Times* website and saw a headline, *"Real House-wives of Beverly Hills* Husband Dead." My heart sunk after I clicked the link and saw the investor's picture. Not only was he dead, but the article showed he was involved in a Ponzi scheme and with the Mafia, whom he owed money to. Had I gotten involved with "his investors" (the Mafia), I probably would not be here talking to you today. I was so impatient and wanted things to happen so quickly that I could have unintentionally gotten involved with some very bad people and into a lot of trouble.

Drawbacks of Impatience

My hope is that you never are put in an experience like that yourself. But you have probably been in lots of other situations yourself where your patience was stretched just like mine was. Here are a few common things impatience does to people like you and me:

1. **Impatience causes us to switch our goals too quickly.** Whether it's a major life or career goal—or even a minor one—impatience causes us to move on when we feel like things aren't going fast enough.

2. **Impatience causes stress.** Impatience releases stress hormones into our system, which contributes to our overall feelings of unhappiness. Even if we achieve our goals while being impatient, we will still feel stressed and unhappy if we reach them.

3. **Impatience increases our irrationality.** When we're impatient, we tend to do things we wouldn't normally do. Darting in and out of traffic, being short and demanding with people, cutting corners at work, and various other things. Some of these behaviors can be deadly, illegal, unethical, or just plain rude. Again, all because we are being impatient.

Why Delayed Gratification Is Scientifically Better for Us

But even though we know we should be more patient, we still might ignore this—especially if we are in a turbo -charged workplace or environment. We might have the mindset that if we don't do anything—and quickly and with aggression—we're not going to be successful. But this idea has been disproven by science.[3]

Studies show that we will be happier if we experience some delays in our goals and gratification.[4] They also show that we will have more satisfaction in our career, relationships, health, and finances.

Here's what Gamaliel, a firefighter from Maryland, told me about his battle with his own impatience:

Gamaliel's Story

I never made Eagle Scout because I was impatient and didn't think I was progressing fast enough. I never finished JROTC in high school because I was impatient and dropped out. For so many things in my life, I was just so damned impatient. I wanted things to go faster. I wanted to accomplish my goals more quickly. I didn't want to wait for anything.

I remember one time where my impatience really ended up costing me. I had bought a season pass to the local ski mountain and, although I had never gone snowboarding before, I decided I would skip the free lessons they gave for first time snowboarders because I wanted to start right away with my more experienced snowboarding friends. What this meant was that, after a couple trips down the moderate slopes to practice, I decided to enter the massive and highly advanced snowboard park because I just couldn't wait to do what I wanted to do.

On my first attempt to go off a medium-size jump I completely lost my balance. I smacked the snow and incredible pain rushed through my body. I was rushed to the hospital and had fortunately only severely fractured my wrist. It could have been much worse, as it had been for others who became paralyzed or lost their lives doing this because they were impatient and didn't want to take the free snowboarding lessons. I could have avoided my pain if only I slowed down a little bit and not tried to be something I wasn't at the time—namely an advanced snowboarder.

After this experience, I became more reflective and started to learn all sorts of things I didn't know before. And as simple as it sounds, learning about exercise and fitness during this time was my most important lesson. It helped heal me of the curse of impatience. I started to appreciate the very slow process of changing and improving my body through regular, methodical exercise.

Once I started to understand the time it takes to make visible progress in my body through exercise, it became easier for me to be patient with other aspects of my life. As a firefighter, military reservist, doctor, husband, and father, I have had a wide range of experiences needing patience. Learning not to rush through exercise is what changed my perspective on patience, and what changed my life. It is what has enabled me to slow down and literally save many other people's lives.

Ways to Overcome Impatience

Just like Gamaliel we can learn to be more patient. Here are just a few helpful tips.

1. **Write down everything that causes us impatience.** For example, if we hate sitting in traffic, ask: Where am I trying to rush off to? Why am I in such a rush to get there? Is the traffic really my problem? Or is it because I'm in a hurry to reach my end goal by a certain time and believe I'll be unhappy or unsuccessful if I don't reach it? If I don't reach my goal, is that a reflection on my self-worth or on how others will perceive me?

2. **Take deep breaths.** Every time we experience impatience, we can take three deep breaths and realize it's going to be ok. This will help us physically understand we will eventually get to our goal or destination regardless of any hiccups.

3. **Refocus our perspective to be more objective.** This allows us to understand that the universe doesn't run on our schedule. We can be more objective about the delays in our lives and make mental and emotional adjustments to them. When we realize it's not all about us, we'll feel much more at peace—and much happier.

4. **Be more patient with ourselves.** This allows us to remove our inner critics that tell us we needed to be faster, stronger, richer, and better like yesterday.

5. **Always weigh costs and benefits.** We can think about if being impatient is really worth the added stress and unhappiness.

6. **Be more empathetic for others.** As frustrating as this is sometimes, developing more understanding of others

who are slow, rude, or incompetent will grow our empathy (and when our empathy grows, so does our gratitude and happiness).

7. **Eat slowly.** Eating slowly increases our patience, research shows.[5]

8. **Find a slow hobby.** Hobbies like painting, knitting, sculpture, and more can help slow our minds and our rushed pace of life.[6]

Review:

Point to Ponder: True Happiness Is Refined in Delayed Gratification

Law to Remember: The Law of Patience

Affirmation to Declare: "Being impatient has been one of my chief struggles. But I don't have to struggle with it. I will take proactive steps to become more patient over time. This won't happen overnight, but I have the tools to do it. This is my declaration of happiness."

For more free resources on this topic, go to www.DrRob.TV/happiness/Chapter11

CHAPTER 12

HAPPY PEOPLE STUDY THEIR PRESSURE POINTS

The Law of Zen

"Speak when you are angry and you will make the best speech you will ever regret."

- Ambrose Bierce[1]

When life gets to us, we can become easily frustrated.[2] And no matter who we are, we experience frustration.

Sometimes our frustrations are expressed through irritation and passive-aggressiveness while at other times they can turn into biting anger and even rage. Regardless, the more often we get frustrated or angry, the less likely we are to be happy.

It doesn't just have to be major things that make us frustrated either. Often, it can be minor things. And I know I don't have to tell you, it's the minor things that can usually quickly get us all bent out of shape.

Minor Things That Often Frustrate or Anger Us

Here are a few minor things that get to most people:

- People eating food with their mouth open.
- Automatic updates on our phones or computers when we need to use them.
- People not replacing toilet paper.
- People who take up the entire sidewalk in front of us who walk slowly.
- Having to see the cashier at the gas station after we attempted to pay at the pump.
- And more.

Although these things are trivial, they are significant enough to alter our mood and frustrate us. They can quickly take us from a state of bliss to a state of miss in zero to sixty seconds. But if we're easily irritated by minor things like these, we usually have deeper issues going on too. I'll get to these issues in a second. But first, it's important to understand that if we're thrown off by small things, we are also likely to be thrown off by major things too.

Major Things That Frustrate or Anger Us

Here are just a few big things that tick most of us off:

- Bad drivers and bad parking.
- People who talk loudly on their cell phone in a public space.
- People who are nosy.

- Being blamed for something we didn't do.
- When a baby cries in an airplane, restaurant, or movie and their parents don't stop it.
- When people don't say thank you when we help them.
- Liars and lies.
- Stubbing our big toe.
- Things that personally anger us.
- And more.

Clearly, this list is small. There can literally be hundreds or thousands of other things that can get under our skin. You know what they are, so I don't have to list them. (Ok, just one more: for me, a big pet peeve is when I see teenagers walking through a crosswalk very slowly using their cell phone oblivious to the traffic they're holding up. This just really irritates me, but I digress.)

The important thing to understand is that some of the things that cause us anger are natural and expected. When we experience unfairness, loss, or pain, for example—especially if it's created by others—our tempers can go through the roof. This is understandable. But I'm not here to make excuses so we stay this way. We've got to empower ourselves so we can overcome this trap in our lives because the reality is that we will always encounter situations that will test and frustrate us. And this is not just every once in a while. This could be every month, every week, or even every day (or multiple times a day). The better we're able to manage our frustrations and even anger at the things we can't control—and we can't control most things in life—the more we'll be able to maintain our peace and happiness.

Here's what James from California wrote to me about his experiences overcoming frustration and anger in his life:

James's Story

My dad wasn't the most pleasant guy to be around. While he could be financially supportive, he could also flip on you in a heartbeat if he didn't get what he wanted. He would assault you with a blizzard of accusations, expletives, and outright hatred. And he could also be quite manipulative, using guilt trips to control you.

I remember when I was in high school how he'd go after my mom and furiously strangle her to retaliate against me if I didn't follow his every order. And I would have to separate them.

The irony is that he was an expert in his field of naval engineering, often chairing subcommittees before Congress, and could get three-star generals on the phone with a single call. He was considered charming and loyal by his friends and many women found him very attractive. You see, none of these people knew about his dark side—his temper was reserved only for those closest to him (his family).

Over the years I learned to keep my distance from him to try to control my own anger toward him. But after my mom passed, I could no longer do this—I had to become directly involved in overseeing his new caretakers.

At that time, he was eighty-six and he badly fell. So I found myself running from Los Angeles to Orange

County daily to address problems he was creating for his caretakers during his recovery. And with every other visit or phone call, I was greeted with the same accusations and blizzard of expletives he would tell me growing up—that I was a selfish, rotten son, who was nothing in his eyes.

I became very exhausted and even angrier than I had been growing up because now I had to nurse somebody who hated me back to health. So I decided to lash out— at God. I would yell at God to tell him to kill my dad, and if he didn't want to kill him, to kill me instead. I actually contemplated sitting my dad down in the dining room and putting a gun to his head. I just wanted all of my anger and frustrations to end. I can't emphasize enough how vitriolic my dad could be and how it was rubbing off on me. Oh, by the way, I was also a department chair at a major university and I didn't need this stuff in my life—or need it to spill over into my students' lives through my interactions with them.

But I would continue to visit my dad and care for him. And during each visit, I would ask God, "why me, when will it end?"

But then one day he passed.

It was hard to process at the time because of all of the anger and hatred he had toward me. But ironically, I didn't feel anger at his passing or even relief—I just felt that I had fulfilled my obligation to him.

I still feel his behavior toward me was a big waste of my life and made it a living hell for quite a long time. But I just somehow knew caring for him was something I was supposed to do regardless of how he treated me or made me feel. I now believe that for whatever reason, we sometimes get assignments from God like this, which test us so that we can learn to be happier regardless of what we're going through. And, I am happy to say that I think I passed the test after failing it for so long…and I think I can continue to learn to overcome the anger that once defined my life so that I can become a completely happy me.

How to Overcome Frustration or Anger

I feel for James and what he had to endure growing up and for so many decades in his life. It caused him incredible anger, not just because it was unfair but because he felt he couldn't control the situation. But there are several proven ways we can overcome our frustrations and anger even in the midst of experiencing them.[3] When we do, we'll be much happier.

Immediate Ways We Can Overcome Our Frustrations or Anger in the Moment

First, take three deep breaths and then count to ten.

Second, look up (people tend to look down and avoid eye contact when they're frustrated or angry which only worsens their anger).

Third, start to make exaggerated facial features (I know this is funny and strange, but if we act like Jim Carry used to in his hit 90s movies it will give us significant emotional release).

Fourth, dance (if you're able—even if you're a bad dancer this will reduce any stress you might have very quickly).

Fifth, do ten jumping jacks (again if you're able).

Sixth, massage the back of our necks or anywhere where we might be feeling tension and sing happy birthday to ourselves while we do it.

Seventh, snap a rubber band.

Eighth, give ourselves a timeout to walk around, do some exercise, and think objectively about solutions to our problems.

Of course, these are only Band-Aid solutions but they can be very helpful when we feel anger and frustration rushing at us in any given situation. Now, let's talk about a few deeper ways to overcome any anger we might be feeling.

Deeper Ways We Can Overcome Our Frustrations or Anger

First, use "I feel" statements instead of "You are" statements. For example, instead of saying "You are a no-good bum piece of scum" for not taking out the trash, say, "I feel irritated that you didn't take out the trash when I asked you to." This will help process anger in better, more constructive ways.

Second, study what makes us frustrated and angry so we can learn how to avoid situations that trigger our anger when possible. Remember, anger and frustrations are emotional, cognitive, and behavioral and we need to see how angry situations are making us feel, think, and behave.

Third, note our feelings in a journal (so that we can reflect on them but not act on them).

Fourth, address the situation (or person) that is frustrating or angering us once we're calm and ready.

Review:

Point to Ponder: Happy People Study Their Pressure Points

Law to Remember: The Law of Zen

Affirmation to Declare: "I get angry and frustrated sometimes. Sometimes I should but a lot of times I shouldn't. If I take steps to lessen my frustrations in the moment, I won't make any bad decisions that could hurt me later. If I study my frustrations, I can develop strategies to manage and overcome them. I will commit myself to not allow the things that used to make me frustrated anymore. And I will commit myself to having more Zen in my life. This will be a process, but I will be victorious in the end. This is my declaration of happiness."

For more free resources on this topic, go to www.DrRob.TV/happiness/Chapter12

CHAPTER 13

HAPPY EMOTIONS ARE CREATED BY A HURRICANE OF ENCOURAGEMENT

The Law of Encouragement

"In spite of everything I shall rise again: I will take up my pencil, which I have forsaken in my great discouragement, and I will go on with my drawing."

- Vincent Van Gogh[1]

Discouragement is an enemy of our souls.

Even if we aren't currently discouraged about something, most of us have been at one point or another—and will probably be discouraged at some point in the future over something.

For those of us who are presently discouraged, maybe it's over a relationship or finances. Or maybe we're discouraged over some aspect of our health or failing to meet a goal we set for ourselves. Or maybe we're discouraged over something else. But regardless of the source or object of our discouragement, it is very real.

Here's the toughest part of it all: If our discouragement grows too strong, it will eventually turn into chronic sadness and depression.[2] This is a reality for hundreds of millions of people, especially women. In fact, young women are 200% more likely to be depressed than young men according to studies.[3] Adolescents are also especially likely to be depressed.[4]

My heart goes out to you if you are currently feeling this way and I'm going to try to help you pull through as best as I can. I know it's not your choice you're feeling this way and that you can't just snap out of it. You deserve better than feeling discouragement or depression, and you can start to overcome these emotions in time. Here are just a few reasons why many of us tend to get discouraged at times:

Reasons We Might Be Discouraged

1. **Our relationships and community ties are not as strong as they could be**. If we're not meaningfully connected to those around us, we're more likely to feel alone, isolated, and discouraged, especially if we receive bad or unwelcome news.

2. **We're more focused on external goals than internal ones**. If we're over-emphasizing external or financial success (or if we have the wrong definition of it), we are scientifically more likely to experience anxiety and depression.[5] In other words, if we tie our happiness to our career success, we are setting ourselves up for long bouts of discouragement and emotional instability throughout our lives.

3. **Our expectations are a little skewed**. If we are unrealistic about how life and the world work, we tend to become disappointed when we don't get the things we want in our artificially imposed time frames. For example, if we are

impatient or don't get the things we want when we want them, we can psych ourselves out unless we develop alternative (and healthy) ways of looking at whatever is discouraging us.

4. **Our emotions are hurt because other people have mistreated us.** If we allow ourselves to take in the negative words and behaviors of other people toward us, we can become easily discouraged. Even worse, we can become even more discouraged if we try to analyze or understand other people's negative behavior toward us, especially when we don't deserve it.

Of course, there are lots of other reasons you or I can be discouraged but these are four of the primary culprits. Here's what Tom from Great Britain told me about his experience dealing with discouragement when he was mistreated by an editor:

Tom's Story

I had been commissioned to write an article for my dream magazine—a world famous magazine I had worked my entire life to one day be featured in. I poured my heart into my piece and, after a lot of blood, sweat, and tears, I loved the end result of my creation. But the editor of the magazine...not so much.

Not only did this editor not love the article, she made it her mission to let me know how stupid I was to even submit what I did. She called my work childlike, derivative, unimaginative, lifeless, and idiotic.

Her comments completely devastated me.

Even though I was a published writer, I couldn't handle what she said. So I absorbed it.

At first, I was angry. Then I found her criticism laughable. Then I was irritated. Then I became angry again—deeply, bitterly angry. And, before long, this bitter anger turned into sadness. I felt like there was nothing I could do about it and like I couldn't "unfeel" the discouragement that was trying to murder my soul.

So for the next few weeks every word I wrote sounded childlike, derivative, unimaginative, lifeless, and idiotic to me. I had let the editor's poisonous words seep into my heart and I couldn't escape the mental and emotional prison she put me in—and that I put myself in.

As I got older, however, I started to realize that the bitter criticism I had faced from the editor wasn't about me at all. It was completely about the editor. I thought to myself, maybe she had a bad morning, or experienced road rage, or got into a fight with her spouse or colleague. Maybe she was going through something else in her life and decided to use me as a pinata to unleash all of her own feelings of anger and self-pity and worthlessness. Maybe she just couldn't control herself or her own emotions.

Today when I remember the pain I felt at that criticism I remind myself to be kind to those around me, and not to take such criticism so much to heart. I realize I can only become discouraged by other people if I let them discourage me. But if I don't let them, I won't feel the discouragement that once almost killed me.

I appreciate these wise and heartfelt words from Tom. Not only did he recognize the source of his discouragement, but he learned that he didn't have to accept what others said to him—or the negative feelings they made him feel about himself. Likewise, you and I can learn to overcome discouragement by using Tim's approach and a few other researched-based methods.[5] Here's how:[6]

How to Overcome Discouragement

1. **Take the long view.** When we stop focusing on our setbacks and put them in a long-term context, we can learn to be more objective and rational about the discouragement we might be experiencing. For example, we can say that while we might be discouraged about something right now, we can see that our lives are bigger than the thing hurting us at this particular moment—and that we have so many other things to look forward to in the future even if we don't know what they are yet.

2. **Keep a "victory file".** This one is really key: It's crucial that we keep a victory file so that we can look back on it over and over again to encourage ourselves with the great successes of our lives. We should read the victories out loud often to remind ourselves of the things we have won and overcome. This will be very comforting in the moments we need to feel protected the most.

3. **Keep an "encouragement file."** We can also keep an encouragement file (similar to our victory file—and similar to compliments journal) of every time someone has encouraged us and what they said when they did. This will allow us to look back to the encouraging words we have experienced in the past for emotional support. If we read our encouragement

files out loud, it will bring even more comfort to us because the voice we trust the most is our own—so speaking encouragement to ourselves will be a very powerful and cathartic tool.

4. **Have lunch or dinner with people who encourage us.** We can invite somebody who is a natural encourager in our lives to lunch or dinner. When we do this, we can confide in them and tell them what's going on with us. They'll help provide the encouragement we need when it's needed most. If we don't know people like this personally, we can bust out YouTube and watch great people like Tony Robbins and Les Brown who will put hope in our hearts in no time.

5. **Encourage someone else.** When we turn our eyes away from our discouragement toward somebody else who is feeling discouraged or depressed, it will naturally lift our own negative mood—just because we helped somebody else.

6. **Accomplish a short-term victory.** We can do something easy like taking a spin class or baking a cake that we can interpret as a short-term victory. This will start to build positive, healthy momentum in our lives—and refocus our minds away from psychoanalyzing the discouragement.

7. **Listen to music, dance, and have fun.** We can move our bodies, shake our hips, and have a little bit of fun, which will release endorphins into our system and start to cheer up our minds and emotions pretty quickly.

Review:

Point to Ponder: Happy Emotions Are Created by a Hurricane of Encouragement

Law to Remember: The Law of Encouragement

Affirmation to Declare: "I've been discouraged before. This is natural. But I don't have to ever continue to be discouraged in the long term because I can learn to encourage myself. I can keep victory and encouragement files that I read out loud to myself, and I can encourage others to help them and make me feel better. This is my declaration of happiness."

For more free resources on this topic, go to www.DrRob.TV/happiness/Chapter13

CHAPTER 14

HAPPY PEOPLE ARE 100% COMPLETE WITHOUT ANOTHER PERSON "FULFILLING THEM"

The Law of Independence

"We live as we dream - alone."

-Joseph Conrad[1]

Loneliness is an epidemic.[2]

Since 1985, the number of people with no close friends has increased 300%.[3] Approximately 46% of men report feeling lonely and 45% of women report the same.[4]

Loneliness is not simply physical isolation; loneliness can be a sad emotional state. We can be surrounded by people and still feel lonely. I remember this feeling in my own life.

I remember being at the Rose Bowl for a football game years ago with 100,000 screaming fans and feeling like nobody understood me or cared about me, feeling like I was all alone. I was going through a tough emotional moment in my life and all the screams around me were drowned out by my own isolating thoughts. I hope you have never felt this way before, but if you have, I completely understand. Just know that it doesn't make you any less of a BEAUTIFUL MASTERPIECE than you already are.

Even if we have loved ones near us—or even if we're in a committed relationship—we can still feel lonely. Even if we have people who tell us how much they love us, we can still feel lonely. Even if we have crowds that adore us, money in droves, fame in spades, and power in abundance, we can still feel lonely. As hard as it is to imagine, it's true. And it's true because loneliness is not just the absence of people or things from our lives. It's due to a few other things too.

The most common reasons we experience loneliness include:

- Genetics[5]
- Moving to a new location[6]
- Physical isolation[7]
- Divorce or separation[8]
- And low quality social relationships[9]

But in addition to this list, there is another major reason for loneliness too: surrounding ourselves with lonely people. That's right, loneliness is contagious. We are 52% more likely to be lonely if we hang around lonely people, for example.[10] And if we're feeling lonely, it's simply not possible to be truly happy.

But unhappiness isn't the only risk we face if we're lonely. We also face serious health risks by feeling disconnected from the people around us.

Health Risks Associated with Loneliness

There are numerous studies that identify how our health is negatively affected by being lonely. Here are just a few of the findings:

- We are more likely to be depressed and commit suicide.[11]
- We are at increased risk of cardiovascular disease and having a stroke.[12]
- Our stress and cortisol levels spike.[13]
- Our memory and learning decrease.[14]
- We start to exhibit antisocial behavior.[15]
- Our decision-making becomes noticeably worse.[16]
- We are at increased risk of alcoholism and drug abuse.[17]
- Our brain functions begin to be altered.[18]
- And more.[19]

Clearly these are horrible things to contend with if we're lonely. Here's what Shana from Boston shared about her experience with loneliness even though she was surrounded by the things she thought she wanted the most:

Shana's Story

My entire family was thousands of miles away because of my dream to study music, sing opera, and perform in musical theatre. I knew that to live my dream I had to be willing to be away from those I loved the most. Some of my friends and family who stayed behind must have thought I was nuts to take such a great leap of faith. But leaving my hometown was the best thing I ever did. I had to get out and explore the world. I had to get out and discover who I was. The funny thing is, however, I never realized that chasing my dreams—and a life of adventure and exploration—would often leave me feeling very lonely.

Now don't get me wrong: I loved my city life. I loved my roommates. I loved everything about what I was doing, seeing, and experiencing. I would go for walks, rollerblade or ride my bike on the Charles River, and listen to music from around the world. I taught myself Spanish and salsa, merengue, the cha-cha-cha, and swing dance. I would socialize and try to make the most of life. But even though I would do all of these things, I would still feel loneliness. Some of my early loneliness was because I wasn't in a relationship. But the strangest realization was that, even when I got into a relationship—and I've been in relationships both good and bad—I still experienced loneliness from time to time.

As I've gotten older and battled through loneliness, I've learned to find strength I didn't know I had. Call it God or your Higher Power or whatever you wish. What I found is there and cannot be measured. I learned to love this new strength. To nurture it. To take hold of it and teach others how to harness this good strength from the Heavens. I've learned to stay busy and not keep idle hands for too long. I've learned that prescriptions, smoking, and vaping, and all the other "happiness substitutes" can never replace finding happiness with a clear mind, sober senses, and a healthy body. I've learned to listen to people, be useful and helpful to others, and be interested in the lives and cultures of the people around me. I've started to work as a caregiver for seniors and realized that what I thought was loneliness was nothing compared to the loneliness they were going through. I've learned to overcome my own loneliness by being positive, staying active, helping others, and relying on outside strength to help fuel my connection to others.

How to Solve Loneliness

I think many of us can learn valuable lessons from Shana's amazing experience. Here are just a few things we can do to overcome loneliness—now or in the future.[15]

1. **Identify the cause of loneliness.** Is it low quality social relationships? Is it being isolated from other people? Is it having our guard up because we feel nobody cares about us? Is it something else? We can identify what it is that's causing our loneliness so we can start to put a stop to it.

2. **Show up in person or online and have a conversation.** If we become genuinely interested in others, the more likely they will become genuinely interested in us. And the more likely they will show us warm feelings and behaviors. Not everyone will, but many people will. We can begin to build high quality relationships by just being present with other people and taking initiative to spend time with them.

3. **Attend meetups.** We can get out of the house and our comfort zones by attending organized meetups with people of similar interests. Not only will we likely make unexpected new friends and acquaintances, but we will have a lot of fun spending time with people who have lots in common with us.

4. Volunteer to help others. When we reach out and help others, we can get our eyes off ourselves and invest in helping make other people's lives better. This makes it impossible to feel lonely when we're truly committed to improving somebody else's life.

Review:

Point to Ponder: Happy People Are 100% Complete Without Another Person "Fulfilling Them"

Law to Remember: The Law of Independence

Affirmation to Declare: "I know that I've felt lonely before and that this has put my mental and physical health in more jeopardy than I realize. But I'm resolving to not put myself in this situation. I will start to be more independent than ever before and go after more meaningful relationships whether I'm feeling lonely or not so that I can be happier. This is my declaration of happiness."

For more free resources on this topic, go to www.DrRob.TV/happiness/Chapter14

CHAPTER 15

HAPPY PEOPLE EMBRACE THE UNEXPECTED

The Law of Resilience

"If you never heal from what hurt you, then you'll bleed on people who did not cut you."

- NotSalmon.com[1]

All of us will experience shock at some point in our lives.[2] No matter who we are or what we do, something will shock us. And when I say shock, I don't mean surprise us. I mean totally catch us off guard.

Now there is both good shock and bad shock. The good shock makes us happy like when somebody does something unexpectedly kind for us that brings us joy. The bad shock, on the other hand, is when we experience the opposite—and this is where our happiness gets seriously tested.

Bad Shock

When we deal with unexpected shock, it can leave us feeling confused and overwhelmed. This is especially true if our expectations are suddenly dashed. When we deal with shock, our emotions get put on the fastest Ferris wheel we have ever seen. We spin around and around, not knowing when (or if) we will ever stop. We often feel frightened, angry, guilty, helpless, embarrassed, or even sad on this Ferris wheel.

But this Ferris wheel of shock can also leave us feeling exhausted; give us brain fogs; and physically upset us, causing insomnia, panic attacks, racing heartbeats, stomachaches and headaches, and more.[3]

Have you ever felt this type of shock? I know I have—I once experienced a shock so strong it knocked me off my feet for weeks, leaving me crying for days, unable to eat or leave bed, and unwilling to even consider thinking a positive thought.

When we experience a shocking incident or circumstance, it can create ripple effects and add additional emotional or physical shock on top of the original shock.[4] And it can come out of nowhere.

Here is what Noor from Malaysia said about her experience with shock:

Noor's Story

One unsuspecting day I found out that I had been manipulated for years by the person I trusted the most: my husband.

When I finally found out the truth of what he did, my chest felt so tight and I couldn't think straight. I cried, I screamed, wishing that this was just a dream—or nightmare. I didn't eat for days and I isolated myself in my pitch-dark bedroom.

My husband ran away after I found out what he did without warning. I'd prefer not to mention what he did for my privacy, however. He turned off his phone and never came back again. I was devastated.

The shock was so immense that I fell into severe depression. And I blamed myself for it. I had known him for eight long years before we got married, why didn't I see this coming? WHY?!

As hard as it was, I sought help and underwent psycho-therapy in addition to taking medication. Although it all seemed pointless at first, I realized that these pro-cedures slowly reset my mind and taught me how to challenge all the negative thoughts I was having.

Now, I've come to accept things and I've healed from the shock—not completely, to be honest. But if not for the support I got from healthcare professionals, my family and close friends, and my cats, I wouldn't be alive today to write this piece.

If there's one thing I learned over the dark years, it's that I'm responsible for my own happiness, not my partner, not others.

Wow. My heart truly goes out to Noor. Such a sad but ultimately triumphant story. For you and me, we can learn very valuable lessons from this. Whether we experience sudden shock over a loved one like Noor or shock with work or finances, health, a traumatic experience, or some other issue, it can be difficult to initially navigate. But not impossible. Here are a few tips on how we too can handle shock in our lives.[5]

How to Handle Shock

1. **Take it slow.** We'll need to give ourselves a chance to mentally and emotionally calm down because we likely will not be thinking straight when we first experience shock. During our healing process, we can talk to friends and therapists who will help us process what we have just experienced so we can become calmer. The calmer and more in control we are the more likely we are to make good decisions in response to the shock in the long run.

2. **Wait for our bodies to calm down.** Because our bodies may experience sudden increases in cortisol and other harmful physical symptoms, we have to wait for these things to calm down before we take any action.[6] The important thing to realize is that our bodies will only maintain a state of shock for a limited period of time before they return to normal.[7]

3. **Embrace the experience and use it as a learning opportunity.** As difficult as it is, we can use our shock as an opportunity to learn about how strong we are; how uncertain life can sometimes be; and about how others treat us regardless of how we treat them. We will gain more insight from our shock if we see it as a lesson and not as a disaster. And we can use it to help teach and empower others later on who are going through the same thing we went through.

Review:

Point to Ponder: Happy People Embrace the Unexpected

Law to Remember: The Law of Resilience

Affirmation to Declare: "I've experienced shock before and it's been overwhelming. I know my emotions were all over the place, but I also know that I can take steps to mentally calm myself down until my body catches up. I will use whatever shocking experiences I experience as an opportunity to learn about myself and to teach and empower others to be overcomers. This is my declaration of happiness."

For more free resources on this topic, go to www.DrRob.TV/happiness/Chapter15

CHAPTER 16

Happy People Learn to Be Content With Who They Are and What They Have

The Law of Contentment

"If I am always comparing myself to others, I will forever be at war with myself. And who needs that?" Khloe Kardashian[1]

ave you ever been jealous of somebody?

Yes, I know: It's a really tough question. But why? Because when we normally think about jealousy it's usually when we think other people are being jealous of us. And rightly so— other people have been jealous of you and me. When we find out we are the object of their jealousy, it's not fun—it's actually quite uncomfortable.

But I don't want to talk about others' jealousy toward you or me. I want to talk about our jealousy toward others. Touchy, yes. But it's absolutely necessary to address for us to learn how to become happier. When we consciously or subconsciously compare ourselves to others we are not only undermining our thoughts (as we saw with the comparison trap in Chapter 3), but we are undermining our emotions.

Whether we're currently experiencing jealousy or have in the past, it is one of the things that will hinder our growth the most. Now I know it's not comfortable for us to acknowledge that we've ever been jealous of others (it seems so inappropriate) but acknowledging this will help accelerate our personal progress. Here are just a few signs that we may have been or currently are jealous of somebody.[2]

Signs We Are Jealous of Someone

- We never seem impressed by them and downplay their accomplishments.
- We think they are lucky and hope that they get what's coming to them.
- We are competitive with them to the point of imitating them and wanting to beat them.
- We bring up bad news if something good happens to them.
- We are secretly happy if they fail.
- We dislike them and become their rival even if they were never ours.
- We try to put them in their place and talk about people who are better than them.
- We avoid them or become overly clingy with them.
- And more.

If we're honest with ourselves, we have felt one or more of these things before about various people in our lives. But the question is: What benefit did we get by being jealous? Is it a good use of our time, thoughts, and emotions? Do we wish we could be more jealous of them? Do we wish we could be less jealous of them?

When we think about these questions, we understand that we gain little by being jealous of them, their looks, their accomplishments, their popularity, or their material possessions.

Here's what William from Toronto, Canada wrote to me about his experience with jealousy:

William's Story

I was always an ambitious person. I tried really hard in high school to get the best grades possible, and when it came time to apply to university, I got into a great program. I studied business and got great grades and participated in all the best extracurricular activities. In other words, my resume was near-perfect. After graduating I got accepted into one of the most prestigious multinational corporations in the world, in a vibrant and big city.

But it was around this time that I started having self-doubts. I tried getting back together with my old high school girlfriend, whom I still loved, but when that fell through it felt like my whole world was crashing down. And this is when my jealousy began. I got diagnosed with a mood disorder and put on medication. The peers that I had grown up with started to surpass me, professionally and personally, and it felt like I was being left behind in the dust.

My life was stagnating. I felt paralyzed, like I couldn't move forward. I was not making money and I was on disability insurance. I just didn't have what it took to make it in the world. Meanwhile, one of my best friends growing up was working for great companies and eventually started his own company. He bought a house with his wife and had a kid. All the while, I had nothing and I couldn't stand it.

Looking around me, I saw success for everyone but myself, which slowly ate my soul with envy. It took a long time, but then I finally embraced a solid piece of wisdom that I had heard for years but never applied to my life: Do not compare yourself to other people. I learned to embrace on an emotional level that as you go through life, there will always be people above you and below you, and you truly have to be ok with that. And your emotions—your feelings—have to be ok with that too.

Steps to Overcoming Our Jealousy of Others

Comparing ourselves to and being jealous of others is an easy trap for all of us to fall into. But we can dig our way out with the following steps.[3]

1. **Acknowledge, accept, and reflect on our jealousy.** In other words, we can admit that we have it, accept that we have it, and think about why we are jealous in the first place. We can see that there is no shame in this, and that this will

actually put us on the path to freeing ourselves from any toxic feelings we might have toward others that we should get rid of.

2. **Examine the beliefs, assumptions, and insecurities we have about ourselves.** By doing this, we can get to the root of the insecurities present in our souls that we are taking out on other people. When we are trying to bring somebody else down—whether in our minds, hearts, conversations, or even other ways—it's because we feel bad about ourselves and are temporarily blinded to just how special we really are.

3. **Develop real self-confidence.** We can look at the good aspects of ourselves and meditate on these things instead of why we don't like somebody else. If we meditate more on what makes us unique and wonderful—if we meditate more on our strengths and gifts—we will take our eyes off other people because we will be focused on living our own lives and running our own races (not watching other people run theirs).

4. **Create a support system.** We can talk to a friend and tell them when or if we're jealous of somebody else—or even if jealous of them (a lot of our jealousies exist in our friendships and other close relationships). I know, I know: This is very scary but if we do it will bring us great relief and better outcomes than we might expect.

5. **Celebrate our victory over jealousy.** When we overcome our jealousy—by admitting it to ourselves, confessing it to others, and beginning to give those we're jealous of the benefit of the doubt—we can start to celebrate. It may not be quick or easy, but celebration can happen in time—and when it does it will be the most powerful feeling we can ever experience on our happiness journey.

Review:

Point to Ponder: Happy People Learn to Be Content with Who They Are and What They Have

Law to Remember: The Law of Contentment

Affirmation to Declare: "I admit it, I've been jealous of others. This is hard for me to admit, but I see that it is necessary. I've been jealous for various reasons but I'm not going to beat myself up for it. I'm going to take steps to stop comparing myself to others and be more content with the BEAUTIFUL MASTERPIECE that I truly am. This is my declaration of happiness."

For more free resources on this topic, go to www.DrRob.TV/happiness/chapter16

PART THREE

MASTERING HAPPINESS IN YOUR MIND RELATIONSHIPS

FINDING HAPPINESS IN YOUR RELATIONSHIPS: Introduction

You're doing great! You're already two sections down with only a few to go. In this next section, let's turn our attention to relationships.

When our relationships are good, life is good. Spending time with the people who appreciate us, that we have fun with, and who inspire and motivate us to go higher can bring us immense satisfaction and happiness. The people that get us—the people that love and protect us—make life more enjoyable and doable.

Unfortunately, however, not everybody will appreciate, love, or support us. Not everybody will care about us or even like us. As you know all too well, some in life will criticize, undermine, and even work against us.

And the crazy part is that sometimes the people who love us the most will criticize us the worst. On the other hand, sometimes the people we think cannot stand us will offer us a helping hand.

Trying to understand people—and relationships—can be quite tricky and confusing. This can make us ask countless questions that we want (THAT WE NEED) to know the answers to. Questions like: Is that girl really my friend? Should I take my ex back? Do these family members always have to put me down?

Is this person dependable? Do these people always have to be so annoying and get on my nerves? Can I trust him? Does anybody really like me or are they all phonies? Why can't they just see how wrong they are and how right I am? And other questions like these can run through our minds and subconsciousness all our lives.

In Part 3, we're going to explore the traps that we face in our various relationships and how we can take them head on so that we can learn to enjoy the people in our lives in a much deeper way—and so that we can learn to be happy in our relationships.

CHAPTER 17

TRUE HAPPINESS COMES FROM LEARNING TO LIVE FOR AN AUDIENCE OF ONE

The Law of Living Your Own Life

"Your time is limited, so don't waste it living someone else's life."

- Steve Jobs[1]

We have been a hostage to other people's opinions. We have been a hostage to other people's approval. And we have been a hostage to other people's validation.

What we think of ourselves and how we behave in our relationships, work, and the larger world have all been deeply shaped by our desire to please others.[2] And this desire to please others—to "over-please" others, really—has unfortunately stolen much of our happiness. Why? Because all the pressure we experience trying to make others happy leaves us unhappy with ourselves because we are often not being true to who we are—and to what makes us happy.

Why Is It So Hard Not to Be a Slave to Others' Opinions?

It is difficult to break free from wanting to please others because of the various obstacles we face in doing so. Some of these obstacles include:

- Fear of being rejected
- Fear of being judged or criticized
- Fear of disappointing others
- Fear of not fitting in
- Fear of losing someone or something
- Fear of being brave
- And fear of [insert fear here]

Our fears are so strong that we would rather keep them than risk living for ourselves—and being happy. We have decided to exchange our happiness for somebody else's because we subconsciously believe if we don't live life trying to please others it will cost us personally, socially, or financially.

Here's what Sakif from Bangladesh wrote to me about his experience with living a life based on other people's opinions:

Sakif's Story

I still remember the day my ex-girlfriend told me that she was completely disgusted at my appearance and everything else about me. She questioned the way I walked, talked, and even ate. We had been together for years and to end on such an unexpected and sad note left me overwhelmingly devastated.

I went to see my mom to tell her what happened to me, hoping to receive lots of compassion and empathy. But instead I got something else: she told me, "Well honey, you could actually dress better and start putting yourself together!" When I heard these words, my heart sunk and I felt like the most worthless person in the world.

After this, everything started to crumble around me. I developed a habit of spending hours feeling bad about myself even if I didn't have anything bad happening in my life. It was a vicious cycle which I couldn't get myself out of. For example, whenever I went out and found someone looking at me, I would make up horrible comments in my mind that I assumed they were thinking about me and my appearance.

So what did I do? I decided to change my situation, but in the worst possible way. I decided to buy more "trendy" clothes and tried to act like the smart person that my ex-girlfriend had by then taken up as her new boyfriend. But despite this, even if someone would compliment me on my style and smarts, I would feel worse about myself—to the point of self-hatred— because it was all an act I was putting on.

I was a caged person living in someone else's skin. I was trying to adjust to the demands and expectations everybody had of me—and trying to live by other people's opinions. I was living to please everybody else but me and tried to maintain the perfect social image just so that I feel accepted by others. But this failed me miserably in the long run.

My saving grace was when I took a course called "The Science of Well-Being." It helped me to learn how to let things go through meditation. It empowered me to observe my negative feelings and just let them go. It showed me that my opinion about myself is the only one that matters. And it showed me that whenever I put someone else's opinion above my own I was choosing to lose myself (and my happiness) in the process.

Breaking the Need to Please

Wow. I appreciate Sakif's vulnerability and how he overcame being a people-pleaser. Just like him, we can become courageous and break free from the need to sacrifice our own happiness just to please others too. And we can do this even if it's scary or costs us things. In fact, it will cost us things but that's ok. Why?

Because when we embrace our truth and announce our authentic selves, it forces others around us to show their true colors. It forces others to show if they are there to love us and support the real us or if they are there to control and manipulate us into pleasing them and their expectations.

The benefits of seeing who our true friends are and aren't will be enormous. When we do start to break free from pleasing others, we can finally stop hiding our true selves or pretending to be somebody we're not. We can finally see who is really for us and who is only for the version of us they think we should be. Here are some steps we can take to break free from the need to please so that we can be happier: [3]

1. Declare independence from other people's opinions. When we do this, we will see that their opinions are just their own

personal preferences, not laws we have to live by. And once we realize their opinions are not laws we have to live by, we will feel much less pressure to please them.

2. Let our true selves organically come out in our conversations and decisions. Our true thoughts and feelings may surprise others at first, but we will minimize their shock if we disclose our real selves little by little.

3. Prepare ourselves to experience inevitable pushback and resistance. For most of us, this will be the scariest and toughest part because others will question us and try to cajole us back into the box they put us.

4. Journal our experiences to reflect how this is making us feel. Even the idea of writing out, "I am a recovering people-pleaser" is healing.

5. Remind ourselves that while other people may start to criticize the real us, they can no longer control the people pleasing version of us—and that they can no longer use their opinions to force us to be less happy than we otherwise could be.

Although this journey might be challenging, it is worth it because you and I deserve to be happy. We deserve to be able to live as our authentic selves. We deserve to know who supports the real us and who doesn't.

Review:

Point to Ponder: True Happiness Comes from Learning to Live for an Audience of One

Law to Remember: The Law of Living Your Own Life

Affirmation to Declare: "It's very easy for me to be a people-pleaser because of fear. I admit it. But starting today I am going to start letting others know what I think, how I feel, and who I am. Little by little. I'm going to start living my own life. Little by little. It will be scary but my happiness is worth it. I do not want to offend others, but I need to know who is really for me. I need people in my life that support me and who I am. This is my declaration of happiness."

For more free resources on this topic, go to www.DrRob.TV/happiness/Chapter17

CHAPTER 18

HAPPINESS DOES NOT SEEK TO DOMINATE OTHERS

The Law of Relinquishing Control

"You can never control or change how others think, feel, or act. You can only change how you think, feel, and act, and lead by example."

- Celestine Chua[1]

As hard as it is to admit, we have all attempted to get people to do what we want them to do—for better or for worse.

Whether personally or professionally, we all think that we're right and so we therefore often feel entitled to tell people what to do. We first learned this behavior as kids and we've continued it throughout most of our lives.

But while making sure our thoughts should be valued by others, if we take this approach to the extreme in our relationships and insist that our opinions become laws for others to follow, we end up causing great unhappiness for others—and for ourselves.

Of course, other people try to get their own way with us—and they even often try to control us—but we're not talking about them in this book. We're not talking about them because we can't change their behavior, we can only change our own.

When we focus on us we can take complete control of our happiness. That way we don't have to wait on others to do what we want in order to be happy; we can focus on changing those things we need to do in our own lives in order to increase our happiness.

I get that you might be thinking BUT THE OTHER PERSON HAS TO CHANGE, especially if you're dealing with somebody who you feel is causing unhappiness in your life. That might be true, but it is equally true that we have to change too. Why?

Because there are some subtle (and not so subtle) behaviors that we also often fall into that causes us to try to control others. And when the spirit of control walks in, happiness walks out.

Below are a few signs that we might knowingly or unknowingly be trying to get people to do what we want to do (aka trying to control other people):

1. When we try to change people to be more like us, we are often trying to control them

One way of trying to control others is to force our beliefs onto them. And it is not just our beliefs about religion, money, or politics, although these are certainly included. It is our beliefs about all the other things we have opinions about (usually our major opinions about society but also sometimes our minor ones about things like movies and sports, food and housework).

We do this because we believe our opinions are almost always right. If a spouse, friend, or coworker does not see eye to eye with us on an issue—especially one that really matters to us—it angers or frustrates us (or we become dismissive of their views).

If this happens, we'll often get defensive and try to prove to them all the ways we are right and all the ways they are wrong. And we'll often try to change what they think and feel to accommodate us because we believe our thoughts and feelings are better than or superior to theirs.

In other words, we'll often want to change them (or control them) so they can think more like us or behave more like us. We have difficulty letting others—especially those close to us—be who they are without us trying to change or control some aspect of them.

2. When we have (hidden) rules we expect people to follow, we are often trying to control them

We'll also often create a series of spoken (or unspoken) rules we expect people to follow if we're trying to control them. These rules are sometimes rules of etiquette and personal boundaries, but sometimes they go far beyond that.

Through our behavior, we reward or punish people around us for breaking our personal, idiosyncratic requirements. And the strangest part about this is that sometimes our rules are not always logical. Sometimes they are, but sometimes they are based on our fears, our past emotional traumas, or our unrealistic thoughts and expectations that we never tell others about.

As a consequence, when we're at our worst we attempt to micromanage others' behavior; repeatedly point out their flaws; give them the silent treatment if we disapprove of their actions; describe worst-case scenarios to them if they do not follow our advice; attempt to invalidate why they should not be feeling the emotions they are if we disagree with them; blow up on them; and more.

I know this sounds extreme, but it is in no way a criticism of us, just an explanation for how we feel and how we sometimes act. I feel it is so important that we empower ourselves so that we can more clearly see the behavior patterns we can all easily slip into even if our motives are good (I know I have engaged in some of these behaviors myself, so no judgment here if you have too). We have all fallen into these tricky behaviors, and it is imperative that we know how these behaviors may be impacting our happiness—and the happiness of those around us.

When we try to tell others how to solve their problems, we are often trying to control them

Finally, when we're trying to control people, we often offer them unsolicited advice about how to solve their problems. We become their self-appointed therapist, life coach, and guru because we truly want to help them. We ironically know how to solve all their issues instantly even if we do not necessarily know how to solve our own problems. And we become overjoyed if they ever follow our advice. But on the other hand, we become disappointed, frustrated, or upset when they don't. This not only increases our unhappiness with them, but it increases their unhappiness with us because they feel like they can't please us.

When Controlling Behavior Gets Out of Control

Because everyone is trying to control everyone else—and because everyone is trying to please everyone else—we often don't see how this cultural behavior can impact the most vulnerable among us if it is being taken to an extreme—especially if that extreme is a controlling or truly manipulative person (i.e., not you or me).

Here's what Andrea from the United States told me about her horrific experience of being controlled and manipulated by someone she thought was her best friend:

Andrea's Story

My last year of high school is when it started. My best friend was a guy and we had been friends for years. He was the most non-threatening presence in the school: He was polite and quiet and, from my time spent with him, respectful. Yet he found an opportunity to manipulate me. You see, as a high school feminist, I was still trying to figure out where I stood on things, especially with my body, and what made sense to me. And this is when he struck.

I told him that I didn't think that boobs were a sexual organ (I felt they were for feeding newborns) and he used this opportunity to agree with me. He said that since my boobs weren't "sexual" in nature, I shouldn't care if he touched mine. To be honest, I don't remember a lot of the conversation that we had at that point—and whether I even agreed or not. I just know that on the drive home he fondled my breasts the entire ride. I neither wanted this nor appreciated it, especially from the guy I called my best friend. But I didn't tell him how this made me uncomfortable because my boobs were not supposed to be sexual—I just assumed it would happen once and that he would drop it so I wouldn't have to deal with my own feelings about the matter. Unfortunately I was wrong.

It didn't matter what I did or what I wore, I would always find myself in the passenger seat of his car with him groping my boobs. Even if I declined rides, he just hit me with his big, innocent puppy dog eyes and told me that I didn't actually care that he touched them and that I would be fine.

It wasn't fine, but I didn't know how to get out of the situation. He knew exactly what to say to shut me up, he was my best friend after all—my very manipulative and controlling best friend. So I thought I should just continue to not say anything about it.

After high school, I stupidly ended up living with him and although he didn't molest me like in high school there was a new air of uncertainty in our relationship. But this time it wasn't him who was the toxic one, it was me. I would drink, snap at him, but would never tell him how I really felt about what he did to me in high school. And after almost two years of this behavior, I couldn't take it anymore.

I told him how I felt about what he did to me. I told him how I didn't appreciate him manipulating me. How I didn't appreciate him controlling me using my teenage naivete against me. How I didn't appreciate how his behavior caused me so much trauma that I couldn't have healthy relationships. How I couldn't look at people without suspicion or stop from wanting to control their behavior so that they could never hurt me like he did.

After this conversation, I decided to move out. I started going to therapy so I could learn how to forgive my former best friend in my heart, so I could set myself free from the pain he caused me. I found someone else who became a true best friend and who understood what I went through. And I stopped drinking to numb my pain. I did what I needed to do to overcome all of the trauma and control issues in my life that were undermining my personal happiness.

Three Ways to Stop Being a Control Freak

Wow, what a truly horrible memory. It took a lot of courage for Andrea to share that and I'm so glad that she did. Fortunately for her, she was able to escape from—and heal from—her manipulative friend who was trying to control her.

If we're being controlled ourselves—or if we're controlling others (even if in small ways that are not illegal or unethical) —we too can overcome this behavior. Here are just a couple of helpful tips: [4]

1. **Learn to accept others' imperfections**. We can begin to understand that people have different life experiences, values, and perceptions than us. They have different flaws than us, and their journeys are different from our own. When we

humbly accept this—and their humanity—we can learn to stop controlling them. I know this is really hard, especially if we really care about or love them, but we can do it.

2. **Stop trying to squeeze others into boxes.** Instead of trying to make others fit into our boxes for them, we can blow these boxes up. If we do not require others to live in our consciously or subconsciously constructed boxes, our desire to control them will weaken. Even if our box for them may make sense to us, it may not make sense to others—so we should definitely get rid of it. Nobody else was created to be a hamster on our hamster wheel—and we will all be better off if we free them from it.

3. **Start learning to forgive.** Part of the reason we want to control others is because we haven't forgiven the people who have hurt or disappointed us in the past. As a consequence, we want to prevent pain at all costs like Andrea did so we resort to behaviors we would not normally engage in if we didn't feel so wounded. If we want to stop being so controlling, we'll have to forgive all of the people who have ever hurt us, even if they never offer an apology. We can simply forgive them in our minds despite our memories or emotions fighting us not to. We'll be so glad that we did, as hard as it might be to do initially, as the act of forgiveness scientifically overrides nasty brain chemicals like cortisol which only makes our pain worse.[5]

How to Overcome When Others' Try to Control Us

At the same time that we are overcoming controlling others, we can also learn how to overcome being controlled. Here are a few tips to overcome people's behavior that may be trying to influence us in negative ways that make us unhappy.

1. **Empathize with them.** People with control issues usually have underlying emotional problems and need the help of a therapist. Instead of judging them, we should recognize this reality and suggest they get the help they need.

2. **Do not react to their bad behavior or argue with them**. Controlling people want to get a reaction out of us, and love nothing more than to argue with us if we do not do what they say. We should not give them the satisfaction of arguing or reacting with stress or anger. We should stay calm so we can make the best possible decisions about how to deal with them.

3. **Establish boundaries with them.** We are not other people's doormats, and no person should be able to walk over us. Just because we might have let some people walk over us in the past, we do not have to continue to let them do it now or in the future. We should set up boundaries with people who may be trying to force us to do or be things we don't want to do or be.

4. **Keep expectations about them realistic.** Controlling people rarely change or they rarely change during the time-frame we would like them to. We should humbly accept this and continue building our patience with them

5. **Remind ourselves it is often not personal.** People who try to control us do so because they are insecure. It usually has nothing to do with you or me. If we helped contribute to some of that insecurity through any shady behavior, we should apologize to them and attempt to earn their trust again. But again, they have underlying issues that they wrongly think they can resolve through their controlling us.

6. **Limit interactions with them.** Most people only have around 30,000 days to live. That is only half a second

compared to how long the earth has been around. We do not have to spend our limited time with people who try to control us.

7. **Walk away if necessary.** If a relationship of any kind is harming us mentally, physically, or emotionally we should walk (or run) away—so that we can reclaim the happiness they are trying to steal from us.

Review:

Point to Ponder: Happiness Does Not Seek to Dominate Others

Law to Remember: The Law of Relinquishing Control

Affirmation to Declare: "I admit that I have tried to control some of my relationships. I usually have had the best of intentions but I realize it was a mistake. I set free all of those I have tried to control, and I set myself free from those who have tried to control me. This is my declaration of happiness."

For more free resources on this topic, go to www.DrRob.TV/happiness/Chapter18

CHAPTER 19

A HAPPY PERSON STOPS VICTIMIZING THEMSELVES IN RELATIONSHIPS

The Law of Personal Responsibility

"When you blame and criticize others you are avoiding some truth about yourself"

- Deepak Chopra[1]

We unfortunately live in a society that loves to point the finger.[2] When something goes wrong, the first impulse isn't to fix it but instead to assign blame. This is especially true in politics and at our workplaces.

But it's also true in our relationships. Be it with a spouse, relatives, friends, or anybody else we frequently interact with, we have been blamed by others for one thing or another. And we also blame others.

On the extreme side of the blame spectrum, we could fall into one of these two categories: We either almost always blame others for things that go haywire or we almost always blame ourselves. If you're like most people, you fall somewhere in between, usually bouncing around from one end of the spectrum to the other.

But in addition to blaming others, we have also sometimes blamed fate, bad luck, God, the universe, or other factors for the messy situations in our lives. All of this blame assigning has caused us to feel like a victim in many circumstances. And the more we feel like the victim, the more helpless and unhappy we tend to feel.

Why We Blame Others

It's no wonder: A blame others mindset is hardwired into us and those around us. Here are a few logical reasons we might do it:[3]

1. *We learned it from our parents or other authority figures.* Blaming others has been modeled for us, and the more we see others do it the more we tend to do it.

2. *Our finger-pointing is a defense mechanism.* Whether it's projection or denial, blaming others helps preserve our self-esteem by avoiding awareness of our own flaws or failings.

3. *We finger-point to attack others.* We engage in destructive name-calling or shaming to hurt others who we feel are hurting us.

4. *It's easier to blame somebody else than take responsibility for our own actions.* Even if we know we're wrong or possibly could be at fault, we assign blame to excuse our own behavior.

5. *We trust our perceptions and knowledge.* We have certain life experiences and background knowledge, and as a consequence, we often make assumptions about a situation even if we don't know all of the facts.

Assigning Blame Causes Conflict

When we blame others, it creates conflict. And almost any conflict leads to stress, which can psychologically and physiologically reduce our happiness.[4] This is especially true if we are being blamed by someone else.

There are usually several types of people who will blame us for the things we may or may not do: the *forever victim* who does not take control of their own life; the *arrogant narcissist* who believes they are never at fault; *those with low self-esteem* who need to bring us low to make themselves feel better; and *control freaks* who never admit to personal responsibility because it would cause them to lose control of a situation.

When we're blamed for something, it's one of the worst feelings in the world. We either tend to feel like a victim or become stubbornly prideful and defend ourselves. Here's what Qurat from New Zealand said to me about her experience with the blame game:

Qurat's Story

For years, I was the girl who would blame everyone around her for her unhappiness. I would rant to my friends and family that I am unhappy because of so and so. This person said this, and it made me unhappy; that person did that and ruined my day.

It continued for quite a while, and deep down, I was happy because I didn't have to take responsibility for my own emotional management. I would put all the blame on others. It made me feel good as I was able to see them as culprits and myself as a victim. To me, always being offended at what others were saying or doing made me feel in control and self-righteous.

But one day, I heard a podcast and it served as an eye-opener. It said that if I don't "choose" to be happy, I will continue to be unhappy because I'm always blaming others. That is when I embraced the fact that I can no longer tie my happiness to what others are or aren't doing to me.

The day when I held myself accountable for how I feel, I stopped blaming others and stopped being offended at every little thing. It's not that I am not bothered by them anymore, but just that I make a conscious effort not to govern my emotions based on the actions of others. Why? Because I realized if I keep blaming others, I will always be at their mercy. I realized that if I wanted to be at peace—and if I really wanted happiness—I had to train myself to be the master of my own emotions instead of letting others be the masters of them.

How to Not Play the Blame Game

What an incredibly courageous thing Qurat has admitted to. I'm grateful she did to help show us the way forward. Like her, we definitely do have to train ourselves to master our own emotions just like Qurat. We also have to train ourselves not to engage in the blame game with others. Here are a few helpful tips to empower us to overcome the blame trap.[5]

1. ***Embrace the "lessons" from every situation.*** If we feel we can learn a lesson from our messy situations, we can search for those lessons. We can try to look as objectively as possible at what we're experiencing to empower ourselves to stop blaming others.

2. ***Try to see things from a perspective other than our own.*** Similar to searching for a meaningful lesson in our

situations, we can try to see things solely from another person's perspective. If we don't discount their thinking and feelings we can better understand where they're coming from and see that maybe they're not 100% at fault—or at fault at all.

3. *Admit when we're at fault.* If we're at fault in a situation, we can take responsibility and admit it. We can apologize and offer positive solutions to fix it.

4. *Accept that we're imperfect.* Inevitably, we will make many mistakes in life. And others will call us out for it. Instead of being defensive or feeling frustrated by their actions, accept that they care about us enough to point out something that we can or should fix. On the other hand, if we have to call out others for their mistakes, we should do it with the right motives and in the right tone—after all, other people are just human beings like ourselves.

Review:

Point to Ponder: A Happy Person Stops Victimizing Themselves in Relationships

Law to Remember: The Law of Personal Responsibility

Affirmation to Declare: "I have played the blame game. I have blamed others for things they've done. I've also been blamed by others, which has sometimes made me defensive and feel like a victim. I'm going to give up the blame game for the sake of my own happiness—and for the sake of my relationships. I'm going to take more responsibility than I have ever before. This is my declaration of happiness."

For more free resources on this topic, go to www.DrRob.TV/happiness/Chapter19

CHAPTER 20

HAPPINESS REJECTS TOXIC ADDICTIONS TO OTHERS

The Law of the Deep Cleanse

"The shattering of a heart when being broken is the loudest quiet ever."

– Carroll Bryant[1]

N o matter who we are, we've experienced a toxic relationship.[2]
It could have been with a spouse, a friend, a coworker, a rival, a family member, or any number of other people. Toxic relationships are about as common as air in modern society.

Relationships that make us feel sad instead of happy, that have caused us emotional or physical abuse, or that have distracted us from being a happy and successful person are toxic relationships, for example.[3]

Relationships that cause feelings of fear, abandonment, and addiction are also toxic relationships.[4]

So, too, are relationships that cause us to need the validation of another person so that we can feel content with ourselves.[5]

Society Is Filled with Toxic Relationships

Looking around society, we can see toxic relationships everywhere. They exist in workplaces, in poor, rich, and suburban neighborhoods, and are always in the news and tabloids. Toxic relationships are even exploited on reality TV shows so that producers can enrich themselves.

Anyway we look at it, society is seemingly filled with and fueled by toxic relationships that are making people very unhappy.

Part of the reason for this abundance of toxic relationships is because everyone—you and me included—have a need for validation, love, and connection that was not validated by some previous relationships. This could have been as a consequence of a lack of validation from a primary caregiver, a significant other, friend, coworkers or mentor, or other relationships that were important to us. As I mentioned in Chapter 6, I never got validation from my biological father because he abandoned me, which caused me some issues in a few of my own relationships later in life.

Another reason our society experiences an abundance of toxic relationships is because we are constantly trying to fix others (or others might constantly be trying to fix us like we saw in Chapter 18). And when others don't change on our schedule or fail to meet our expectations, a chaotic relationship usually ensues in one way or another.

Sometimes the toxicity is invisible—and we just give up and don't say anything, thereby causing a one-sidedness to the relationship.

But other times it's passive aggressive—and we think, say, or do things to express our feelings or anger in subtle ways in hopes that the other party will get the clue.

And other times it's overt: It's in-your-face disagreements, arguments, power moves, and other manipulative tactics to fix or control others.

Another reason there are so many toxic relationships is because people may have never learned to fully love themselves. And if they can't love themselves, they are incapable of loving another in a healthy way. When two lonely hearts get into a relationship, for example, the likelihood of one or both of them having a toxic addiction to that relationship is very high.

Wrong Beliefs About Relationships

The reality is that many people have the wrong idea about both love and happiness. They think romantic relationships have to complete them and that other relationships have to fulfill them. But they never stop to analyze what the purpose of every relationship they have is.

No relationship is the same, and every relationship should have a rhyme and a reason. Yet too often people have trauma from past relationships—romantic relationships, friendships, or work relationships—and they are bringing their baggage from their old relationships into their new relationships. They do this because they misunderstand the real reason for the various relationships in their life.

The sad fact is our toxic relationships are probably the things bringing us the most unhappiness in our lives. So it's important that we know how to deal with them.

To start, we must deal first with our thinking about our relationships, particularly our assumptions and expectations for them. If we assume we need another person to make us happy (in a romantic relationship or even friendship), for example, we are already going into a potential relationship with a toxic mindset.

If we assume other people need to behave certain ways to make us happy we are choosing to adopt a toxic mindset.

And if we assume we can just fix things about somebody else (however small), we are choosing a toxic mindset that in the end will leave us unhappy.

Toxic Mindsets and Behaviors

Toxic thoughts in relationships often produce not only destructive behavior, they also produce destructive thought patterns. If we're constantly trying to understand the motives or reasons why somebody is doing something, for example, we will drive ourselves crazy. Thinking why did she say this, why did he do that, why can't they just be this way is one-way ticket to unhappiness.

So, too, is romanticizing any relationship we have, being in denial about who people really are, bargaining with ourselves that others will change, and having a victim mentality when it comes to our interpersonal interactions.

All of these thoughts and feelings stemming from a toxic mind-set will leave us feeling isolated, frustrated, anxious, addicted, and with low self-esteem. They will leave us desperately chasing the people who are not validating us in the way that we want. And, as importantly, they will lead us to internal suffering, unhealthy relationships, and unhappiness.

Here's what Paul from Great Britain told me about his experience overcoming a toxic mindset and relationship.

Paul's Story

I realized I was obsessed with Debbie (or Debs as we all called her) after I had spent several chapters writing the perfect Valentine poem that would win her over. I'd known her since the start of term the year before and it had been love at first sight, at least it had been for me. It was painful to be around her. Painful to be away from her. I could not live, could not breath without her. She was at the center of my every thought. But, she only ever saw me as one of the gang. A friend.

This went on for an entire year and I knew I was obsessed. The gang spent almost all our time together. Debs, Tom, Bill, Daz, Anna, Kate, and me. Some of the gang lived in a shared student house and that was the hub of our social world, because they had a big living room and Nintendo. But we'd spend time almost anywhere; the park at 2 am, playing Frisbee in the dead of night, really anywhere.

But my obsession with Debs was making me unhappy. So I started to withdraw, slowly at first, until I took myself out of the gang completely.

I decided to play my guitar more often. In fact, I spent an entire winter in my tiny single-room flat playing the guitar. And I failed all of my college exams as a result.

Even though I temporarily distanced myself from the gang, I returned to them a few years later. And I returned to my obsession with Debs.

Looking back on it, I realize how foolish this obsession was. I was toxic and I didn't even know it. I'm glad that I later learned that I didn't need Debs to make me happy—or any other person for that matter.

I really appreciate Paul's honesty about his toxic obsession with Debs. It takes a lot to admit what he just did. But he could because he has healed from his experience. Here's how we all can heal from any type of toxic relationships we may have had in the past, any we currently have, or any we might have in the future.

Healing from Toxic Relationships

1. **Start loving ourselves more.** The only reason we put up with toxic relationships—or toxic pursuits of relationships— is because we don't love ourselves enough. We devalue how special and important we are—we devalue that we are BEAUTIFUL MASTERPIECES—and as a consequence, we find ourselves in toxic relationships or situations more often than we would like.

2. **Stop "romanticizing" relationships, especially romantic ones.** We should realize that while relationships are here to help support and allow us to grow, no person should be our god or source of happiness or validation. When we romanticize somebody (no matter how great they

are) the other person ultimately ends up controlling bits and pieces of our happiness (which is very unhealthy for us).

3. **Take inventory.** We can, like in so many other things in our lives, journal the good and bad things about our various relationships, their purpose in our lives, and who needs to stay and go. We should be super honest with ourselves about this if we decide to use this approach because it can become an accelerated path to our healing.

4. **Stop trying to fix others.** We have ninety-nine problems but fixing somebody else shouldn't be one. We have our race to run, so we should let others run their race. If we feel like we can't be happy until other people change, we will continue to be unhappy—because they are likely to never change, at least on our arbitrary timetables.

5. **Give ourselves permission to enjoy our relationships.** Instead of griping about the negatives of others, we can give ourselves permission to enjoy the best and most positive parts of every person and relationship around us and take them for what they are worth. We will see just how amazing and special the people are around us if we only stop and look at them for who they really are.

Review:

Point to Ponder: Happiness Rejects Toxic Addictions to Others

Law to Remember: The Law of the Deep Cleanse

Affirmation to Declare: "My understanding of toxic relationships has really changed. I realize that maybe I had a toxic mindset because of the culture I've been living in. But

I can start to love myself and stop trying to fix others so that my relationships can improve and so that I can derive more satisfaction from them. I can start to cleanse myself from all of the toxicity I've absorbed from the society around me. This is my declaration of happiness."

For more free resources on this topic, go to www.DrRob.TV/happiness/Chapter20

CHAPTER 21

HAPPY PEOPLE UNDERSTAND
THE GIVE AND TAKE

The Law of Interdependence

"You can't depend on anyone else to be happy; no relationship will give you the inner peace that you haven't created"

- Anonymous

We are meant to be in healthy relationships with others.

But in today's world, the mantra is: The only person we can depend on is ourselves. And in some cases, this is true. We are responsible for our own motivation. We are responsible for the goals and dreams we pursue. We are responsible for the work we produce. And so on.

Yet having the mindset that we can only depend on ourselves is a double-edged sword. On the one hand, it allows us to pursue the things we want and to take control over our own destiny. But on the other hand, if this attitude is taken too far it can prevent us from building loving, nurturing, and trusting relationships that we need to grow because we will only be looking out for ourselves.

Whether in our personal or professional life, it is imperative to build genuine relationships with people we can be open with and rely on. But it is also imperative that we don't build relationships that cause us to be overly dependent. It's a tricky balance, I know, but we can learn how to walk it.

The best kinds of relationships are neither too dependent nor too independent. The best kinds of relationships are interdependent.

We'll discuss interdependent relationships shortly, but before we do let's take a quick look at the qualities in relationships that make us too dependent. When we're too dependent, we will not be as happy as we could be.

Dependent Relationships Bring Us Unhappiness

Here's how to recognize if we're in a dependent relationship.[1] This could be a romantic relationship, but it could also be a relationship with a family member, friend, coworker, or some other person in our lives.

1. **We give up our power by allowing other people to assume responsibility for areas of our lives.** In this dependency, we claim we can't do or be something unless the other person does or becomes something. We give up our power to other people as if they're responsible for us, our circumstances, and our happiness. This often happens when

somebody says they can only be happy when the other person does something or changes.

2. **We tend to shy away from disagreeing with others out of fear.** In this dependency, we prefer not to disagree because we fear abandonment or rejection by the other person. We keep our opinions to ourselves not to keep the peace, but to keep the relationship. We are full of fear and can't bear the thought of the unhappiness we might experience if the other person challenges our opinion or exits the relationship.

3. **We make ourselves responsible for bad things that happen in the relationship.** In this dependency, if something goes wrong in the relationship we immediately blame ourselves. For example, we believe we deserve mistreatment because of what we did or because of who we are. Many domestic violence victims have unfortunately had this mindset literally beaten into them.

4. **We feel responsible for fulfilling the expectations of others.** In this dependency, we want to fulfill the expectations of others not because it makes us our absolute best but because we don't want to experience negative repercussions from others.

5. **We struggle to create or maintain personal boundaries.** In this dependency, we do not know how to tell others when and how to speak to us, treat us, and what buttons not to push. We become a pushover to please them and we don't know how to enforce any type of boundaries.

6. **We need the validation and approval of others.** In this dependency, we crave the approval of others because we will feel unfulfilled, unworthy, or unwanted without it.

Here's what Michael from Lagos, Nigeria wrote to me about his issues with being too dependent in relationships.

Michael's Story

I'm twenty-seven, and for much of my life, the one word that defined me accurately was scared. Growing up in a home where my dad battled cancer for years, and where my mom had to do everything for him, my idea of what human relationships should be was warped. I grew up afraid of facing the world on my own, so much so that I always needed someone to lean on. In fact, I would argue that I would have been a beanstalk if I were a plant. I don't know the term for it, but nowadays I call it my beanstalk complex.

In college, I was part of a clique that I one day aspired to lead, but in all honesty, I was the most disposable member. With such insecurity, it's easy to think that I was unattractive by conventional standards, but I wasn't. I'm over six feet tall, muscular, and have a nice beard. In other words, I had the goods, and I knew so, but somehow I never really felt like I did or could be my own man. I always looked for validation from others, and I took this insecurity into my intimate relationships. Suffice it to say that I was always getting dumped.

In my ex's words, "You're choking me, Mike! I can't do this anymore."

I never understood her and to be fair, I think I was expecting her to be like my mom—always giving and giving and never really receiving anything in return. I cried and cried after she left me, but it wasn't until I talked to my mom about it that she opened my eyes to reality.

Before the cancer, my dad was the strongest man she had ever known, and he helped her through a lot. He still helped her through her PTSD from her years growing up as an abused child, but I just couldn't see it. I could only see his physical dependency on her but not her emotional dependence on him.

My conversation with my mom was short, but it turned me around. Slowly, I started to see the world differently and the people in it as more than just shoulders to lean on. I realized that if others could stand up to the world, I could too! Literally!

Here's the moral. We all have our struggles, and while we may need people to help us get through, sometimes we must learn to be independent—or better—interdependent. We need to learn to give and take in our relationships if we want to be happy.

How to Build Healthy, Interdependent Relationships

I appreciate Michael's wise words and remember having to learn how to break from being too dependent on others as well. Here are some steps all of us can take to build healthy relationships that are neither too dependent (or too independent) that will grow us socially, emotionally, and even spiritually:[2]

1. **Visualize ourselves in honest, caring, growing relationships.** This first step will help give us a better

understanding of what healthy relationships are. We need to visualize what common ground, synergy, responsiveness, communication, awareness, tolerance, and evolution look like for each of our relationships. We can write it out or even talk about it with those we're in various relationships with, and then put into practice what we feel we should do to build and maintain healthy, mutual beneficial relationships. And we can do this regularly.

2. **Identify any roots of addiction we might have to others.** If we are making somebody else the source of our happiness or some other need in our life, we are addicted to or dependent on them. We should accept it, admit it, and take proactive steps to move away from our addictive mindset. In some cases it will just require an attitude adjustment, but in others it will require us to exit the relationship altogether for our own protection and well-being (and the protection and well-being of the other person).

3. **Expand our social circle.** The more deep, meaningful friendships we have the happier we will be. We shouldn't just rely on one or two people to bring us all of our social fulfillment. We should get out there and meet different people who can bring good things into our lives in different ways.

Review:

Point to Ponder: Happy People Understand the Give and Take

Law to Remember: The Law of Interdependence

Affirmation to Declare: "I know it's possible to build healthy relationships that will grow me emotionally, socially, and even spiritually. I will commit myself to understanding what that means for me and take steps to do that in all of my relation-ships. This is my declaration of happiness."

For more free resources on this topic, go to www.DrRob.TV/happiness/Chapter21

CHAPTER 22

HAPPINESS IS CULTIVATED IN EMOTIONALLY INTELLIGENT COMMUNICATION

The Law of Communication

"The single biggest problem in communication is the illusion it has taken place."

- George Bernard Shaw[1]

H appy relationships are defined by great communication.

But our communication with others is often a complicated thing because of who we are as individuals. The education and experiences we have had, for example, and the values we carry, our current stress levels, and our mood all dictate how we communicate with others.[2] Our communication is also complicated by our perceptions of others.[3]

We often treat others based on how we view them through our own limited lenses, for example, and not based on who they actually are. We ask ourselves, are they important to us? Do we trust them? Do we like them? Do we agree with them? Are they just another face in the crowd? Are they somebody who can help us? Are they somebody we could care less about?

But other people are asking the same questions about us and viewing us through the same distorted lenses. And the complications that arise from the way they perceive and communicate with us (and how we perceive and communicate with them) is causing a lot of miscommunication that is, in turn, damaging many of our relationships.

I know this has happened to me before. I can recount many occasions when people have spoken to me roughly or condescendingly simply because they were viewing me through their own limited perspectives. I know others have done the same to you because they have failed to see the BEAUTIFUL MASTERPIECE that you are and have mistreated you as a consequence.

Unfortunately, the sad reality is most people are not aware of how they communicate—or how easily they fall into the miscommunication trap. As a result, they frequently do not communicate in healthy or intelligent ways, and they do not communicate to address the needs of others or to truly connect with them.

Instead, they only communicate to speak their minds (and insist on their agendas) and end up disregarding the feelings of others in the process. Because of this, emotionally intelligent communication is often lacking in many relationships, which has resulted in increased conflict and greater unhappiness throughout society.

Poor Communication Habits

But I do not believe most people intentionally want to communicate poorly. I believe they communicate poorly as a result of what they've seen modeled for them at home and in society. Here are just a few examples of poor communication we may have experienced first-hand (or may have inadvertently caused).[4]

1. **Interrupting others.** When people interrupt us when we're talking, it makes us feel disrespected and undervalued. If we feel undervalued, our happiness walks right out of the door because we feel stripped of our agency.

2. **Multitasking during a conversation.** If others are on their phone while at lunch or dinner or when they are hanging out with us, it leaves us feeling unimportant and irritated. If this goes on too long, we will become unhappy very quickly.

3. **Rambling too much without a point.** When people use words carelessly and without a point—that do not educate, inform, empower, connect, or entertain—they are straining our relationship because they are eating up our limited time—and driving us crazy in the process. How many times have you avoided "that friend" because they called or texted but all you knew they would do is ramble on and on and waste your time?

4. **Invalidating others' feelings.** When people discount, belittle, minimize, ignore, or negatively judge us or our feelings—even if unintentional—they communicate with us that we don't matter to them. This can cause serious harm, especially if this happens in very important relationships.

5. **Being tough on the person and soft on the issue.** This happens when we make an innocent mistake but instead of discussing the mistake, the other party attacks us personally. For example, if you forgot to take out the trash they might say, "you're such an idiot" when they could have instead said, "you forgot to take out the trash." I have definitely been attacked in this way and I know you have too.

6. **Overusing the word "but."** When people say one positive thing to you but then say "but," it acts as a negator of what they have previously said. How many times have people said something positive to you but then immediately used the word "but" and canceled everything they said before that by speaking something negative?

Of course, these are only a few examples of poor communication habits people use that create irritation, disrespect, frustration, and unhappiness in our lives and relationships. You and I could easily list many more. But the point is, we have all experienced poor communication that has negatively impacted us.

As mentioned earlier, if poor communication occurs in our very important relationships—or if it occurs when we're especially young—it can impact our self-image, cause us to be withdrawn or timid (or in some cases very rebellious and angry), and make us feel unwanted, unappreciated, and unhappy.

Here's what Rachel from the Philippines wrote to me about her experiences with a family that communicated poorly with her growing up:

Rachel's Story

When I was younger, I always tried to be a good daughter. People around me always thought I had the "perfect life" because I went to the best schools, was an honor student, went to church every Sunday, and didn't have any issues with money. My grandmother "spoiled" me, giving me everything she thought I wanted. My parents and grandmother always had their way when it came to deciding what is good for me. I never really had a choice in expressing myself or doing what I wanted to do.

Growing up, I was shy, timid, and would never start a conversation. I was taught to never talk back to my parents and family members who are older than me. I was told my opinion didn't matter and so my opinion was never asked about anything—because my family always saw me as a "little girl" even in my twenties. Over time, I grew afraid of speaking up.

When I got older, decision-making and speaking up were very difficult tasks for me. I always got anxious whenever there was a need for me to talk to someone about what I think. When relatives would ask me for favors (mostly asking for money), I did not know how to say no—I was just taught to do whatever my family needed me to do because my opinion was meaningless. I couldn't even call out someone when they had done something wrong to me—my lips were sealed because I was too scared to talk.

But everything changed when I met my husband. He was the complete opposite—he is straightforward and will say what he wants to say. He made me realize that some people were manipulating me through their poor communication. He kept encouraging me to say what I really felt. It was hard, but over time, I finally learned how to. Also, being a mom somehow helped. NOW, I CAN COMMUNICATE WHAT I FEEL AND I'VE NEVER FELT HAPPIER.

Ways to Improve Our Communication

I'm sure Rachel's experience of not feeling like her voice matters has been experienced by many of us. But even if we didn't experience what happened in her relationships, we've all been in relationships (or home, at school, at work, or in society) where we felt we could not be ourselves because others were communicating with us that our opinions didn't matter as much as theirs.

On the flip side, we've all probably been in situations where we also fell into the miscommunication trap ourselves, which ended up not only causing the other party unhappiness but us unhappiness too. If we ever find ourselves falling back in this trap—or if we're currently there right now—here are a few techniques to get out of it so we can get back to being better communicators.[5]

1. **Focus on people's needs.** We can ask ourselves, what does the listener need to hear the most from us? What kind of mood are they in? Are they emotional and do they need a sympathetic ear? Are they confused and need guidance? Are they just looking to connect in a low-key way? What do they need the most and how can we provide it in that moment? When we stop and focus on others' needs and not just our own, we will stop communicating in a one-sided and transactional way in our relationships society has taught us to communicate in.

2. **Adjust our assumptions.** Even if we speak the same language, we should never assume we are speaking the same "language." In other words, certain keywords may be very different for us versus someone else. Always ask people, especially the important relationships in our life, if there are certain words or phrases that seem to make them uncomfortable so we can adjust our communication with them to make them feel valued and comfortable.

3. **Be curious about other people's perceptions.** Even if we're an expert in one thing, our expertise is always limited. Therefore, we can learn to be curious about how others perceive things so we can relate to them on their own terms. We'll not only understand them better, but we'll also be more likeable—and learn a thing or two.

4. **Use positive, affirming, uplifting language.** We can make sure that the words coming out of our mouths are always positive and encouraging. People have lots of stress and discouragement in their life, and we can be an antidote to this. A happy person always seeks to lift up others through language. As happy people, we can use our words to heal and to build others up so that they can be happy too.

Review:

Point to Ponder: Happiness Is Cultivated in Emotionally Intelligent Communication

Law to Remember: The Law of Communication

Affirmation to Declare: "Communication is so important and as a result, I'm going to make every effort to be an emotionally intelligent communicator. I'm going to focus on others' needs, and I'm going to be more consistently positive and encouraging with my words. When I do, I will build strong, healthy, and happy relationships. This is my declaration of happiness."

For more free resources on this topic, go to www.DrRob.TV/ happiness/Chapter22

CHAPTER 23

HAPPY PEOPLE LET NEGATIVITY SLIDE OFF THEIR BACK LIKE WATER

The Law of Positivity

"Stay away from negative people. They have a problem for every solution."

- Fearless Soul[1]

Other people can drive us crazy.

Not only are there negative people all around us, but they often have a specific "negative agenda" for us too.

Their negative agenda—which is sometimes known to us and oftentimes unknown—is undermining our happiness. Part of their agenda includes trying to manipulate and control us, trying to force us to see things from their perspective, and trying to bring us down to a level where they can put us into a nice little box.

Our happiness is not their concern. Sometimes they might say it is, but it really isn't. Us following their agenda is their concern.

The negative family, friends, acquaintances, and coworkers in our lives have been stealing part of our happiness. And every time we have let one of their negative comments or actions make us feel bad, we have given away a little part of our happiness to them. In other words, we've let them knock us down a rung or two on our Happiness Spectrums.

During our time on the earth, there will be critical people who come into and out of our lives. These are negative voices that we must learn to recognize and deal with. If we don't learn how to properly deal with them now we will never learn to be truly happy because these negative Nathans and Nancys will keep popping up in our lives.

Ten Negative People in Our Life

Here is just a small sampling of the negative people we will encounter throughout our lives.

1. **The big mouth.** This person is a gossip or instigator and can't tame their tongue. They often spread fires, and somehow we end up the worse for it.

2. **The bad influence.** This person's values are no good. They appeal to the worst instincts inside of us and can undermine our goals, success, character, and reputation. They usually are very fun or persuasive, but they have all sorts of destruction within them that stops our progress.

3. **The betrayer.** This person gains our confidence over a period of time. They may even actually be a true friend or confidant. But when the moment strikes, they turn on us. Sometimes it's planned and sometimes it's not. They often use all sorts of rationalizations and excuses for why they

turn on us, but it does not negate the fact that they're still a betrayer.

4. **The chronic downer.** This person is always sad, always miserable, always the victim. They see the worst in everybody and everything, and the worst in life usually happens to them. They suck our energy fast and usually require great amounts of attention. Even when we help them, they do not change; they simply glory in their sorrow and the attention that it brings them.

5. **The critic.** This person would rather tear somebody or something down than build it up. They are not dreamers looking to create something new and great. They are looking to find our flaws or mistakes and magnify them.

6. **The flake.** This person always says one thing and then does the opposite. We can only sometimes rely on them, and they leave us disappointed frequently.

7. **The narcissist.** This person thinks they're better than us, and cannot stop thinking about themselves. They're highly manipulative but can also be likeable or boastful, or both.

8. **The rival.** This person fears us and competes to try to be better than us. Sometimes this is a family member or coworker. They will stop at nothing to beat us.

9. **The underminer.** This person is a real shark. They want to undermine our goals and plans simply because it brings them joy or gives them something to do. This person usually is somebody within our office. If we just thought of a specific person, it's probably them.

10. **The enemy.** This person is anybody who willingly stands in the way of our dreams. They often show up in the form of family or friends who try to hold us back from doing something we want by speaking "logic" and "reason" to us.

As we can see, there are lots of potential negative people in our lives. And all of these people are seeking to control or manipulate us in some way. I don't say this to scare you or make you feel overwhelmed. I say this to be real. I also say this because we have to learn how to deal with them so that we can be happy. But in all truth, how have we reacted to them in the past? Let's be honest with ourselves here.

If we reacted in anger, stress, disbelief, worry, panic, or anxiety to the negative people in our lives they have some level of control over us.[2] And they have already undermined our happiness in various ways.[3] Here's what Tiffany from Ohio wrote to me about her experiences dealing with negative people.

Tiffany's Story

My parents love me. I've never questioned that part of my story. But growing up, life was difficult and complicated. My mom worked around the clock, and my dad often held two jobs. I only remember going to the dentist a few times in my childhood because we didn't always have health insurance. Fights over money always happened. My mom had a very jealous disposition and despised anyone who appeared to have a better lifestyle than her.

My family had access to more money, but they never wanted to ask for it. My dad's parents had plenty and were willing to help us any time, but my dad was too proud to even mention it. His dad, my grandpa, was not someone we wanted to owe money to. He was ruthless and a felon. So instead of asking for money, my dad did work for my grandpa.

One day, I walked in on my dad beating my mom uncontrollably. This came at a time when my family was being investigated for running a criminal drug operation out of my house and after my grandpa was arrested on an unrelated charge for soliciting a prostitute. I saw my life playing out in the local news and felt like I wanted to have a meltdown. I even had $1,000 I secretly stored up and a "go" bag if I ever needed to leave. I was angry with my family, especially my mom and dad. I blamed my mom for being so stupid to stay with my dad and my dad for being so backwards. Why were these people so negative, I thought, and why did I have to suffer the consequences of their actions and choices?

For all of my parents' flaws, though, I never doubted they wanted the best for me and did the best they knew how to provide it. So I worked hard, left to go off to college—education was my ticket out—and I never looked back. I then had my own husband and family, and tried to distance myself from my childhood as much as possible. Decades went by and everything was going great until I got a call from my dad. He told me that my mom's dad—my favorite and beloved granddad—was a pedophile who sexually abused my mother for years. My world came tumbling down and I was sucked back into the childhood I tried to escape.

I paced, I stewed, I pulled every single photo of my granddad out of the albums. I put them in a resealable bag and told my husband to put them where I would never find them. I wasn't sure what I wanted to do with them, but I wasn't sure I wanted to destroy them either. I was confused. I didn't want to believe that a person I had loved was one of the most despicable kinds of people that walk this earth. I didn't want to think that my grandmother would live with this person and expose her children and grandchildren to his evil. I didn't want to accept that not believing it would mean my mother is the vilest liar that could ever exist. It had changed everything I thought I knew.

After this experience, I realized I was not in control of my emotions. I was suddenly aware that my behaviors that I thought I had tamed were oozing out of me in a seething, angry manner. I could no longer say that my hot-temper flare ups were because I had a Scotch-Irish heritage. I was shaking my legs uncontrollably at random moments. I was snapping at my staff and children. I was selfishly throwing myself into my doctoral work so that I could curate the identity I had created in one space where nobody knew how unraveled I was becoming.

I wish I could say that I went to counseling, but that is a distorted truth. I went to counseling by proxy. My youngest daughter had picked up on some of my unconscious behaviors. She was exhibiting signs of significant anxiety, and I knew medication wasn't the path I wanted to take for her. Plus, she already took medication for ADHD. She needed to learn ways to manage stress appropriately through more conscious techniques. She participated in cognitive behavior therapy for a few months, and I watched closely. I realized that the strategies were working for me as much as for her and that I probably needed these coping methods all along. It was humbling but necessary.

As my emotions regulated, I knew that the life I wanted to live was not the life I was living. I am not at peace with my childhood, but I do accept that it is my truth as I see it now. I also know that my future is mine to design. My upbringing—and the negative people and circumstances involved in it—do not have to define my destiny or my happiness.

How to React Positively to Negative People

When Tiffany first shared her heartbreaking story with me, I was stunned. And I cried. I had known her personally and never knew her upbringing was so harsh and negative. I'm sure we can all learn from her strength for how to deal with negative people. If you're dealing with a negative person right now—even if it isn't anywhere near as extreme as Tiffany's case—here are a few proven tips you can take so you can hold onto your happiness.

1. **Be mature and do not reciprocate a person's negativity.** This is easy to say, but how many times have we lowered ourselves to a negative person's level and reciprocated their vitriol back at them? As happy people, we are mature and do not need to change our thoughts or emotions to put somebody else in their place. Leave that for other people to do even if we think it will feel good for us. We should

consistently maintain our composure no matter what is said or done to us by negative people.

2. **Smile and use positive body language, words, or text.** When we smile and are positive, it is difficult for a person who is negative to remain critical of us. If we are not defensive and do not say nasty things back to them, it is difficult for them to remain nasty to us. When we remain positive in all of our communications with them, and maintain the moral high ground, we will know we've done the right thing—and shocked them too.

3. **Voice our opinion.** While it is good to overlook an offense, if it is repeatedly aimed at us, we must say something. We have courage inside of us, so we must let ourselves be heard at the right time. The truth is most of the time negative people don't even know they're being negative. When we share our perspective with them, they just might change theirs. If they don't, we'll know they are just trying to control us because they are unhappy with themselves and that they should probably see a therapist.

4. **Separate from negative people if necessary.** If a negative person becomes too overwhelming, we must separate ourselves from them like Tiffany did with her family. We have the right to peace and happiness, and we have a right to a similar environment. We should not allow anyone close to us to undermine us or our environment on a regular basis.

Review:

Point to Ponder: Happy People Let Negativity Slide Off Their Back Like Water

Law to Remember: The Law of Positivity

Affirmation to Declare: "I recognize there are all kinds of negative people around me. Most of them are trying to manipulate and control me, even if they don't know it. I won't respond negatively to these people. I will maintain my composure if they try to undermine me, and I will exit their presence if they try to repeatedly do me harm. I choose to be happy and positive even if other people make it hard for me to do so. This is my declaration of happiness."

For more free resources on this topic, go to www.DrRob.TV/happiness/Chapter23

CHAPTER 24

A HAPPY PERSON ACCEPTS THEIR HATERS

The Law of Haters

"Do your thing and don't care if they like it."

- Tina Fey[1]

Some people don't like us.[2]

In fact, a lot of people don't like us. I know this is hard to hear. But it's true. Statistically, 25% of people we meet will never like us.[3] Ever.

That means that if you look at the whole population of the earth (currently 7 billion), 1.75 billion people would not like us if everyone knew our names.

But on the other hand, 25% of people - or a different 1.75 billion people - in the world would like us if everybody knew our names.[4]

And about 50% of people—a little over 3 billion people in the world—would neither like us nor dislike us (they would simply have no opinion of us and can be persuaded to like us or dislike depending on what they hear about us).[5]

These statistics are stunning. Why? Because it goes to show you that no matter who we are, no matter what we do, no matter how much we accomplish or what we look like, we will have people who do and don't like us. And they will or won't like us based on who they are—not on who we are.

We just have to accept this reality if we want to be happy. We cannot base our happiness on the approval of others because we can never become what some people want us to be.

For the 25% of people who don't like us, here are just a few reasons why they don't:

Why People Don't Like Us

We remind them of their failures. If we're good at something and they aren't, they will hate us because of who we are and who they are not.

We remind them of what they lack. If we have something— looks, talent, money, relationships, status, etc. —that they don't have, they will be jealous.

We remind them of their past. If we remind them of the negative things they once did (or experienced), they will instantly dislike us and be tormented at our presence. Ever meet somebody who had the same name as that "horrible" ex? You get the picture.

We remind them they feel worthless inside. Many people are very insecure, and those who don't like us usually fall into this category. They feel worthless and they project their self-hatred onto us without even knowing why.

We remind them of themselves. Sometimes, we remind others of exactly who they are and if they don't like who they are, they won't like us.

They think we are a threat. We scare them in some way, and they think we will undermine their life, so they don't like us.

We're not like them. We may not look, think, or speak like them and people often fear and dislike the unknown or the unfamiliar.

These are just a few unfair reasons why people may not like you or me. But there may also be a few legitimate reasons some people have not liked us that we can change today if we're trying to grow into the best and happiest possible versions of ourselves. Here are just a few:

Why People Don't Like Us Continued

- We might brag too much.
- We might try to manipulate or control people.
- We might be selfish at times or tell little white lies (or even big black lies).
- We talk too much and take up too much energy.
- We have little self-awareness at times.

I know, I know. This is difficult to point out. But I want your and my happiness so badly that I have to humbly show us all the reasons why people may not like us—both the good reasons and the bad. Here's what Thomas from Brazil wrote to me about his experience with not being liked.

Thomas's Story

When I was younger, we moved to a new house every year, in a new city. Nobody knew me and it was hard to make friends. The other kids wouldn't talk to me and would exclude me from every activity. I remember one time I was the victim of bullying and had no one to help me. Needless to say, it sucked. But it also made me feel fear and anxiety whenever I entered a new school.

As a result, I had very low self-esteem and this made me want to stay at home locked in my bedroom away from everything and everybody. And I blamed my parents for this.

My parents never listened to me. I begged them to stay in the same city for another year, yet they sacrificed me to the wolves of new school after new school because I thought they didn't care about me; I thought they only cared about my dad's job.

But when I learned I would be going to yet another new school, I had an idea that I believed would change my life forever: I decided to change myself and become a "new me" in the next school. I figured I would become the coolest kid in school because at least then I would be liked. At least then I would be accepted. At least then my anxiety and low self-esteem would be eliminated.

But do you want to know what happened? That school year was actually the hardest year of my life because, to prove my worth, I had to put in more effort than anybody else. And not only did they not care, I still felt unliked, unaccepted, and full of anxiety and low self-esteem.

Later that year, I had a big realization that helped me see the truth of my situation, though. My parents told me why they would keep moving and why I kept having to switch schools. They told me when I was born I had to go through a major surgery that cost a lot of money and so my dad had to take up a job that required him to travel often just to pay for my surgery and to support the family. Instead of them trying to torture me by uprooting my life and keeping me on the road, they did it because they were only trying to make ends meet because of something that happened I wasn't even aware of.

In the end what I learned was that even during the times when I was being bullied and disliked at all of these new schools, I was still learning. I was learning how to overcome my fears. I was learning how to overcome my anxieties. I was learning how to overcome my desire to fit in. I was learning how to be strong without all of the Band-Aids society tells you you have to have to be acceptable. Now I feel I'm on my way to being the best and happiest version of myself simply because I no longer care about whether I'm liked or not—and I have my parents to thank for that.

Review:

Point to Ponder: A Happy Person Accepts Their Haters

Law to Remember: The Law of Haters

Affirmation to Declare: "I recognize that some people will never like me. I used to let this bother me, but I'm not going to anymore. Even if I tried to get them to like me, they won't so I'm just not going to let this change my life or impact my happiness. I will choose to be happy even though I've got haters. This is my declaration of happiness."

For more free resources on this topic, go to www.DrRob.TV/happiness/Chapter24

PART FOUR

MASTERING HAPPINESS
IN YOUR CAREER

MASTERING HAPPINESS IN YOUR CAREER:
Introduction

Let's continue on our journey and focus on the work that we do to make a living because our work should be bringing us happiness. I know, I know: You might be thinking, "if only." And that is completely understandable.

The overwhelming majority of people struggle with finding happiness and satisfaction at work. Even people with a dream job and dream income still struggle more than we might realize. But these struggles can be overcome

I do realize this is a very big statement. After all, all of the meetings we must attend and emails we must answer can leave us feeling stressed out and overwhelmed. Many of the mindless bureaucratic procedures we must go through to get anything done can leave us bored and frustrated. And some of the negative coworkers or clients we have had to deal with can sometimes leave us feeling a mix of cringeworthy emotions.

Despite all of these issues—and more—we can learn to be happy at work. We can learn to be happy in the midst of stress, pressure, deadlines, bureaucracy, and negative coworkers. And we can learn to be happy right now even without switching jobs or organizations. In this section, we're going to repeatedly hit the themes of money, status, success, "destination disease," and difficult workplaces from different angles because these are the areas most people face the biggest traps in becoming happy.

CHAPTER 25

A HAPPY PERSON SEARCHES TO DISCOVER THEIR DESTINY

The Law of the Assignment

"Leave your ego at the door every morning, and just do some truly great work. Few things will make you feel better than a job brilliantly done."

- Robin Sharma[1]

The happiest people on earth love their jobs.

But the sad reality is most people don't. In fact, a full 80% plus of people hate or are dissatisfied with their jobs.[2] This is causing them to be less productive, more stressed out, and more unhappy.[3]

But the question is: Are you part of the 80% of people who dislike their jobs?

Why People Dislike Their Jobs

If you are a part of the 80%, it is probably for one of the following reasons:

- You feel stressed out
- You have an unreasonable manager or boss or unproductive employees
- You have unlikeable, disagreeable, stressful, or slacking coworkers
- You find your work uninteresting or boring
- You are working in the wrong organization
- You are working in the wrong career
- You have not found or are ignoring your true assignment and calling
- You might be misunderstanding the purpose of the challenges you are facing in pursuing or maintaining your dream job or career

This is by no means an exhaustive list, but you might have found yourself identifying with one or more of these things like I used to when I was unhappy with my work in the past. But the real question is why have most of us chosen to stay in jobs that we haven't liked?

Why have we chosen to stay in careers that haven't brought us fulfillment?

Why have we chosen to stay in organizations that haven't made us happy?

Although our answers will vary, we usually put up with work we don't like for the following reasons:

1. It is a steady job
2. We need the money
3. We cannot find other work
4. We are too afraid to get into the industry or organization we really want
5. We used to have dreams but failed at them so we settled for second best
6. This is only a side gig or temporary job until things really line up for us
7. We are disillusioned or let down by our dream job or company
8. And we are just doing this now so we can do the things we really want to do later

Regardless of the reasons why we might be unhappy in our jobs or careers, we must know that we are wasting our valuable time and forfeiting our happiness if we are not doing anything about it. We must know that we will never be truly happy unless we solve this workplace issue. Why?

Because you and I will work an average of 2,000 hours this year and over 90,000 hours over our lifetime.[5] We will work 1,000% times as many hours as we will spend seeing our family and friends.[6] Let that sink in for a minute.

That is a statistic and not hyperbole. And in fact, consider this statistic too: Most of us will only spend a little over 5% of our total time on earth with our loved ones.[7]

Here is what Jonathan from the United Kingdom told me about dealing with a job that didn't make him happy:

Jonathan's Story

"Do I have to do this all day?" I asked as my colleagues laughed. They thought I was joking, but I wasn't.

It was early on a winter's morning. I'd been with the company for just over a year and I'd just seen my list of tasks for that day. Ugh.

It was simple work but the pay was good because it was very dangerous.

But careful working practices and constant training were designed to keep us safe. The slightest diversion from the company's strict policies, though, like any unsafe handling of the machines, any wrong color shoe lace, etc., would result in a snap note. Three snaps and you were out.

There was plenty to be unhappy about in this company. I honestly only took the work because I needed something quick. A previous job had ended suddenly and this company was a large local employer. And the worst part was my supervisor. I swear he was physically attached to his clipboard. He would notice every minor infraction like an unhappy drill sergeant. He gave me a snap note for having an unbuttoned shirt cuff while on the machine floor once. Ugh.

I wanted out and I wanted out bad, so I worked toward getting another job to no avail.

One morning I was at the coffee machine in the break room when I heard a loud bang from the machine floor. Then another bang! Bang! Bang!

Before I could turn around the room was empty. Everyone was outside, standing near the railing. I saw a machine had jumped clear of its red zone and was wedged into the machine next to it. My coworker Jeff was being escorted off the floor by the supervisor, one hand on his red clipboard and the other over Jeff's shoulder. I instantly knew exactly what had gone wrong. It was an operator error. That resulted in three snaps in one. Jeff wouldn't be stepping onto the machine floor again.

"He was late this morning. He looked tired," one coworker said.

"No, he hated it here," I said. I'd been talking to Jeff in the breakroom only a few days before and knew how much he despised the job and the company. But then someone shot back to me, "we all hate it here." But in this moment came my eventual epiphany.

I drove home that day tired and worried. I thought about how dangerous the work was. I thought about how loud it was. I thought about how boring it was. But I wondered if there was something redeeming I could find in it? Was there a way I could actually learn to enjoy my work and not hate it like everybody else? For the sake of my job and for the sake of my sanity?

I decided to come in a little early the next day. It was very quiet as I stood next to my coworker Nathan and marked out my tasks. Nathan and I had started at the same time at the company and had been on the training machine together. Of the six of us who had started the day we did, only Nathan and I were left. I nudged

Nathan as he wrote, deliberately jolting his pen, messing up his duty sheet. He responded angrily, shoving me hard. He took a new duty sheet and started writing again. I jolted his pen again. He shoved me again, but not so hard, and he was laughing. "I've got enough to do without dealing with you too," he said.

Then I saw the supervisors offering coffees to the team. "No sugar, double cream for you," the supervisor said as he handed the drink to me. I didn't know he knew how I liked my coffee. Has he actually been paying attention to me and what I value? I thought.

I took the coffee with me onto the machine floor. "I can't believe I get to do this all day," I said.

Then the supervisor started walking toward me, his clipboard in his hand. He gave me a friendly smile before uttering, "Don't put that coffee down in a red zone. Work safe."

I knew I wasn't going to be doing the job forever, but I started to see the positive in my job and in my supervisor. And it was just that tiny change in my attitude that made all of the difference for me and my happiness at work.

Why We Need to Make Happiness in Our Jobs a Priority Right Now

Whether we are working in our dream job right now or in a job like Jonathan was, we should make being happy at our *current* workplace one of our highest priorities. We are losing too much time, enduring too much stress, and sacrificing too much happiness.

But we are also doing more than this, as terrible as these things are. We are also harming our health, workplace relationships, productivity, and bottomline by being so unhappy.

Research shows that our unhappiness at work is costing us more than we think.[8] It is physically releasing toxic hormones (cortisol) into our system; undermining our interpersonal relationships with coworkers; decreasing our focus and ability to successfully complete our tasks and perform at our highest level; and causing severe financial losses for our organizations.[9]

This has to stop. We cannot keep poisoning ourselves this way. We have to decide right now that we will make happiness in our current jobs—defined as perceiving our current work and colleagues as meaningful and necessary—a top priority.

We have to do it even if our coworkers are not doing this (and even if they are cranky, unreasonable, lazy, and even if we find our work boring).

We have to do this even if we're planning to eventually quit because we think some other job (i.e., a better job or dream job) will make us happy in the future.

If we don't, we will continue to slowly cut our wrists. Because the reality is this:

We will never step into our next level of happiness in our "dream job" until we master happiness at our current job.

For example, did you know that most doctors are unhappy and that doctors have the highest rates of suicide in the world (even though they are working in a "dream job")?[10]

Did you know that statistically most lawyers are miserable mentally and emotionally?[11]

Did you know that most rich investment bankers are unhappy?[12]

All of the research shows this.

Although certain jobs seem like a dream from the outside, if we are not pursuing happiness before we get these jobs we will be filled with misery. These are "dream" jobs and professions, but they have become nightmares for millions of people despite their status. And it's not just the stress or responsibilities of these jobs that is causing people unhappiness either.

It's also the disappointment people experience in many cases once they finally get what they want. In many people's quest for money, power, fame, or success, for example, they worked so hard because they believed that once they achieved their dream careers they could then relax and be happy. But when they did achieve their dreams and all that came with them, they experienced one of the biggest disappointments of their lives: They realized that most of their success was not really making them happy (or as happy as they could be).

For you and me, we have to take a different path to our happiness than just going after dream jobs and success as important as these things are. We cannot wait to be happy until we achieve all of our dreams. We have to choose to be happy in the work we are doing right now with the people we are doing it. If we don't, happiness could elude us all of our lives because there is no dream job that will automatically fill us with the joy we long for.

How to Be Happy at Work Right Now

Having said all that, there are a few simple ways to become happier in our workplaces right now.

1. Write out a list of all the things we appreciate about our current jobs (i.e., that it provides a paycheck, helps us get groceries and pay bills, etc.) and put that list in our wallets. We can pull it out often so we can reflect on the good things about it. Like with anything else, gratitude will cause us to look differently at the jobs we're in (and invite more happiness into our workplace experiences as a result).

2. Smile more at our coworkers, customers, and bosses. Smiling releases dopamine in our brains and makes us feel good and other people feel good.[14] Most people will reciprocate and the whole office (or Zoom) will feel better when we do this.

3. Get a work "bestie." We can find somebody at work that we can genuinely talk to. But we have to make sure this person is positive and not just somebody we complain to or gossip with (which is normally the people we gravitate toward when we're unhappy at our jobs). Whenever possible, we should surround ourselves with happy, uplifting coworkers.

4. Perform at our highest levels of excellence in everything that we do. When we do, it'll make us take pride in our work and appreciate it more than ever before. When our performance and appreciation rise so does our happiness.

Of course, there are other things you can do to become happier in your current workplace. And if you're not in a field or role that is truly your heart's desire, I encourage you to go after that dream and that role (the subject of the next chapter). But in the meantime, you don't have to sacrifice your happiness. You are a BEAUTIFUL MASTERPIECE and you don't have to let anything get in your way.

Review:

Point to Ponder: A Happy Person Searches to Discover Their Destiny

Law to Remember: The Law of the Assignment

Affirmation to Declare: "I can no longer tolerate disliking my job or being unhappy with any part of my job. It is costing me my time, health, relationships, and productivity. So instead, I choose to be happy. I choose to use my time wisely at my job and appreciate what I have. I choose to go after my assignment. I will stop making excuses for why I cannot be happy at work, why I cannot pursue my dreams, and why I cannot enjoy my dreams once I achieve them. This is my declaration of happiness."

For more free resources on this topic, go to www.DrRob.TV/happiness/Chapter25

CHAPTER 26

HAPPY PEOPLE STOP COMPROMISING THEIR DREAMS

The Law of Commitment

"Talent or intelligence don't matter. It's your dreams that will decide how big a person you become."

- Imran Khan[1]

Nothing makes us come alive more than chasing our dreams.

Our dreams can give us hope, direction, and connection with others. Achieving our dreams can fill us with satisfaction, purpose, and deep meaning. In short, pursuing and attaining our dreams can bring a sense of great happiness to our lives.

Destination Disease

But if you are anything like I was, you might be struggling with "destination disease" when it comes to your dreams.[2]

Destination disease is when we believe our dreams only matter when we achieve them.

It's when we believe that the journey of our dreams is less important than the destination of them.

It's when we fail to recognize the lessons we learn in pursuit of our dreams are the primary reason why we should be chasing our dreams in the first place.

And it's part of the reason so many people are unhappy in their lives. They never realize that life is 90% journey and 10% destination. They never learn to enjoy themselves during the journey and reflect on what they are experiencing in the day-to-day of it. They think they can only be happy once they get to their destination.

This might sound like you sometimes. I know it was me once. I would think I could only be happy "later" on—once I finally reached my dreams.

So I worked very hard and succeeded, but looking back on things, I didn't really find tons of happiness in the process (or I didn't find as much happiness as I could have). And when I would achieve a dream, I was temporarily happy but then became quickly dissatisfied because I needed a new dream that I thought would make me finally happy (because my old dream didn't make me happy like I thought it would). And subconsciously I believed I couldn't be completely happy until I reached the new dream even though I had reached my old dream(s). This vicious cycle went on and on until I learned how to escape it.

Now don't get me wrong: Achieving our dreams does bring us great joy. But we cannot put off our happiness in the process of reaching our dreams. We cannot put off our happiness until we finally "make it." We must enjoy the process. Contrary to popular opinion, we don't have to be constantly dissatisfied with what we have to pursue for greater goals, greater success, and greater happiness.

The Right Dreams

But there is another reason why we should not put off being happy until we achieve our dreams: We may not actually be pursuing the right dreams in the first place!

I know that is surprising, but it happens all of the time. I've seen countless talented people around the world who were not pursuing things that interested them. Why? Because of family pressure. Because of social expectations. Because of financial security. Because of prestige and ego.

I've seen countless people pursue the things they thought they were "supposed" to pursue. I've seen countless people who convinced themselves they would "one day" be happy once they achieved a certain level of success or a certain destination. I've seen countless people who convinced themselves that they couldn't really be 100% happy today, but that someday they will be once they get to a certain point in their careers or lives. I've seen countless people pursue their "dreams" —or other people's dreams they've accepted as their own—while often sacrificing their happiness.

Compromising Our Dreams

But even though I've seen some people pursue their dreams, I've seen even more people who don't. And they don't pursue them because it's not easy to. So what do they end up doing? They often end up sacrificing both their dreams and the happiness that comes from pursuing and attaining their dreams. Here are just a few reasons why people don't pursue the dreams in their hearts:

- They fear losing status, money, or perceived security
- They have never turned their dreams into practical, step-by-step goals
- They have not sought out proven mentors (people, books, etc.) to teach them how
- The fear of starting is causing them anxiety
- They are distracted
- They are afraid of being judged for failing
- They let people talk them out of it
- They have overcommitted themselves financially
- They feel it is not the "right timing"
- They feel they are too young, too old, or do not have the right experience or connections

In short, there are many reasons why we may be compromising on pursuing our dreams. There are many excuses. But consider what Sadia wrote to me from Pakistan. She had every reason in the world—and every excuse in the world—to not go after her dreams, but she decided to anyway:[3]

Sadia's Story

Growing up as a girl in Pakistan means from the moment we're born a set of expectations is thrown at us. We spend our life living up to them one by one until we become a stranger to ourselves. From birth to death, our life is not our own.

Here's a glimpse of what these expectations look like:

- Get the bare minimum education necessary until we get marriage proposals from men.
- Once we have the bare minimum education at age seventeen and are eligible for a wedding, then we work toward winning the "star wife" badge, which means learning every domestic skill under the sun (because taking care of the house is solely a woman's responsibility). When we do this, we will make our "auntie" fall in love with us so that she makes us her daughter-in-law. After all, we are nice and polite girls who know their place.
- And before we know it, we're a bride.
- Now we're our husband's property.
- And what this means is that we can't get an education once we marry. We can't pursue a career once we marry. And we can't have any individuality once we marry.

This is the culture I grew up in. A culture that didn't allow girls like me to pursue our dreams. If a girl did, she would be shamed, guilt-tripped, and suffer abuse. She would also become an outcast: too much education would mean she was no longer marriage material because a girl would make a boy look stupid in comparison. Too many goals would mean a girl wouldn't be a good homemaker. Not committing herself to a lifetime marriage at seventeen would mean a girl would be too old to be valuable.

In my culture, girls were sucked into the pressure of society and wound up in loveless marriages of abuse and living lives they hated. But not me. I refused to be one of them. I know I cannot surrender to society. I know I need to fight for the life I want. I know I can't bury my dreams by taking the easy way out.

As Jane Eyre said, "I am no bird and no net ensnares me. I am a free human being with an independent will."

And so I will continue to chase my dreams. I will continue pursuing what I love, build a business that I love, and I will travel the world so that I can take care of myself. And who knows, maybe I'll find love along this journey. But love is not my final destination. Marriage is not a box I have to check off my list before I die.

There's so much more to life than what people told me growing up. And there's so much more to life than what people are telling you. We don't have to accept everything that's thrown at us. The life of our dreams is worth fighting for because our happiness is worth fighting for.

Write Down Our Excuses

Sadia is so courageous and her example can give us so much inspiration to reach toward our dreams. But we can also do something else that is practical that will help us get past any blockages we have when we reach toward them.

1. Right now, write out every excuse imaginable for why we might not chase our dreams. Think of as many as possible.

Once done, find a red sharpie and make a giant circle around it. Proceed to put a giant "X" through the list. Now post it somewhere it can be seen as a reminder we are terminating past excuses once and for all.

2. Next, write down all of your dreams. Think of dreams for every area of your life. Then write down the top three to five baby steps needed to take to make each dream happen. When done, make a few copies of this list and post a copy on the fridge, put one in the car, or wherever it will be seen daily. And finally, give a copy to two trustworthy people so they can hold us accountable. (If you don't know anybody trustworthy, you should keep your lists to yourself and get some new friends!)

Review:

Point to Ponder: Happy People Stop Compromising Their Dreams

Law to Consider: The Law of Commitment

Affirmation to Declare: "I recognize that I have compromised on some of my dreams. But now I am going to commit to focusing on pursuing my dreams, step by step, with the right motives. The more I can do what I feel called to do, regardless of the results I get, the happier I will become. This is my declaration of happiness."

For more free resources on this topic, go to www.DrRob.TV/happiness/Chapter26

CHAPTER 27

HAPPY PEOPLE MAKE IT THROUGH THE FIRE ALIVE

The Law of the Potter's Wheel

"Sometimes you just have to put on lip gloss and pretend to be psyched."

- Mindy Kaling[1]

No matter who we are, our workplaces will challenge our happiness—over and over again.

Even if we are pursuing our dreams or taking steps to be excellent in a job we're not that interested in, our working conditions will not always be perfect. In fact, they will often be the opposite of perfect.[2] We will almost never have a perfect position with a perfect portfolio and perfect colleagues and perfect customers. That simply doesn't exist.

We'll have to embrace the fact that our romanticized versions of perfect workplaces—of perfect jobs—are just fantasies. Even if we work for the places considered to be "the best places to work on earth," all of them are far from perfect.

We will have to deal with inevitable problems and politics, some of which we won't want to deal with. But we will have to and this could stress us out and cause us to be unhappy even in our dream jobs and organizations if we're not careful.

The more we get stressed over time—even while chasing dreams—the more our resolve to be happy and successful will weaken and change. We can easily enter a job for the right reasons because it was a dream but easily just stay in it for the paycheck after we burn out.

This happens a lot. Even people with mission-driven careers begin to burn out over time because of the stressful or negative conditions in their workplace. So instead of being happy and content in their dream job, they become disillusioned and complacent. And work becomes a chore.

This happened to me time and time again. I would work in dream roles with some of the most famous people in the world but because there was a bad apple or two, I would let them stress me out. I let the bad apples strip me of my unhappiness. I didn't know that my focusing on their negativity or my complaining about it in confidence to others was turning what I loved to do into something I hated.

We must resist this urge to allow our happiness to be undermined by the cranky people in our lives who do not care about us. But this is very difficult sometimes, I know. Here's what Hannah from the UK said about her unfortunate experience dealing with a difficult working environment (which happened to be her first job):

Hannah's Story

I started my dream job and I was dumped right into the middle of a mess I had no way to prepare for. How was I supposed to anticipate untrained staff, rude supervisors, and a manager who had it out for me? I couldn't have.

At first I thought, hey, this isn't so bad. The pay was good, and it had the experience I desperately needed, so I stuck with it. But, as always happens with blind naivety, things went downhill fast.

I was the youngest on the team by almost a decade, one of only a handful of women, and I didn't exactly have the no-nonsense attitude that most of them did.

But don't get me wrong, I was good at my job, but being good wasn't enough—and there was always one manager willing to remind me of that.

Pretty soon, constant criticism began and it became a physical drain. I was criticized for every little thing— arriving on time meant I was late, smiling too much meant I was being unprofessional, but frowning meant I was being unprofessional too. Everything I said or did offered up some kind of critique, always with an undertone of sneering.

While I realized I didn't have to stay in what I thought was my dream job forever and that I could always quit, I needed to learn how to enjoy the good parts of my job—and the few good people. I needed to learn how to change my perspective and count my blessings. Yes, there were parts of the job that sucked, but I still had a paycheck, was still healthy, and could still focus on the redeeming things. And this is what made all the difference for me.

Even though I eventually ended up getting a new "dream job," I was still able to be happier in my old dream job once I made an attitude adjustment toward it. I knew I couldn't change my negative coworkers but I could change myself—and my reactions to them.

If you're in a dream job with a few negative coworkers like I was, I offer you the same advice. First change yourself and see if you can handle your situation. If it is still too onerous to work there after you do this, then change your situation and leave.

Things That Will Challenge Your Happiness Even in Your Dream Career

If our workplaces do get to be too much like Hannah's, we can always leave.[3] We should never allow anyone to continuously abuse and disrespect us. But we should realize that no matter who we are or where we go—and no matter how "ideal" our perfect workplaces could be—certain things will always challenge our happiness at work. Here is a brief list.

1. **Boring work.** There will be some aspects of our jobs (even our dream jobs) that are just plain mundane. It might be 10% of our work, 25%, 50%, or more. We have to accept this and not lose our drive. Even people in the most exciting careers do not feel excited 100% of the time because of the

sometimes dull routines of their jobs. In my work as a film-maker in Hollywood, there are parts of my job that I loathe but I have to do it nevertheless.

2. **Lack of connection.** There will be some people who don't want to talk to us at work. There will be some people who don't like us. This could be supervisors, coworkers, or even employees we oversee. We may not feel "connected" to everybody. This is ok. We can still find meaning and connection with the right people and do not have to concern ourselves with others. Even if those others are on our teams, we can use the techniques from Chapter 25 to try to brighten their day (and our own).

3. **Bullying behavior.** In almost every workplace, there is at least one bully. People who mock or demean or mistreat others. People who make it unpleasant. People who are cynical or skeptical or who bring down our moods. There is usually an underlying emotional problem these people have for doing this. We shouldn't take it personally and shouldn't let it distract us from completing our (dream) work with happiness.

4. **Inequality.** Every organization has a hierarchy. That is, every organization will allow specific people to make certain decisions because of their title or seniority. But the problem is that these people often let their work hierarchy substitute for a real-life social hierarchy, and this artificial hierarchy creates a separate and unequal work environment. While we should accept the protocols of our workplaces, understand the people within it are not superior or inferior to us—job title notwithstanding. If our workplace is very unequal, study to see how we can change it. Or leave.

These are just a few of the many issues that we will encounter in almost any (dream) organization we work with and for. Even if we start the company and are the "boss," you will encounter some of these situations so be prepared for what you will inevitably encounter.

Review:

Point to Ponder: Happy People Make It Through the Fire Alive

Law to Remember: The Law of the Potter's Wheel

Affirmation to Declare: "I have to remember that no job is perfect, not even my dream job. I will encounter challenges in the workplace but I can still choose to be happy and overcome them. I can temper my expectations and adjust my perspective so I won't lose my positive motivations for pursuing my dreams and achieving my goals. I realize I'm on a potter's wheel getting better and better and that's ok with me. This is my declaration of happiness."

For more free resources on this topic, go to www.DrRob.TV/ happiness/Chapter27

CHAPTER 28

A HAPPY PERSON SEES THE GLASS AS HALF FULL

The Law of Grace

"No one ever injured their eyesight by looking on the bright side."

- Anonymous

Our workplace relationships can make or break our happiness.

Research shows that a positive workplace can empower us mentally, emotionally, and physically.[1] It can make us feel alive, productive, and put extra pep in our step. It can make us look forward to getting up in the morning and to completing tasks throughout the day. And most importantly, it can contribute to our overall sense of well-being and happiness.

A negative workplace, on the other hand, can do the opposite.[2] It can drain us emotionally, mentally, and physically. It can make us stressed out, anxious, and cause us to engage in destructive behavior, possibly even revenge. In fact, nearly 50% of people have admitted to seeking workplace revenge at their organizations.[3]

This is not because people are just mean, though some are. It's because people feel underappreciated, overworked, or like there's been political maneuvering going on. Maybe you've felt this way at times (I know I have). And whenever we feel this way, it decreases our happiness.

Our workplace happiness—and the relationships we have at our workplace—are a big deal. Statistically we will spend a lot more time with these people than our friends and family.[4] Who they are and how they treat us is an important part of what is contributing to our happiness or unhappiness.

Types of Negative Coworkers

If we're unhappy at work, it is usually because of one or more of our coworkers.[5] If they're negative, they can make life miserable affecting our entire day and even our home life. Negative coworkers usually fall into one of these types:

1. ***The gossipers.*** These people believe anything they hear without fact and spread rumors around the office. Sometimes they know they're a gossip but many times they don't. They can also be drama kings or queens.

2. ***The pessimists.*** These people will respond to good news with skepticism or cynicism. They'll also often thrive on negativity and love to point out the mistakes people make.

3. ***The victims.*** These people believe that everything negative is being done to them and will latch on to anyone who provides a sympathetic ear.

4. ***The conquerors.*** They are there to impress us, beat us, and rule over us. We exist for the purposes of their ambition and are a pawn in their game. Or so they think.

Of course, there are other types of negative coworkers but
these are a few common ones. Here's what "Sly" from Hawaii
said about his experience with negative coworkers:

Sly's Story

Some time ago, I was entering a special time in my
military career. I just renewed my enlistment contract,
and I reported to a new command. I settled into my
corner office and promptly put up family pictures and
framed quotes. I love the sound of flowing water, so I
put a tabletop Zen waterfall on my desk. Life was good.

A year into my tour, my command merged with
another command. Instantly, our staff doubled in
size. I was ordered to give up my office, and, at that
moment, I was not feeling very Zen-like. However, I
needed to control my happiness and find the positive.
So, I embraced the idea that our combined commands
would benefit most from an awesome team of two specialists instead of one.

My counterpart, Jamie, reported onboard, and initially, our interactions were cordial, pleasant, and
professional. But then, Jamie's attitude and behavior
toward me became antagonistic and occasionally vin-
dictive. I was confused by this hostility, and I began
to question whether I did something. Instinctively, I
became defensive, because, in my opinion, there was
no reason for Jamie to be this way with me. From
that point on, the tension between us grew, and our
coworkers began to notice. Life was not good.

Imagine two pilots attempting to fly an airplane and build it at the same time while fighting over who should be the pilot and co-pilot. That's a serious problem that ultimately benefits no one. So, as the senior service member, I had to take control of the situation. Jamie was a smoker, so during every smoke break, I would take a "walk break." It was during one of

those walk breaks that I decided to take the lead and fix our workplace team, purposely.

I invited Jamie to lunch to discuss a plan of action related to an upcoming high-profile project. However, my true intent was to find some common ground between us. During lunch, we discussed business, but I was also able to ask about Jamie's evening. Surprisingly, I discovered that Jamie was a Walking Dead fan. I was a Walking Dead fan. Then, it hit me. That's it! Time passed, and Jamie and I bonded over the Walking Dead franchise. We shared our process for prepping zombie apocalypse "bug-out" bags, and our mantra became "Stay ready, so you never have to get ready." We applied that mantra to everything. In the end, I made a connection with a person I know will help me survive during a zombie apocalypse. Lastly, we turned out to be a pretty good team of specialists because our efforts helped the command earn a high-profile award for excellence. Life was good again.

In this situation, I learned that I could not allow someone to highjack and hold my happiness hostage. I had to take control and fly the plane. I took the steps necessary to land on common ground. The moral of the story, if you're dealing with difficult coworkers, is to take control and fly the plane to land on common ground.

Overcoming Negative Coworkers

These are very wise words from Sly. We can all learn to overcome negative coworkers so that we can have more happiness in our workplaces. Here are a few steps how:

1. ***Resist office politics.*** Every office has them, and they are easy to get sucked into. We should focus on ourselves and our jobs and not other peoples' personalities, performances, or rumors.

2. ***Spend time with positive coworkers.*** By connecting with people who understand and are positive, we'll naturally not engage with the negative people. We can do this during our breaks and lunchtimes, or even happy hours. It's even better if they work directly with us or our team, but this may or may not be the case.

3. ***Set boundaries.*** If we're dealing with a "gossip," for example, we can ask them if the innuendo and rumors they're telling us about others come from facts or just something they heard. If we're dealing with a "pessimist," we can challenge them to point out the good in a situation. If we're dealing with a "victim," we can ask them to name some good things in their life or work that make them happy. If we're dealing with a "conqueror," we can ask them if they've truly evaluated other people's feelings and opinions about their proposals. The more we set healthy boundaries, the more negative coworkers will either respect us and act positive around us or just leave us alone—both good outcomes.

4. ***Never say an unkind word about anyone.*** In Congress, they often use formal language to address each other (at least they used to!). For example, they might say the distinguished senator from Montana or the gentlewoman from California. They do this to remain cordial. It doesn't always work but it does improve inter-personal relationships. If we resolve never to speak an unkind or critical word about any of our colleagues—no matter how irritating or incompetent they might be—we will keep ourselves free of office negativity and set ourself up for workplace happiness.

5. ***Look for the best in others.*** When we remember that everyone is struggling in some areas of their life—just like us—it will make it easier to look for redeeming qualities they have and focus on those instead of their flaws.

In short, we can make or break our workplace happiness with some of these simple behaviors.

Review:

Point to Ponder: A Happy Person Sees the Glass as Half Full

Law to Remember: The Law of Grace

Affirmation to Declare: "My workplace is a battleground for my happiness, and I choose to be positive at it. I choose not to let negative coworkers bring me down, and I choose to only speak kind and graceful things to others. I won't engage in workplace revenge as tempting as it is, and I will continue to focus on me and my performance so I can get to the next level. This is my declaration of happiness."

For more free resources on this topic, go to www.DrRob.TV/happiness/Chapter28

CHAPTER 29

HAPPY PEOPLE REJECT THE CULT OF BUSYNESS

The Law of Balance

"It's not enough to be busy, so are the ants. The question is, what are we busy about?"

- Henry David Thoreau[1]

Our busyness is killing us. And it's causing us deep unhappiness.[2]

But in today's society, being busy is a badge of honor. And in some circles, it's a badge of superiority.

This is a shame. Being overly busy should be considered a badge of dishonor.

If we're overly busy, that means we haven't learned to prioritize what's most important to us. If we're overly busy, that means we haven't learned self-love and self-care. And if we're overly busy, that means we haven't learned one of the greatest lessons of life: saying no.

Yet, in far too many of our conversations if somebody asks how we're doing we say, "Oh, I've just been really busy." And the person who asks usually walks away impressed. Likewise, if we think others are really busy we are impressed with them and all they are supposedly accomplishing.

But the reality is, most of this busyness is just a waste of time. It's a waste of time because there is a big difference between being a workaholic (or overly busy) and being a high performer. These two phrases are synonymous in our lives but they are in fact very different things.

The busiest people on the planet are often the most stressed and the ones with the least amount of power and control over their own lives, for example. They are often running from job to job to pay bills, or from activity to activity to climb the ladder.

High performers, on the other hand, may have full schedules but they are targeted toward only the most important things that matter. They're in control of their lives and what they say yes to and what they say no to. Everything is very strategic for a high performer.

Why People Become Overly Busy

In today's society, most people aren't in charge of what they say yes to and what they say no to. They unfortunately add tasks to their plates without thinking about their capacity to take them on. Here are a few reasons why we might be falling into the trap of being overly busy:

- We think this is what we're supposed to do.
- We don't want to fall behind compared to our friends, coworkers, and neighbors

- We think it will lead us to the success that will supposedly bring us happiness
- But mostly we become overly busy because we don't like the idea of being alone with ourselves and our own thoughts (and research shows this).[3]

I know I just laid this on strong. I certainly don't want to stress us out or judge us—my goal is to help build us into becoming even more BEAUTIFUL MASTERPIECES than we currently are. But I do want to be very clear because this book is meant to empower you and I to be better—and happier. I myself have been guilty of being overly busy for the reasons above. But it got me nowhere in terms of my happiness or productivity. We must break free from this rat-race that we're in if we really want to be happy.

But there are also other reasons that we should want to break free from this: busyness has terrible effects on our health, relationships, and professional life according to numerous studies.[4]

Busyness and Our Health

- Being overly busy leads to emotional exhaustion.[5]
- Being overly busy puts our body in fight, flight, or freeze mode.[6]
- Being overly busy weakens our immune system, which can lead to blurry vision, headaches, ulcers, digestive problems, muscle spasms, insomnia, anxiety, bowel problems, and weight gain.[7]
- Being overly busy can produce stress leading to heart disease, cancer, and even death.[8]

- Being overly busy can produce stress hormones that are passed down to our children and grandchildren.[9]

Busyness and Our Relationships

In addition to busyness negatively impacting our health, it also negatively impacts our relationships. For example:

- Being overly busy statistically causes us to dislike more of the people around us.[10]

- Being overly busy causes us to become emotionally unavailable to loved ones.[11]

- Being overly busy leads us to take a transactional view of people.[12]

- Being overly busy creates negative memories for those closest to us.[13]

Busyness and Our Professional Life

And finally, busyness negatively impacts our professional life as well. For example:

- Being overly busy leads to multitasking, which reduces our productivity.[14]

- Being overly busy decreases the quality and quantity of our work.[15]

- Being overly busy gives us lower satisfaction for our professional outputs.[16]

- Being overly busy leads us to feel our accomplishments mean little.[17]

Of course, there are many more negative effects of being overly busy for each of these areas above. But the main takeaway should be that our busyness is not helping us; it's hurting us. And it's stressing us out and making us unhappy.

So why are we doing it? Why are we choosing to be overly busy?

Here's what Bora from South Korea told me about her experience with being overly busy.

Bora's Story

On one January morning, I collapsed on the subway in Korea. I lost all consciousness and was immediately rushed to the emergency room. I had been incredibly busy—typical me—and had overloaded my schedule with work. I was so physically exhausted that my body literally shut down on me. I thought I could handle a full-time job, two freelance consulting gigs, and going to school at night full time. Boy, was I wrong.

I was just trying to be superwoman and, for a while, it worked. But looking back on it I realized I was just committing suicide indirectly. I was so busy that I often forgot to eat and slept maybe a couple of hours a day. All my life I loaded up my schedule so much because I wanted to get ahead and impress people. I was told this is what I was supposed to do to be successful and happy. But if I'm being honest with you, the reason I really loaded up my schedule is because I felt deep insecurity, like I wasn't good enough. And the more I thought about it, the more I realized that maybe I didn't have to try to save the world, but just contribute to it.

Laying in the hospital forced me to rethink things. I sent a "rescue email" to my friends in Korea and in the United States letting them know what was going on with me. This was a deeply humbling and embarrassing experience for me as I wanted people to think I had it all together. But for the sake of my health, I needed to confess that I didn't. Me being superwoman was hurting me and I needed to take off my cape and show my friends and family that I am human too. To my surprise, my support network responded with so much love, empathy, and compassion and I now wonder why I didn't ask for help sooner. I now realize that I am accepted even when I'm not overbusy, that I'm accepted even when I'm not superwoman.

I really appreciate Bora's honesty, vulnerability, and inspiration. She fell into the trap I've fallen into numerous times and perhaps you have too. It is very easy to because sometimes we will have seasons where things are hectic and we're sacrificing to get ahead. But often this goes from a temporary season of overbusyness to two years, five years, ten years, and even longer. It becomes our lifestyle and identity. And it is killing us and our happiness.

We can like Bora learn to overcome this so that we can enjoy our lives, become happier, and even live longer. Here are a few ways to do it:[18]

Overcoming the Trap of Busyness

1. **Create a system to evaluate which projects and activities to say yes to and to say no to**. Create a system that ranks the projects and activities we are going to take on. For example, create a sheet that lists all of our projects and then rates them from one to five (with one being the lowest and five the highest) in the following categories: Strategic Purpose, Personal Fulfillment, and Time Sensitivity. We should choose only the one or two projects with the highest score. If we are already on a couple of projects, we need to make a trade off to either keep the project we're currently working on or take on the new projects we are excited about. We should empower ourselves to stop doing too many things.

2. **Read daily.** Find time for at least 30 minutes every day to read actual books (this could include e-books or physical books). This does not include online articles or anything we read for work. Numerous studies have pointed to the relaxing effects long-form reading will give us, not to mention how reading will make us a more creative thinker and a higher performer.[19] Reading will give us the ability to slow down so we don't feel as much pressure to say yes to things we should be saying no to.

3. **Schedule 30 minute lunch or dinner meetings.** We should schedule 30 minute lunch or dinner meetings with our family or friends without any devices. This will help us stay connected to the people who matter the most to us, and give us a reminder that we are not a human-doing, we are human-being. It will also show the people around us that we really care about them.

Review:

Point to Ponder: Happy People Reject the Cult of Busyness

Law to Remember: The Law of Balance

Affirmation to Declare: "I recognize the negative effects of an overly busy schedule. Today, I'm going to start taking steps to declutter my schedule so that I can focus only on the things that matter. This will make me healthier, happier, and improve my relationships. I choose to say no to the cult of busyness. This is my declaration of happiness."

For more free resources on this topic, go to www.DrRob.TV/happiness/Chapter29

CHAPTER 30

HAPPY PEOPLE DON'T NEED THEIR NAME
IN LIGHTS TO BE FULFILLED

The Law of Fulfillment

**"The fame you think you need to become happy will
quickly become your nightmare once you get it."**

- Anonymous

We've all dreamt of what it would be like to be famous.

We've all wondered what it would be like to have everyone know our names.

And we've all thought about how others would treat us if we were among the most popular or admired people in the world.

Growing up in Los Angeles—and working as a writer and director in the entertainment industry—I've had a front seat to this type of magical dreaming most of my life. I have worked with or met many of the top stars in the world, and I can say without a shadow of a doubt that they are not happier than most non-famous people I know. Nor are their assistants or agents or lawyers or entourages happier either.

But despite this, the dream of fame—or at least some level of status—still tugs at people's hearts and they can sometimes still blindly pursue it unfortunately. Even if people don't feel called to Hollywood per se, many want to achieve notoriety through social media or within their workplaces or industries. While this is not a bad thing, when the desire for some type of low-level or high-level status gets out of control—which it often does—it can be very detrimental to our happiness.

The reason it's detrimental is because when we start to tie our happiness and self-worth to the number of likes we get online, to the number of followers we have, and to whether other people are "talking about us" (or admiring us or envying us) we wind up in very dangerous territory. If we don't have enough of these things, we can feel like we're not good enough (for ourselves and for the world) and so we become insecure. And the more insecure we become the more desperate we are to chase these things—regardless of their costs—until we get them.

Status-Oriented People Are Unhappy

But if we get that fame or status (or success), the ironic thing is most of us would become very disillusioned by it. Here's what a couple of celebrities who did gain the highest levels of fame have to say about it (and how that fame affects their happiness):

"You get to Hollywood, you achieve something and then you realize, 'S--t, it didn't actually bring me the happiness I thought it was going to. It didn't fix anything.'" - Chris Hemsworth, Hollywood movie star.[1]

"You might not make it to the top, but if you are doing what we love, there is much more happiness there than being rich or famous." Tony Hawk, champion skater.[2]

These are only a couple of quotes of numerous quotes that exist from rich, powerful, famous, or successful people who discovered that fame and success did not lead to the happiness that they thought it would.[3]

In fact, research shows that famous people are more unhappy than "everyday" people.[4] And they're unhappy because they romanticized what success would do for them and became disappointed when it left them feeling more emptiness than joy.

But are we doing the same as these rich and powerful celebrities? Are we chasing after fame or online notoriety or status (through our jobs, accomplishments, or associations) because we feel it will make us feel happy (or respected or secure)? Do we subconsciously believe it will fill the holes in our hearts of not feeling good enough if we get the attention we think we need?

Even if we aren't chasing after fame, are we chasing after our goals so strongly (whether they be goals of money, status, comfort, or security) that we are not enjoying our present lives or valuing the people around us as much as we could?

Here's what Arianna from Nairobi, Kenya told me about his experience chasing status and success, which shows us how people everywhere (not just in the United States and Europe) are doing it:

Arianna's Story

Growing up in Africa I could smell the sweet morning dew. I would usually wake up after my parents who were always out working before the first cocks crowed. But seeing them work so hard caused me to want something different. It caused me to want success very badly not only because I wanted a better life, but because I wanted the money and the status I never had growing up.

So I wrote out a list of my goals and began checking them one by one. I did well in school, got a university scholarship, and before I knew it achieving my goals became addicting.

I became so successful that I figured I no longer needed to take the calls of my close family members. I thought, "Why should I? I have my own money! I have my own place! I don't need them!"

It was then I realized I built a huge social wall between me and my parents. But I didn't really care. I was succeeding. My lifestyle skyrocketed and I was living the success that I knew others envied. And this made me feel good. Arrogant. Invincible. Indestructible.

But then something happened.

One morning I woke up and I lost the job that for so long had become my identity. The money stopped flowing in. And my so-called superior superstar status evaporated into thin air. And who was there to pick me up? I became so focused on myself and my success that I never stopped to realize that in my chase for success—in my chase for happiness—that I was living for all the wrong reasons (for all the reasons society and the media tells you that you have to live for). And I was hurting the people I loved the most.

I knew I had to stop thinking the way I did otherwise I would risk wasting my whole life and building
walls between myself and other people that ironically
would continue to keep my happiness out.

How to Stop Chasing Status and Success

I know many people can identify with Arianna's experience. I
know I used to. But we can all learn from him so that we can
truly realize that success (fame, likes, followers, notoriety, etc.)
will not bring us the happiness we have always thought it would.

Now, this doesn't mean we should give up on our goals or give
up on being "successful." It just means we should learn to realize that when we shift from chasing status and success to simply
enjoying our journeys on the way to our success—like we discussed in Chapter 26—we will multiply our happiness. Here's
how we can do it:

1. Appreciate who we are and what we have right now by
   practicing meaningful gratitude exercises daily (i.e., expressing gratitude in the morning, at lunch, and in the evening
   to constantly keep it at the top of our minds). Setting gratitude reminders on our phones can help us do this. The more
   grateful for what we already have in our lives, the less we will
   lust after what we don't have (and probably don't need).

2. Start to celebrate our daily progress in the various areas of
   our lives, which will show us just how successful we already
   are and make us feel more fulfilled and content with ourselves
   regularly. Doing this will show us that the idea of progress =
   happiness really is true as the research says.[5]

3. Accept that fame, notoriety, status, and recognition are
   not substitutes for happiness—and are not multipliers for

happiness either. The more we let this sink into our souls the less importance it will take on in our lives. According to studies, superstardom on any level brings more stress, pressure, anxiety, depression, pain, lower self-esteem, and unhappiness into our lives than we might realize.[6] If we stop chasing after status we will stop unintentionally allowing these negative things to multiply in our lives.

Review:

Point to Ponder: Happy People Don't Need Their Name in Lights to Be Fulfilled

Law to Remember: The Law of Fulfillment

Affirmation to Declare: "I admit I have gotten caught up from time to time in the world's idea of notoriety and success. I have become a little too concerned at times about the number of likes I get, the number of followers I have, and the number of people paying attention to me but I'm not going to continue to act this way. I don't need fame, popularity, notoriety, status, or even recognition to be happy because I know that I am a BEAUTIFUL MASTERPIECE without them. I'm going to start being happier with who I am, what I have, and the daily journey that I'm on. This is my declaration of happiness."

For more free resources on this topic, go to www.DrRob.TV/happiness/Chapter30

CHAPTER 31

HAPPY PEOPLE BECOME SUPERIOR TO MONEY AND POWER, NOT DRIVEN BY IT

The Law of Superiority

"You're not rich until you have something money can't buy."

- Unknown

Our success has little influence over our happiness.

Beyond securing our basic material needs, having more money and power are no guarantee for happiness. In fact, they usually guarantee just the opposite.

In a study published in Nature Human Behavior, results showed that having higher income is associated with lower life satisfaction and lower well-being worldwide (i.e., lower happiness).[1] Although the research didn't say why, one reason for this may be that our emotions are truly indifferent to material wealth.

Looking at lottery winners, studies show that winners are no happier (in the long run) than non-lottery winners, for example.[2]

Even those in the top 1% of wealth holders globally are not statistically happier than those who are not.[3] And if the 1% with all the toys and all the gold in the world are not happier than most people, why do most people think getting that next raise or new BMW will make them happier? Like most people who get something new for the first time, their happiness will increase for a few days or few weeks and then it will dramatically fall again—back to their default happiness.[4]

I really want to drive this point home.

The dollars we may be chasing, the power we may be craving, and the status we might be desiring (whether that status is to fit in, be admired, grow followers, or even gain local or global fame) will not make us happier.

This is scientifically proven.[5]

These things are nice for a moment but it's just for a moment. When we get them it's scientifically the equivalent of getting a lot of likes on social media for a picture we post—we will feel happier in the moment but in a week or two those likes won't mean much to us.[6]

Let's think about that. Gaining traditional material success will have the same influence on our happiness as getting likes from one of our social media posts in the long run.[7]

But it has been so programmed into us that our happiness should be correlated with money, power, and status that it's not going to be easy to drop this type of thinking. That's why I've emphasized it from different angles for a few chapters. We live in a culture that adopts the golden rule—he or she who has the gold rules—so the message from this chapter and in this book will not be driven home very often to us.

Of course, it's important for us to have basic necessities and even save money. But if we let these things become the focus and goals for our lives, we will never reach peak happiness. We will just end up like everyone else who felt that money, power, and status would make them happy but didn't.

Living in Los Angeles, I see this constantly. People are trying so hard to gain these things and I try as often as I can to counsel them that these things will not make them happy.

But even if people say they don't care about money, power, or status and are only interested in being "comfortable" and being "secure," they fall into the same boat. Why? Because comfort and security really don't make people feel comfortable and secure (or happy).

People might have a certain dollar amount in their heads for what they think they need to be happy. But even if they get it, they won't feel more secure or any happier in the long run. It'll just force them to get a new dollar amount in their heads about what they feel they will need to feel secure and happy (after they realize the old dollar amount didn't). I've seen this over and over again.

The point is, money, power, status—and security—will not bring us to the promised land as far as our happiness is concerned. What will bring us to the promised land is being superior to these things, not driven by them. In other words, not emotionally relying on them to make us happy or content.

Here's what Bryan from Wisconsin told me about his experience with this trap:

Bryan's Story

It's hard to be in the corporate world without being focused on money. After all, the point of business is to make money for yourself and your shareholders. Early in my career, power and status seemed to be the best way to get it so I went all in. I was going to get my money—and I was going to use power and status to do it.

Every chance I got I fought for more and more power. Then I had a chance to achieve what I had long been aiming for: "c-level" status. So naturally I fought. But this required a high-level fight with the CEO of the company I was working for at the time. I knew I needed to take it. The CEO was a numbers guy and I was a sales and operations guy. We were like oil and vinegar. But I arrogantly believed that in a conflict between us, the board of directors would surely choose me, the business generator, over the back office CEO. I was wrong. They didn't choose me and I ended up leaving the company.

My failure wasn't simply in engaging in a conflict with a higher-ranking CEO to try to take his job; my failure was in what I thought was important: money, power, and status. I decided to create a risk for the board to gain the things I had always wanted for myself. I was blinded by lots of glitter and lots of gold as so many businesspeople are.

When I looked back on this, I realized my drive in life was for all the wrong things. So I made up my mind to change. I started investing in people rather than power, I started investing in teamwork rather than positional status. And to my surprise this was making me happier. Realizing true happiness in business comes from the success of others truly changed me.

I used to hear that you must first fail before you succeed. I now believe this to be true. I had to experience a failure to shift my focus away from money, power, and status. I had to learn from pain to find what I valued most in life.

Review:

Point to Ponder: Happy People Become Superior to Money and Power, Not Driven By It

Law to Remember: The Law of Superiority

Affirmation to Declare: "I see that money, power, status, and even security cannot truly make me happy. They have not made other people happy and I will not fool myself into thinking they will make me happy. I will still pursue and succeed in my goals, but I won't be driven by material things or thinking I need my bank account to have a certain amount in it to finally be happy. I will choose to be happy whether I have a lot of money or no money at all. This is my declaration of happiness."

For more free resources on this topic, go to www.DrRob.TV/happiness/Chapter31

PART FIVE

MASTERING HAPPINESS IN YOUR BODY

MASTERING HAPPINESS IN YOUR BODY:
Introduction

Phew! How are you holding up? We're more than halfway through the book and you're doing great. Now let's shift our attention a bit and start talking about our looks. I know it's a touchy subject, but we're brave enough to go there.

As people, all of us want to feel attractive. We want to be confident in our bodies and how we're portraying ourselves to the world. Yet, most of us aren't as confident—or as happy—as we could be with our looks so we tend to be pretty hard on ourselves. We tend to notice things about ourselves others don't and sometimes magnify those things, causing us to be insecure or dissatisfied or unhappy with them and with ourselves.

But these aren't the only challenges we face with our bodies causing us to be unhappy. We also can face health challenges too. From minor illnesses and injuries to major diseases and substance abuse, there are many things that can potentially rob us of our health and happiness when it comes to our bodies.

In this section, we're going to explore the common traps we face with our bodies and how we can power through them—and run them over. Here we go.

HAPPINESS IN YOUR BODY BEGINS THE MOMENT YOU REALIZE YOUR FLAWS CANNOT HOLD YOU BACK

The Law of Relative Beauty

"You have been criticizing yourself for years and it hasn't worked. Try approving of yourself and see what happens."

- Louise Hay[1]

Our appearance does not define us.

Yet over 50% of people believe that it does.[2]

Approximately 61% of people believe that being better looking will allow them to live better and happier lives, and more than 50% of all men and women are very critical of their looks.[3]

On average, women rate themselves as a "5" on the "hotness scale" and men rate themselves as a "6" (on a scale of 1 to 10).[4]

And about 80% of people say they want to be better looking.[5]

Similarly, most people—over 80%—said that they judged people based on their looks.[6] And when asked about the topic that people lie the most about, they admit it is other people's looks (and their own).[7] In fact, people lie about other people's looks more than they lie about titles, salary, age, and test scores.[8]

So what in the world is going on here when it comes to our looks?

An Artificial Standard of Beauty

Of course, everyone wants to be as attractive and presentable as possible. That is human nature. But what is not natural is the lengths to which people are now going because they are dissatisfied with their looks.

Since the early 2000s, for example, there have been over 225 million voluntary plastic surgeries in the United States alone.[9] Breast implants, lipo, eyelid surgery, and more. This does not count Botox or all of the over-the-counter, non-surgical cosmetic enhancements.

Both men and women are chasing this standard of beauty that is not only artificial, but that is also fleeting. Beauty and attractiveness is defined differently in different cultures, for example.[10]

In Europe, especially France, beautiful is defined as being very thin. In Korea, beautiful is defined as being very tan. In Hawaii, beautiful is defined as being very dark. In Kenya, beautiful is defined as being very heavy. In the Middle East, beautiful is defined as wearing a lot of jewelry and makeup. In Venezuela, beautiful is defined as having large breasts (and getting breast implants if you're a woman who doesn't have naturally large breasts).

Likewise, beauty and attractiveness does not just change depending on the culture we live in but it also depends on our exposure to what others tell us is beautiful.

For the last 100 years in America, for example, "beautiful" has been represented in the media as thin, white, toned, and symmetrical. Because of the American media's global influence, it has caused millions of people around the world to believe the one standard of beauty is thin, white, toned, and symmetrical.

As a consequence, in the United States, many people, especially young women, report having lower self-esteem after being exposed to this definition of beauty if they do not personally look like it.[11]

But it is not just lower self-esteem impacting them; many young women are resorting to starving themselves, getting surgery, or even ending their lives because they do not meet this made-up body type that is considered "beautiful."

The same is true in places like Africa and Asia. Because America's influence is dominant in those places, millions of young people—who naturally have darker-hued skin—have resorted to skin-lightening products so they can match the image they see on their screens. But these images and standards of beauty are not just because Africans and Asians naturally believe that lighter skin is more attractive; it is because that is what they have been told is attractive (it's all they've ever been exposed to through the media).

In one explosive study, researchers visited an isolated village in Nicaragua—where no electricity, television, Internet, or mobile phones were present—and presented a group of natives with two sets of pictures.[12] They asked the natives to describe the ideal body type over about 15 minutes.

One set of pictures (seventy-two in total) was of plus-sized models presented to one group (group A). The other set of pictures (also seventy-two) was shown of thin models to the other group (group B).

The group that was exposed to the plus-sized models (group A) said that the ideal body type was plus size while the other group who was exposed to the thin models (group B) said the ideal body type was thin. Each group changed their standard of ideal beauty based on what they were exposed to and told was beautiful.

Why We Feel So Down About Our Looks

Based on studies like this and many others, you and I may be feeling down on our looks simply because of what we have been exposed to.

On average, we are exposed to between 5,000-10,000 advertisements per day.[13] These ads do not count television or movies, or internet videos. Most of these ads are for consumer products, and many of them feature the "ideal-looking" model or body type according to profit-hungry executives often based in New York or Los Angeles who are looking to capitalize on the public's own body insecurities.

This means that every year we are exposed to millions of images of what a small group of people are telling us is attractive. So subconsciously we believe these images are attractive. And if our body does not match up with these images, we experience cognitive dissonance and unhappiness. We negatively judge our own looks, the looks of others, and view ourselves as average or unattractive as a result.

Here's what Taly from Los Angeles told me about her experience with body image issues:

Taly's Story

Strength, dexterity, agility—these are words I did not think applied to me. I was born with cerebral palsy, and have limited use of my right hand and right leg. I walk with a noticeable limp and use only my left hand for everything—dressing, eating, opening anything. It is often something I do without even noticing. I always sit on my right hand to keep it steady, tie my shoe one loop at a time or pull out my daughter's juice box straw with my teeth. Who knew Capri Suns could be so challenging?

At the same time, I know there are things I will never be able to do. I love dance, but am often hesitant to do it myself unless in my own living room. I want to do yoga, but fear I will fall and look silly every time. Disability was a word I feared for years. I did not want to look at myself as a girl who was challenged or disabled. Yet, I have always been and will always be fiercely independent. Almost to a fault. I always try to do things on my own first, even when I know it is out of my reach. I walked along a wall as a seven year old, unbalanced as I was, only to fall off and break my shoulder. While for some, this might be a sad story, for me, it was a great one. I wasn't going to let a little wall stand in my way. I swam in a cave in Cancun and made it down the ladder to my husband—even though I was terrified on the way down. I hike, and never noticed until my husband pointed it out, I speed up the mountain when I get to the steepest part. For better or worse, I want to reach the top on my own. I look at my daughter, and pick her up, despite the fact that it is getting harder the bigger she gets. I want to be the one who will hold her and hug her when she's proud or sad. In that, I am learning I am strong. I am agile. I will always keep trying things on my own despite how my body looks and what it tells me I can't do—that is my happiness. Even though I don't look like those made-up "air-brushed" models, I know I'm beautiful.

How To Break The Media's Stranglehold on Our "Beauty" Perceptions

Taly is a friend of mine and I asked her to share her incredible story. She didn't let society's standard of beauty stop her from loving herself, finding her happiness, or doing the things she wanted to do in her life. Neither should we. Here are a few more ways to break the artificial standard of beauty we have been indoctrinated into:[14]

1. Accept our looks and bodies for what they are, and know that if we consider ourselves to be beautiful— we will be beautiful (and many others will think so too). It is that simple.

2. Stop obsessively focusing on only a few specific body parts of ours to judge our attractiveness. We are a whole person and bigger than our perceived flaws.

3. Become a critical consumer of the often airbrushed and manipulated images in advertising, television, and especially social media. They are not real, so we should not compare our reality to their technology.

4. Expose ourselves regularly to images of beauty different from that of our own culture's. This is easy to do—we can just pull out our phones and search for it.

5. Embrace the fact that we can go somewhere in the world right now (perhaps a different culture) that will view our specific looks—our faces, bodies, skin tones, and the like—as beautiful and even perfect.

6. Realize that the most important aspect for our success and happiness is not our looks, but our attitudes! Our looks cannot be controlled (unless we go under the knife), but our attitude can be and it is considered the key ingredient to attractiveness and personal success.[15] No matter what we think our flaws are, they really cannot hold us back unless we want them to.

Review:

Point to Ponder: Happiness in Your Body Begins the Moment You Realize Your Flaws Cannot Hold You Back

Law to Remember: The Law of Relative Beauty

Affirmation to Declare: "I now realize that my standard of beauty was being manipulated by the media and advertisers. I realize that beauty is relative, and because it is I choose to believe I am beautiful. I know that what I perceive as my flaws truly cannot hold me back from being happy or living the kind of life I want to live. My own perceptions will now define my beauty and my attitude will determine my success. This is my declaration of happiness."

For more free resources on this topic, go to www.DrRob.TV/ happiness/Chapter32

CHAPTER 33

HAPPY PEOPLE TREAT THEIR BODIES AS BEAUTIFUL TEMPLES

The Law of Consecration

"I have come to believe that caring for myself is not self-indulgent. Caring for myself is an act of survival."

- Audre Lorde[1]

Our bodies are sacred.

It is where our brains, hearts, and souls reside. It is where our memories are stored. And it is the object that allows us to experience pleasure and pain while we're living on the earth.

Over recent decades, more and more people have been realizing this. Yet despite this epiphany, people are less healthy than ever before.

Obesity and diabetes are at an all-time high.[2]

The use of antidepressants has increased over 400%.[3]

A majority of men and minority of women are addicted to pornography, and rates of STDs are doubling in many cases with the majority of Millennials carrying some sort of sexual disease or infection.[4]

Drug use is becoming an epidemic for both illicit and prescription medications.[5]

And alcoholism has increased over 50% overall, with it increasing by 83% for women and 92% for African Americans.[6]

All of this is happening because people are unhappy in their lives so they are searching for unhealthy escapes. Let's look at a few things people do to their bodies that contributes to their unhappiness. Think about if you fall into any of these categories.

Eating Poorly. Research shows that not only do people eat poorly when they are sad, but that they are sad because they eat poorly.[7] Diets composed of higher calories, sodium, and saturated fats, for example, result in negative moods two days later. They also result in larger waists and poorer health across a variety of areas.

Lack of Sleep. Just like eating poorly, not sleeping properly can decrease people's happiness.[8] It used to be that insomnia was linked to people who were depressed, but modern studies have shown that people who sleep less (for whatever reasons) are at higher risk of becoming depressed after never having been depressed before.

Alcohol. Alcohol temporarily releases dopamine into people's systems and elevates their moods (causing them to have fun in the moment), but then it does the reverse: It lowers the serotonin and norepinephrine levels in their bodies, which increases their likelihood of becoming sad and depressed.[9] Alcohol can also activate their genes linked to depression and negatively alter their thought process (after the "buzz" has gone away).

Pornography. Like alcohol, pornography temporarily releases dopamine (pleasure chemicals) into people's system, but it also increases mental anxiety, feelings of loneliness, and depression over the long term.[10] Research has shown that those who view porn frequently have a 300%-400% increased likelihood of becoming depressed or severely depressed.

Casual sex. Studies show that those who engage in casual sex are at higher odds of not only contracting an STD, but of becoming depressed and experiencing lower self-esteem.[11] In other words, casual sex leads to negative emotional consequences that last much longer than the original hook-up.

Drugs. For non-addicts, drugs can alter brain chemistry leading to higher levels of depression. This is true for people who were depressed before drug use and those who were not.[12]

Of course, there are other unhealthy behaviors that people engage in that cause them to experience more unhappiness than they should be but these are just a few common ones. Here is what Lauren from South Africa wrote to me about her experience with not treating her body well:

Lauren's Story

The raw honest truth is that I never treated my body well from a very young age. I started cutting myself at around fourteen, and I also started smoking cigarettes. A few years later I went on to drinking and smoking marijuana. I would also have sex with almost any male that looked half decent and showed me attention. I just didn't care.

I would sleep with hard-core drug addicts who were much older than I was. It was almost like I was trying to punish myself. I would also drink till I blacked out and then do it all over again the next day. In terms of food, I would usually eat take-out and only after not eating for the entire day.

But right before I turned thirty everything changed for me. I gave up both smoking and drinking. And I joined a gym and educated myself on what it meant to be truly healthy. I opened my eyes to the fact that even though I had studied psychology when I was younger, I lacked insight into my own self-destructive behavior that was clearly damaging my body. I started to realize it was my own lack of self-love that caused me to engage in unhealthy behaviors for a very long time.

Once I woke up, life became easier. I met a healthy partner who loved me just the way I was and I have been with him ever since—and with none of those men who would only use me to fulfill their sexual desires and fantasies. My partner helped me to love myself for who I was. And he helped me to start really valuing my health and making it a huge priority in my life.

I finally treat my body well and when I see people mistreating their bodies I just want to shout out to them as cliche as it may sound: "Self-love really is the greatest love of all".

Overcoming Abusing Our Bodies

I know it wasn't easy for Lauren to share this story, but it sure is powerful. If you happen to find yourself abusing your body in any way, there's hope to overcome your pain—you are going to pull through whatever is holding you back, you BEAUTIFUL MASTERPIECE. Here are a few helpful suggestions below.

1. ***If you're over- or undereating:*** You can start to eat well! You can start making moderate adjustments in your diet today and build on them each week so you can change the way you eat. Look online as there are lots of free or low-cost solutions to guide you on your way.

2. ***If you're having trouble sleeping:*** Try to go to bed at the same time every night. And be sure not to consume food, drink, or media before bed either if possible. Also be sure not to go to the gym, check email, or get into a phone or text conversation. Try to get into a relaxing state and read, reflect, meditate, pray, stretch, or even take a bath—you'll put yourself in a more sedative state by doing this.

3. ***If you're abusing alcohol:*** You can learn to cut back. Try not to drink every day or even every week (drinking weekly actually increases your risk of cancer). If you do happen to drink, try not to have more than one or two beverages. If you feel you are addicted though and can't cut back easily, try joining Alcoholics Anonymous or an equivalent group so you can live the healthy life you deserve.

4. ***If you're addicted to porn:*** You can get an accountability partner you can talk to so you can admit your challenge with watching it. There is no shame and condemnation in this. You can also filter your computer and smartphone, and avoid sexually explicit movies and images online. If it's hard to do this, try joining an online or local support group for

help—you'd be surprised at just how supportive these types of groups can be for those who want to break their addictions so they can be healthier and happier.

5. *If you're engaging in casual sex:* Take the same steps you would to break pornography, but also try not to physically put yourself in a position to engage in sex casually. If you do find yourself in a position like this, try to leave immediately. I know this is drastic but the temptation may be too great when feelings, hormones, and neurological chemicals start to kick in and take over.

6. *If you're using drugs, cigarettes, or vaping:* Commit to quitting for good. Join a group like Narcotics Anonymous or similar. Get a long-term accountability partner to help you stay sober after you get out of the program so you can put yourself on a strong path to ultimate victory.

Review:

Point to Ponder: Happy People Treat Their Bodies as Beautiful Temples

Law to Remember: The Law of Consecration

Affirmation to Declare: "In the past, I have mistreated my body in one way or another. I was doing it to have fun and feel better but I now realize that I was also making myself unhappier. I will start to proactively take steps to treat my body as a temple. This is my declaration of happiness."

For more free resources on this topic, go to www.DrRob.TV/happiness/Chapter33

CHAPTER 34

HAPPY PEOPLE REALIZE TRUE HAPPINESS IS NOT THE ABSENCE OF PAIN

The Law of Overcoming

"Don't let pain define you, let it refine you."

- Tim Fargo[1]

Pain is inevitable.

When we were kids, we ran and played and fell down. We got cuts, bruises, and scratches. We lost teeth. Some of us may have had broken bones, gotten stitches, or needed major or minor surgeries. We went to the dentist who stuck a giant needle in our mouths. We lost friends. And some of us were even physically or verbally abused by bullies or family members.

At the time we experienced pain as kids, the physical, mental, and sometimes emotional stings were overwhelming. But we still got through these things. And for the most part, unless we experienced a traumatic incident—like when I did when I fell off the side of a mountain—we no longer feel the pain of most of the past things that once hurt us. Most of the pain in our lives came and went, and most of us moved on without a care in the world.

But as an adult, the carefree perspective that helped us overcome—and helped us forget a lot of our pain as kids—has been beaten out of us by life.

People Are Stressed to the Max

Recent research has shown that most of the pain people are experiencing as adults is happening because of stress.[2] Or because of people's reaction to stress. People are not processing the negative things that happen to them in the same way they used to as kids. And the consequences are pretty brutal: Between 90%-95% of all illnesses and diseases, for example, are being created by stress (and according to cellular biologists, only 5% of diseases are occurring because of genetics).[3]

In other words, most adults who are experiencing sickness are experiencing it because they're making themselves sick. The fatigue, overeating, headaches, increased allergies, hypertension, diabetes, cancer, and various other illnesses are hitting people hard because of their response—or lack thereof—to the stress in their lives.[4]

But even if people aren't experiencing pain because of stress, it is still causing them major unhappiness. A chronic illness or disease can also be torturous and end up leaving people feeling very unhappy with the cards they were dealt in life. But it can also cause them to look at their pain in a different way.

Here's what Jess from Los Angeles said to me about the ongoing pain she's experienced in her life as a kid and as an adult:

Jess's Story

I have anemia. I have arthritis. I get hypoglycemic, and I get sad sometimes because of the pain. But let me tell you a little more about me, let me tell you about why I'm not defined by my sicknesses or pain.

I'm a successful psychotherapist and non-profit entrepreneur. I've learned to make time to live life and enjoy it. I love to travel and have learned that my life is only a vessel to create things and help people. There are many reasons why I've gone through what I've gone through.

Last year, I almost died because my iron and blood levels dropped dangerously low. I was getting dizzy and irritable all the time, and didn't know why I had to fight this battle. But I remembered there are many reasons why I've gone through what I've gone through.

Before my near-death experience last year, I was driving on the freeway when suddenly two cars slammed on their breaks, causing me to swerve to not hit them, only to lose control of my own car. I spun around the freeway three times, smacked into a pole, and literally almost took a nosedive off of the freeway. There are many reasons why I've gone through what I've gone through.

When I woke up from the shock in the ambulance and realized the EMTs were going to take me to a different hospital than the one I worked at, I said,

"Really? You see my badge... take me there!" referring to my own place of employment, my own hospital. When my coworkers saw me they said, " You are supposed to be helping patients, not be one!" There are many reasons why I've gone through what I've gone through.

Before this, at age twenty-four, I started to lose the feeling in my legs, and so I had my-then boyfriend carry me into his car to take me to the hospital. I had officially lost the ability to move my legs. Soon thereafter, I had officially lost the ability to walk. There are many reasons why I've gone through what I've gone through.

At age eleven, I suffered a dislocated hip. As a consequence, I've had to have many surgeries that have made me like a walking, talking cyborg. There are many reasons why I've gone through what I've gone through.

And here are the reasons. You can look to my story and my crazy issues and realize that you can still smile, laugh, and live life like me despite any pain you or your loved ones are experiencing or will ever experience.

You can look to my story and realize you have the strength to go on too.

You can look to my story and realize you don't have to take your life or your health for granted.

You can look to my life—all of my battle scars—and realize that life happens and that negative situations help us learn and level up.

And you can look to my story and learn to trust God if you never had, as he will literally always have my back and yours.

There are many reasons why I've gone through what I've gone through and why you're going through what you're going through. These reasons help us to become the amazing, strong, and bionic human beings we were designed to be.

Increasing Happiness When Fighting Sickness or Disease

Jess is such an inspiration and I know many people look up to her around the world. She has shown such grace under fire and serves as an example that people can be happy even when they're battling major pain and health crises. Here are a few lessons you can learn from Jess if you're facing a physical crisis such as a terminal disease like she is.

1. **Fight it with a smile**. Although you can't choose whether you have an illness, you can choose how you response to that illness. You can choose to be happy or sad, so you should just choose happiness with a smile.

2. **Try to search for meaning**. Even though life can sometimes be mysterious, you can try to see what lessons you can learn from this and teach others.

3. **Resolve to enjoy yourself as much as possible.** Nobody is going to make it out of this life alive, so you should enjoy your time while you have it just like Jess has done. And if you're mobile, you should engage in your favorite activities and spend time with your loved ones.

4. **Be an inspiration.** You can use your pain to be an inspiration to others—both those who have a sickness and those who don't. If you're able, you should spread your positive mood, volunteer, and show others that your illness doesn't define you.

Healing Chronic Stress to Increase Happiness

Even if you're not facing a terminal illness like Jess, but are instead encountering major stress like millions of other people, you can also overcome your stress so that you can become happier in your life. Here are a few ways:

1. **Walk barefoot on the beach or the grass.** This will calm your nervous systems, improve your blood circulation, and reduce any inflammation you might be experiencing in your body.[5]

2. **Do something pleasurable for yourself everyday** like a foot massage, salt bath, or other things that bring you pleasure.[6]

3. **Go to sleep by 10pm** to increase the functioning of your healing hormones (those positive brain chemicals) and cellular restoration.[7]

4. **Adjust your diet.** Whenever possible, you should cut back on and avoid caffeine, processed foods, sugar, fried foods, carbonated drinks, and unhealthy foods you might be addicted to. Instead, you should eat whole foods like sweet potatoes, carrots, and chicken—it will make you feel better, less sluggish, and believe it or not will actually improve your happiness.[8]

Now, doing some of these things may be difficult, but your health and happiness are worth it. I've made the same adjustments for my health and it's made all the difference. When we realize that we have the tools to become happy regardless of the stresses or physical pains in our lives, it should give us all the motivation we need to use them so that we can grow into a better—and happier—us.

Review:

Point to Ponder: Happy People Realize True Happiness Is Not the Absence of Pain

Law to Remember: The Law of Overcoming

Affirmation to Declare: "Many of the physical symptoms I sometimes deal with are caused by my stress, but I now know how to reverse this. I can walk back some of my unhealthy habits so I can physically feel better and happier. If I keep the right perspective on my health, I can be happy, unstoppable, and overcome anything thrown my way. This is my declaration of happiness."

For more free resources on this topic, go to www.DrRob.TV/happiness/Chapter34

CHAPTER 35

HAPPY PEOPLE LEARN A THING OR TWO ABOUT BODY LANGUAGE

The Law of Body Language

"The human body is the best picture of the human soul."

- Ludwig Wittgenstein[1]

Our body language says everything about our happiness.

On the one hand, it's easy to spot people who are happy based on their body language.[2] They have big smiles on their faces, they're walking and speaking confidently, and there seems to be a special grace to them. They have more energy and seem to be brimming with life. They exude a warmth and compassion that lifts the environments they enter, which is often contagious.

On the other hand, it's also easy to spot the people who are not happy based on their body language. They often walk glumly, have unfriendly or sour faces, and seem to have very weak and defensive body language. They permeate negativity, and we can sometimes even "feel" their energy. When they walk in a room, we want to leave it as fast as we can.

Research shows that our happiness can influence our body language—but also that our body language can influence our happiness.[3]

In our modern culture, the way we sit, walk, talk, and engage in the physical environment around us can influence the moods we're in, for example. And the moods we're in can in turn influence how we perceive ourselves (i.e., whether we see ourselves as happy or sad), how we interact with others (i.e., if we are acting openly or defensively with people), and more. When mom told us to sit up straight it turns out it wasn't just about having good posture—it was also about our happiness—whether mom knew she was encouraging that or not (more on this in a second).

Here's what Dennis from Kenya said to me about his own experience with his body language:

Dennis's Story

One great advantage to being raised in Africa is the vastness of our cultural heritage. I was lucky enough to experience a rich culture growing up, but this rich culture also drained me in ways that, truthfully speaking, took me to rock bottom.

I was twelve years old and at the onset of experiencing puberty. It was the law in my community that each household's male members had to undergo circumcision. I had nothing against this right of passage as my elder brother had already participated in the act and so I didn't think much of it other than to embrace it.

The day came, and my father took me to the hospital. But before undergoing the medical procedure, the doctor on duty had to examine me first. He gave a worried look on his face as he exchanged glances with my father. Something was wrong. I was missing a testicle.

Growing up, I thought I was normal and healthy, and therefore missing a part of my manhood never bothered me. So I decided to undergo circumcision as planned. I had no idea this wouldn't be my last visit to the hospital.

The doctor recommended that I undergo an additional surgical procedure and I went in for more discussions with him. But my parents disagreed with the doctor. They thought it would damage me and that I would not be complete if I "corrected" my situation.

As this thought grew in me (that I needed to be fixed) it impacted my body language and my self-confidence more and more. I felt so damaged— worthless, really—and I let it show on my face and in my interactions. My social life became a nightmare. I couldn't make eye contact with women. I became insecure, defensive, and unhappy because I was meditating on what I lacked—on how life had done me wrong, had done my sex life wrong. It just wasn't fair.

But I realized something as I continued to complain about how unfair it was—and as I continued to push others away, including women, through my closed off body language. It forced me to embrace more of my spiritual side over my physical reality. It forced me to accept who I am. It gave me the strength to fix my insecurities (on the inside). It allowed me to overcome thinking of myself as a victim. And it gave me power to be happy—and to show my happiness through my body language, which I hadn't done since before I visited that doctor years ago.

Happiness Poses You Can Use to Increase Your Happiness

I know it was not an easy thing for Dennis to share everything he's been through regarding his health, insecurities, body language, and unhappiness. But there are so many silver linings in it. Even if things aren't perfect in our lives, Dennis shows us that we don't have to allow these things to bring us down—or impact our self-confidence, happiness, and interaction with others. Here's how to break negative or defensive body language in case you are currently experiencing it or if you ever experience it in the future:

1. *Smile more.* The secret to smiling more is smiling more.[4] You heard that right. Smiling more releases endorphins into your system and rewires your brain. If you purposely smile for 60 seconds in the morning it can transform your mood. If you purposely smile at different times throughout the day, it can also increase your mood (not to mention improve your immune system!). Smile, smile, smile!

2. *Walk "happy."* Researchers who study walking show that if you walk depressed, you will feel depressed.[5] But if you walk happy, you will feel happy. If you walk with wide and with quick steps, for example, you will feel more confident and happier versus if you walk with small and slow steps.

3. *Sit and stand upright.* Research shows that when you do this, it is difficult to recall feelings of hopelessness, helplessness, powerlessness, and negative emotions.[6] In other words,

sitting and standing upright can boost your self-esteem and self-confidence, and improve your happiness. So if you slouch just know it makes you a grouch (mom was on to something here)!

4. ***Talk more.*** Speaking more to others can boost your happiness, science has found.[7] Talk to friends, family members, coworkers, baristas, and people you see during your daily living.

5. ***Talk about more meaningful things.*** Likewise, if you talk about deeper things your happiness will increase (not just small talk, gossip, sports, or chores).[8] Talk about deep things. The rule that you can't talk about politics or religion—or esoteric or controversial things—needs to go if you want to be happier.

The good news is you can begin doing all of these things starting right now if you don't currently do them. They're easy to do, free, and in your total control. Initially it might be weird to do some of these things if you're not used to them. But eventually they will become habits and you will train your brain into being happier. By mastering your body you can master your thoughts and emotions.

Summary:

Point to Ponder: Happy People Learn a Thing or Two About Body Language

Law to Remember: The Law of Body Language

Affirmation to Declare: "I will take direct control over my body language. I will implement happiness poses starting right now. I will tell my mind and emotions how to feel because I'm in charge now. This is my declaration of happiness."

For more free resources on this topic, go to www.DrRob.TV/
happiness/Chapter35

CHAPTER 36

HAPPY PEOPLE MONITOR THE JUNK FOOD SOCIETY THROWS AT THEIR SOULS

The Law of the Filter

"Who shall watch the stars when we close our eyes to the truth?"

- Anthony T. Hincks[1]

What we choose to consume will end up consuming us.

Our thoughts and emotions are directly affected by what we're paying attention to. And in an era of unlimited access to information, mind clutter has never been more of a danger.

We have access to almost any television show, movie, song, or video in the world.

We have access to almost any piece of positive or negative news in the world.

We have access to almost any video game or app in the world.

And we have access to billions of web pages and millions of opinions of bloggers, friends, and crazies through social media and the Internet.

The information we choose to focus on will influence what we believe, how we feel, and our happiness. So the real question becomes: How are we protecting what we feed ourselves?

Negative Ways to Feed Ourselves

There are countless studies that demonstrate the negative effects of what we are voluntarily consuming in our lives:

- Watching too much news will make us fearful, cynical, and skeptical.[2]
- Spending too much time on social media will increase our anxiety and unhappiness.[3]
- Binge watching television will increase our chances of weight gain, sleep deprivation, depression, and diabetes in the long term (after the temporary "happiness" endorphins fade away from watching).[4]
- Watching traumatic content strongly affects our mood in a negative way.[5]
- Heavily playing video games increases depression, anxiety, and social phobias.[6]
- Listening to music that validates any negative emotions we are feeling makes us worse off in most cases.[7]

I'm sure parts of this list don't surprise most of us and also parts of this list can make us uncomfortable in ways. That is, seeing that research says we will become less happy if we binge watch television over the long term or listen to certain kinds of music is not necessarily welcome news we are hoping to hear. But I just want to report the truth, not judge it. If we are serious about becoming happy, we will honestly look at everything we're consuming and evaluate if we should be consuming it so that we can empower ourselves to make the best decisions.

But it's not only media sources we're being exposed to that are influencing our happiness. The people we're around day in and day out can have just as much—or more—influence on how we're feeling than the images and sounds we're digesting on a regular basis. What they're saying to us can impact us in very profound ways too.

Here's what Irah from the Philippines told me about her experience dealing with absorbing many negative words growing up:

Irah's Story

I was raised in a household where discipline meant punishment and love was supposed to be earned. My father was authoritative about everything. He wanted us to be prim and proper. He wanted me to be the best and when I wasn't, he erupted in anger. As the eldest in the family, he had very high expectations for me, even when I was still too young to understand what success actually means. He said he was grooming me for the future, but I was young and very frightened.

The most hurtful words I have heard in my life all came from the mouth of my dad. It was his daily routine to call out every mistake in the household and somehow throw all the blame on me. He would call me dumb, irresponsible, careless, and many more nasty things. It was as if I could never be good enough at anything for him. His words and pressure filled me with anxiety. That's why I never believed that a daughter's first love is her father—I actually felt he was my first vicious heartbreak.

My father's nagging filled me with fear for many years. It was an inescapable trap, because he was my family. Fortunately, my mother's guidance and encouragement has enlightened me to overcome my inner struggles with hope and optimism because she believed in my capabilities.

As I grew older, I played to my strengths. I stopped being a coward and faced everyday with the promise of pursuing what makes me happy. I transformed my pain into power by inspiring people to use their words wisely through Spoken Word Poetry. While I may never be able to fully control the environment that surrounds me and with the realization that there will always be people I cannot please, I will choose to radiate positive energy. I will bring compliments everywhere and speak kindly. Yes, words may be destructive, but words can also heal.

Positive Ways We Feed Ourself

So many people like Irah have had people who have used words to poison them. Whether it was family, friends, coworkers, enemies, or even strangers, people have used words to harm. But you and I don't have to let these words bring us down.

We don't have to let them make us unhappy.

And we also don't have to let the negative words, images, and sounds of the larger world bring us down either if we choose to shut more of these poisonous things out of our lives.

Here are a few proactive ways you can start feeding yourself in more positive ways if you aren't currently:

1. If a family member, friend, coworker, or Internet troll is saying negative things to you, you can try to ignore it by connecting to positive influences (i.e., people, books, online videos, music, etc.) that will feed you with the right words you need to hear to help lift up your soul. Whoever said "sticks and stones will break my bones but words will never hurt me" was lying—words do hurt, words do scar, and words do poison.

2. If you're binge watching too many hours of TV per week, you can cut back on the overall amount of television you're watching. For example, the average person watches 4 hours of TV a day (or 112 hours of TV a month).[8] If this is you, you can cut this back so that it can help you improve your happiness. Instead, you can read a book, plan a meal with friends, or do something else that brings you joy like attending a sporting event or karaoke night.

3. If you're addicted to social media like I was, you can remove the apps from your home screen or phone altogether and resolve to check them no more than once or twice a day for a few minutes—and no more than a few times a week.

4. You can also curate music that inspires you and dance to it, work out to it, and rock out to it.

5. And finally, you can listen to audiobooks to feed yourself uplifting knowledge and information on your way to and from work or the store.

Review:

Point to Ponder: Happy People Monitor the Junk Food Society Throws at Their Souls

Law to Reflect On: The Law of the Filter

Affirmation to Declare: "According to the research, some of my media consumption habits may have brought me unnecessary unhappiness. Some of the words other people have spoken to me may have also brought me unhappiness. As hard as it is, I'm going to take steps to make sure that I'm consuming the right content and listening to the right people every day so that I can be the happiest possible version of myself. This is my declaration of happiness."

For more free resources on this topic, go to www.DrRob.TV/happiness/day36

PART SIX

MASTERING HAPPINESS IN YOUR CIRCUMSTANCES

MASTERING HAPPINESS IN YOUR CIRCUMSTANCES: Introduction

Now let's shift gears a bit and turn to looking at the traps we face in our circumstances because, no matter who we are, we face many of them. And the reality is we can't really control most of them. Let's look at a few examples.

We can't control the weather, for example, or the traffic we sit in, or the long lines at grocery stores or sporting or music events. We can't control natural disasters, gas prices, or war. We can't control what others think, say, or do, and we can't control the past or the future. We can't control growing old, who is in our families, or whether we inherit a genetic disease. We can't control the reality that we will die one day, or that we are just one accident away from our lives changing forever.

In short, there is very little we can actually control.

Even if we have millions or billions in our bank accounts, have teams of people working for us, are powerful in our industries or have worldwide fame, we have very little control. But even though we have very little control, sometimes it's hard not to try to control situations or circumstances (or even people) around us, which can really impact our peace of mind and happiness. Let's take a deeper dive into how we can be happier regardless of the circumstances we're in—and regardless of the circumstances we may not be able to control.

CHAPTER 37

HAPPY PEOPLE RESPOND TO THINGS
DIFFERENTLY

The Law of Perceptions & Reactions

"Miracles are a shift in perception."

- Kenneth Wapnick[1]

Our happiness is decided by our perceptions of and reactions to our circumstances, not our circumstances themselves.

But how many people truly believe this?

Many people who end up living unhappy lives find a litany of excuses for why they are unhappy. For example, they usually say they are unhappy because of some other person or some unfortunate incident or some circumstance they could not overcome.

They usually say they are unhappy because the events of their lives turned out differently than they expected.

They believe they would have been happier if only this person would not have hurt them.

If only that situation would have turned out differently.

If only the stars did not say this or karma did not say that or fate decided differently.

If only they were born with a different personality, with different looks, with different parents, with a different zip code.

If only their circumstances would have been different.

If only, if only, if only.

Unhappy People See Themselves as Victims

The people who think this way—the "if only" kind of people in the world—usually see themselves as helpless or powerless. They have given away whatever power they have as human beings to other people or to mysterious circumstances, and just let life happen to them.

You and I have certainly been in seasons that have made us feel like this. But what separates us from unhappy people is that unhappy people choose to remain in these unhappy seasons for a lifetime.

Do We Feel in Control of Our Own Lives?

Now, I am definitely not trying to blame any of us if we have been through a rough patch or have felt like a victim. As we talked about early on in this book, I have been through some very difficult seasons myself so I know exactly how people feel during these moments. I've felt like a victim before, I've felt powerless before, and I've even felt hopeless in the past. Feeling this way when life is tough is normal and natural. When I was mugged by two people coming back from a house party in Brooklyn, New York, for example, I definitely felt this way. I felt like two strangers could have taken my life so quickly and easily and I felt incredibly helpless in that moment. I also felt this way when I was run over by a car in a hit and run when I was walking across the street on Sunset Blvd. and left for dead.

But regardless of how I felt or how other people have felt whenever bad things happen to them, I know that it's easy to "blame the victim." I do not want to do that here. It is not always easy to get out of difficult circumstances (in fact, it is often only possible with the help of family and friends, community, or other supportive social resources).

But what I am saying is that regardless of what we are facing or have ever faced, it is up to us to choose how we perceive our circumstances and how we respond to them. It is up to us to decide whether we think our happiness should be based on our circumstances or if our happiness should be <u>immune</u> to our circumstances.

To help you figure out where you currently stand on this— whether your circumstances dictate much of your happiness or not—think about some of the following scenarios and how you might choose to perceive and react to them. Would you choose Response A (the negative response) or Response B (the positive response) if these things happened to you in the long run? That is, after experiencing the initial shock of the scenarios, how would you still be perceiving and reacting to them months (or even years) later?

Scenario 1: My partner has been cheating on me and has run away with another person.
Response A: Why did this happen to me? I didn't deserve this. I sacrificed everything for them. Why me? I can't be happy now that they ruined my life.

Response B: Thank goodness this person revealed their true character so I can move on with my life as hard as this is and find somebody better.

Scenario 2: **I just got into an accident, wrecked my car, and cannot afford this right now.**

Response A: Ugh, nothing good ever happens to me. I don't know what I'm going to do. This is horrible. I'm so stressed out.

Response B: Thank goodness I'm ok. It sucks for my car but I'll get it fixed or make my transportation work one way or another even if I don't have the money for it right now.

Scenario 3: **I just lost my job and my home.**

Response A: This is the end of the world. I'm ruined. I can't recover. This is the worst thing that could have ever happened to me.

Response B: Well this is bad, but I will eventually get another job and another place to stay. I never wanted this to happen to me, but I will get through it like millions of others have as well.

Scenario 4: **I just lost a loved one.**

Response A: I'm so overwhelmed and don't know if I can keep going without them. I'm past my breaking point.

Response B: They are in a better place, and even though I'm really going to miss them I will find peace and strength from this to continue on in my life and make them proud.

Scenario 5: **I was just diagnosed with a major disease.**

Response A: I'm scared and think I'm going to die. Life isn't fair. Why me, God? Why me?

Response B: Whether I'm cured or not, I'm going to now do the things I want to do with the people I want to do them with in whatever time I have left.

As we can see, if we choose to react to each scenario with Response A (the negative response) we are most likely perceiving the event or circumstance in a negative way—which usually makes us feel like helpless victims powerless to change our lives. If we consistently choose Response A in the long run in most scenarios, we will never be truly happy because with this mindset, our perceived powerlessness = our very real unhappiness.

On the other hand, if we choose to react to each scenario with Response B (the positive response) we are most likely perceiving the event or circumstance in a healthy and empowered way (which makes us feel like we are wise and determined overcomers who will learn from our experiences so that we can be better and stronger in the future). When we feel like we can overcome anything, our happiness will skyrocket because we feel in control of our attitudes and reactions (even if we're not in control of our circumstances). With this mindset, our power over our reactions = our very real happiness.

But please do not get me wrong: The reactions that matter the most are not our initial reactions to our circumstances (especially potentially crazy ones); the reactions that matter are our long-term reactions that we choose after we have time to seriously reflect on whatever scenario we are in. If we choose to think negatively over the long run about our circumstances—as bad as they can be at times—we will never be truly happy.

But regardless of if we have ever dealt with these specific scenarios above—or dealt with other negative scenarios—we should realize that our perceptions and reactions to these scenarios will decide whether we will bounce back and ultimately be happy. Our response to be a powerless victim or an empowered overcomer is completely up to us. We can choose Response A (the negative response) or Response 2 (the positive response) in any circumstance we face in life. Our response (and our happiness) is really up to us.

If we are consistently choosing Response A (the negative response) for most of our negative circumstances, we have to ask ourselves if it's worth it? That is, we have to ask ourselves if choosing to respond to a problem in a stressful, negative, or unhappy way is actually going to help us get out of our problems more quickly. We have to ask ourselves if our response is adding unnecessary stress on top of our problems. We have to ask ourselves if the juice (our reactions) is really worth the squeeze (the added stress).

At the end of the day, it's really up to how we are perceiving and reacting to most of our circumstances that is determining how happy we are within them. Here's what Jessica from Great Britain told me about how she perceives and reacts to the things in her own life.

Jessica's Story

I was feeling down. The kitchen window was leaking again. The rain was somehow forcing its way in and was making a puddle on the windowsill. I'd tried to seal the frame but the rain was still forcing its way through.

This made me feel very unhappy. But I knew it wasn't just the leaking window that was causing me to feel this way. Work was hard. Some hobbies that once gave me joy had lost their appeal. I had bills. Life was hard. And I honestly couldn't really remember when I was last happy.

I had to think back to a time when I was a young woman living alone in a small studio apartment in the city. I had my twenty-first birthday in that apartment, almost a dozen friends crammed in, and I was as happy as I could be. I remembered that I had a fun job in a city center bar. And I remembered I could barely make rent some months. But despite this, I was still happy.

Back then I had holes in my socks. I had no money. I had no car. I struggled to keep food in the cupboard. I didn't have a telephone and I barely had a working TV. But I was happy.

As I reflected on this, I wondered how I could have been happy back then? After all, I had practically nothing. And I started to wonder what was the difference between the old happy me and the new, unhappy me?

When I asked myself this question, I realized that being happy wasn't so much about what I have in my hands, but instead about what I have in my head.

I realized I had become a person who didn't see the positives in her life—or who at least wasn't always grateful for them. And I had become a person who was addicted to feeling sorry for herself.

So I decided that I needed a change. But I knew that change wasn't just in my circumstances. It knew that change was in my head. That change was in my heart. I knew that I had to start having the right perspective about everything that was happening to me in order to be happy like I used to be.

How You Are Making Decisions

I agree with Jessica. How we decide to perceive and respond to what's happening in our lives is completely up to us. We may not be able to change our circumstances right away (or at all), but we can change our perceptions about and reactions to them.[2] Ultimately, we can choose to be positive overcomers in every area of our lives or to stay stuck as unhappy victims. The choice is really up to us.

Review:

Point to Ponder: Happy People Respond to Things Differently

Law to Remember: The Law of Perceptions & Reactions

Affirmation to Declare: "I may not be able to control all of my circumstances, but I can control my perceptions of and reactions to them. Even when things seem out of control I will choose to be an overcomer, not a victim. I will choose to have the right perspective and be the best possible me, as hard as this might be at times. This is my declaration of happiness."

For more free resources on this topic, go to www.DrRob.TV/happiness/Chapter37

CHAPTER 38

HAPPY PEOPLE BECOME COMFORTABLE WITH MYSTERY

The Law of Embracing The Unknown

"We do not fear the unknown. We fear what we project onto the unknown."

- Teal Swan[1]

You and I don't know most things.[2]

And that's completely ok. We don't know how many unknown species there are in the world, for example. We don't know most of the thousands of languages spoken around the earth. We don't know most academic subjects in depth even if we are an expert in one of them. And we don't know much about our own genealogies even if we have taken tests, among the literally millions of other things we don't know about.

The reality is we just don't know a whole lot. Even with advances in science, literature, technology, and society, as individuals in particular (and as humanity in general) we only know a tiny fraction of existing knowledge there is to know. That's why a wise person will be the first to tell you they don't know much—because the more they have learned the more they realize they haven't learned much in the first place.[3]

But perhaps the place that is hardest for us not to "know" something is when it comes to our own lives. When it comes to our own well-being or interests. In our day-to-day living, our natural impulse is to want to know as much as we can so that we can be certain about the things that matter to us.

For example, we want to be certain about our safety; certain about our health; certain about our money and bills; certain about our family and relationships; and certain about a lot of other things. Even if we like variety, we still crave certainty about many things and if we don't get it, we will often experience anxiety and stress. This is why we often come to fear the unknown.

Fear of the unknown is one of the greatest destroyers of our happiness. Although it is wired in us, the worry and doubt it feeds our minds and souls can be unbearable when taken to the extreme.

Even if it is not taken to the extreme, it is still pretty detrimental and why we have to learn to come to grips with it. For me, this was one of the most difficult lessons to learn growing up. As a "recovering perfectionist" as Brené Brown might say, I needed to know the outcome to everything under the sun. I needed to control things. I needed things to go or be a certain way. And I was driving myself—and others—around me crazy. It got so bad to the point where I was calling a friend for reassurance about something (as I had done several times that same day) and they told me that I just needed to stop being so insecure about not knowing what was going to happen.

The reality is that for my life and yours, we won't know the outcome for many things. And when we don't have certainty about these things (especially if they are important or confusing things), this can really eat at us. But we don't have to let it. Listen to this story from Dara from New York and how she learned to deal with her uncertainty when she didn't know whether she was going to live or die (the biggest uncertainty of all).

Dara's Story

The year I had cancer was the most joyful of my life. I said this to my friends one day, and they scoffed (with a particularly sarcastic tone) in disbelief. Such a bold and incredulous statement felt hyperbolic and dishonest to them. So, with a bit of righteous indignation I sought to correct them, convincing them this was indeed my truth.

First, I reminded them that I really did think I was going to POTSA (Pass on to Something Awesome). POTSA is my alternative term for dying.

I had stage 2 breast cancer and an irky feeling that I wasn't going to make it through. I thought this was it. So when I accepted my fate, it came with it a sense of total freedom that I hadn't had before. And I did what many strategically thinking cancer patients do—I used the "Cancer Card". I used it hard.

I posted on Facebook asking for housing near my chemo and radiation treatment centers, and new and old friends lined up to open their homes to me.

I demanded that people in my presence bring ONLY positivity. If they wanted to be negative, they could do so outside of the room. I was shocked that EVERY-ONE honored my positivity bubble—even the Debbie Downers.

When I was feeling good, I spent my time doing super-fun art projects and took walks with friends. When I wasn't, I watched TV and movies that had been on my list for years.

I approached and got to sing on the sidewalk with celebrities who made me laugh my a** off and helped me get through the roughest days. (Google Ilana Glazer, Dara Barlin, and Abbi Jacobson for a fun snippet.)

I got a guitar and strummed it next to a babbling brook.

I asked for and received endless cascades of YouTube videos of cuddly owls, playful elephants, and words of encouragement, which kept me in a good space when I felt myself going dark.

I learned how powerful crying is for helping to move through and past bad feelings when I did go dark.

I created a professional-level chemo karaoke video, with all of my friends dancing and cheering me on in the hospital. (Google chemo karaoke and you'll see me there too.)

I conquered my fear of POTSA, of pain, and of doctors all in one fell swoop, and became more courageous than my anxious disposition ever thought possible.

Long story short, there were good days and bad days. But I became a master at honoring and moving through the bad as quickly as possible, and taking the good days up to the highest possible altitude.

And that made it the best year of my life. In a cocky tone, seeking vindication, I turned to my friends and said "there—now do you believe me?"

One friend quickly responded, "And you didn't even need cancer to do it."

I must admit I felt a pinch of frustration, feeling like she was dismissing me at first. And then I took a moment to reflect and the truth hit me like a cascade of sycophants choosing to retire. She was 100% right.

How to Become Comfortable with the Unknown

We can learn so much from Dara about how she took the fear of the unknown head on. We can learn from how she became free. How she became positive. How she did everything she wanted to do. How she gave herself permission to be happy when she didn't know what was going to happen to her—or when she expected the worst to happen.

But even if we aren't facing life and death like her, we can learn a lot from her experience regarding how we too can become more comfortable facing important or confusing situations that we don't know the outcome for. Here are just a few:

1. **Focus on the process and not the outcome.** Like Dara, when we focus on the things we can know, do, and learn—during the process of our uncertainty—the more comfortable we are going to feel not knowing the outcome. Happiness is all about the journey, not the result. If we are going to be comfortable with uncertainty, we should focus on the path and not the destination.

2. **Adjust our perspectives.** Our expectations—how we view reality—are contributing to our stress or our peace, our happiness or our unhappiness. How we are thinking about what we don't know may be stressing us out. If we are thinking negatively, we might want to reprogram our thoughts. So for example, if we feel fear about not winning a court case just speak, "I may not know the outcome, but soon enough I will know. Whatever happens, I will learn how to deal with it. So I'm not going to stress in the meantime." You can substitute whatever situation you are going through using this statement.

3. **Accept that we are not in control.** This is the hardest of all, because we all want to be in control. Especially of our own lives. When we aren't, it's frustrating. But it is truly ok that we cannot be in control of everything. When we accept this, our lives will be filled with a lot less stress. There is no such thing as a highly controlling person who is also a very happy one.

Review:

Point to Ponder: Happy People Become Comfortable with Mystery

Law to Remember: The Law of Embracing the Unknown

Affirmation to Declare: "There may be some things in my life I am struggling to control. I used to believe that I needed information to make me feel safe and secure. I used to believe that I needed to know that the outcome of certain things would be to my advantage. I no longer believe this. I will embrace the fact that I don't and can't know everything, but that I will eventually have a conclusion to the uncertain situations and struggles in my life. And whatever conclusions I receive, I will learn to live with them. This is my declaration of happiness"

For more free resources on this topic, go to www.DrRob.TV/happiness/Chapter38

CHAPTER 39

HAPPY PEOPLE TURN ON THE FLASHLIGHT WHEN IT GETS DARK

The Law of Testing

"Grief is like the ocean; it comes on waves ebbing and flowing. Sometimes the water is calm, and sometimes it is overwhelming. All we can do is learn to swim."

- Vicki Harrison[1]

W e're all in a major test.

In fact, our lives have been a collection of tests.

A collection of battles.

A collection of victories and defeats.

In short, our lives have been a series of experiences meant to stretch and grow us. And the more we grow as people, the happier we will become.

Right now, we're on a potter's wheel called the "wheel of life." This wheel is meant to refine us. It is meant to improve our character and make us better in every area of our lives. No matter who we are, our mind, emotions, relationships, ethics, and happiness will be tested at various times on this potter's wheel.

And at no time is this more true than being tested with the issue of "trauma." The loss of a loved one, for example (and the accompanying indescribable grief), can be overwhelming. So can breaking up with somebody you care about, losing your job, or the ending of a friendship. Sometimes this grief can be so overwhelming that it is possible to experience negative physical (and even deadly) symptoms.

Physical Symptoms

A lot of research has been done about the effects of grief on the body.[2] Here are just a few things you could experience if you ever go through the grieving process.

Fatigue. You're tired all of the time and feel drained. Even if you nap or sleep, you still feel fatigued.[3]

Aches and pains. Your muscles can start to tense up so much so that it is possible you feel like you have the flu.[4]

Shortness of breath. You can experience tightness in the chest, an increase in anxiety, and waves of shortness of breath that can be triggered by the memory of your grief.[5]

Headaches. The number one source of headaches is stress, and grief is a major stressor. Your head could be throbbing because of your grief.[6]

Forgetfulness. You will sometimes forget basic things like where you placed your keys or meetings or appointments you forgot you had.[7]

Lack of focus. You zone out and become distracted easily.[8]

Appetite changes. You might not have an appetite to eat anything at all, or you gorge on everything in sight. But either way, your appetite changes in extreme ways.[9]

Increase in sickness. Your grief will take a toll on your immune system, increasing your likelihood of getting sick.[10]

Any way you look at it, trauma can take a very heavy toll on our health. This could last for only a few moments in the best case or for years or decades in the worst case. It's all up to how we respond to it. It is not possible to live in grief on the one hand and in happiness on the other. We must overcome grief in order to be happy.

Here's what Myles from Amsterdam told me about dealing with and overcoming grief in his own life.

Myles's Story

Even today, over fifteen years later, while most of adolescent life seems like a blur, I remember the day quite vividly. It started by me waking up in an empty house, finding a note from my father about how I didn't have to go to school. Instead, we would go to the hospital later that morning to say goodbye to my mother whose body had given up overnight after a five-year battle with breast cancer turned MDS (leukemia). By the time the rest of my family flew in from out of state later that afternoon, all that was left to do was to begin the mourning process.

The following months, which quickly turned into years, were difficult for my family. My mom was the glue holding us together, and family life would never be the same again. My father and myself turned to alcohol to numb the pain, my brother to drugs, and slowly the separation of a once-tight family unit began to ensue. Everyone went on their own separate paths, and I'm grateful for friends and life opportunities that presented themselves to piece together my unconventional upbringing.

While the devastation hit the family quite hard, I always seemed to keep my head above the water the most. In her final years, my mom would always repeat the mantra "what doesn't kill you makes you stronger." Taking this to heart, I eventually was able to realize that while, of course, I missed her dearly, I had survived the tragedy and was a stronger person because of it. At the age of fifteen, I had dealt with, as far as I could foresee, the toughest life event that I would ever have to deal with and came out on the other side. Based on her wisdom, my mom would want me to be the rock of the family and become the strong, caring, and intelligent man she always knew I would become. I was left with no other choice than to continue to try to make her proud.

I would go on to live a unique life, starting by touring with an indie rock band for the last two years of high school until today, where I run my own nut-oil processing business in Kenya (the first of its kind). The transition from phase to phase, much like everyone's journey, has brought new hardships and life lessons at every step of the way. Throughout it all, I remind myself that "what doesn't kill me makes me stronger" and that I have already dealt with situations much, much harder than anything I am going to face in the future. This acceptance of my mother's death and adaptation into inner strength which I created from it has been a key element of my being for my entire adult life.

I am grateful for my mom's foresight that allowed me to turn a tragic event into a transcendent one with the careful choice of words and values which she instilled in me.

The Five Stages of Grief

Myles is brave for sharing the devastating loss of his mother. He is brave for sharing his grief. If you're ever experiencing grief yourself, know there are five stages to help take you from tragedy to triumph.[11]

The process of grief often follows the same pattern. First, when you learn of loss you are so shocked that you usually **deny** it as a defense mechanism.[12] You are so overwhelmed with emotion that you can't easily process everything.

Second, you will experience frustration, helplessness, and ultimately **anger**.[13] You may direct your anger toward other people, God, the universe, or life in general. Sometimes you even direct this anger toward a loved one who has died or exited your life.

Third, you play the "**what if**" game.[14] What If I did this? What if I said that? What if I could go back and change things?

Fourth, you experience **sadness** and sometimes **depression** as reality kicks in.[15] Feelings of loneliness and regret are common.

Fifth, you embrace the truth and **acceptance** about your loss.[16] It might still be difficult, but you're ready to move forward.

Bouncing Back

How quickly you move from the first stage of grief ("denial") to the last ("acceptance") in the grieving process will depend on your personality, age, beliefs, and support systems. But in general, the happier you are the more quickly you will bounce back because you have developed resilience. Here are a few tips to help you bounce back if you are currently grieving or if you ever experience grief in the future. I know you can because what makes you a BEAUTIFUL MASTERPIECE is all of the strength you've developed in yourself over all of these years.

1. Be patient with yourself. It's going to take a little bit of time and that's ok; you don't have to beat yourself up in any way, shape, or form in the meantime.

2. Adjust your expectations. You are much stronger than you think and can make it through the tough times even if you feel scared and alone. You are a fighter and you can do it.

3. Accept what you can't change. When you accept that you can't change your situation mentally and emotionally, you'll give yourself freedom from trying to control the things you wish you could (especially the past).

4. Find strength in others. As difficult and personal as your situation is, you don't have to experience it alone. You have friends and family to support you (and if you don't have them, there are other people in your community who would love to be your rock if you need them to be even if you don't currently know who they are).

5. Don't get stuck in negative emotions. When we go through grief or trauma, the world always looks dark. But just know there is still good and light in in that you will experience again.

6. Create meaning from this experience. Even though things may not make sense, you can use this to grow stronger and wiser and teach others how to grow stronger and wiser too.

Review:

Point to Ponder: Happy People Turn on the Flashlight When It Gets Dark

Law to Remember: The Law of Testing

Affirmation to Declare: "I recognize that life is a test and that I'm on a potter's wheel. Things will not always go my way, and grief is sometimes the result of this. I will start being more patient with myself and will also give myself permission to heal from any grief in my life. I will always try to find meaning during the darkest days of my life. This is my declaration of happiness."

For more free resources on this topic, go to www.DrRob.TV/happiness/Chapter39

CHAPTER 40

HAPPY PEOPLE QUIT THINKING THEIR SUCCESSES OR FAILURES DEFINE THEM

The Law of Good Success

"Never let success get to your head; never let failure get to your heart."

- Anonymous

There are many seasons in our lives.

We experience seasons of success and seasons of failure, for example.

We experience seasons of peace and seasons of war.

We experience seasons of action and seasons of inaction.

We experience seasons significance and seasons of insignificance.

And so on and so forth.

The point is, our lives will be marked by various seasons we enter and exit. A season can last for a short period of time or even for years or decades.

But the reality is, all of us experience rotating seasons and we're not always in control of them. But we must learn to recognize the ones we're in and adapt to them—in real time.

Our ability to adapt will be what helps us not only be victorious in these seasons but helps determine whether we will experience happiness in them too. The more quickly we can learn to emotionally exit low points or difficult seasons (such as seasons of failure) the happier we will become.

Misunderstanding Success and Failure

This is such a tricky concept to understand, though. And that's because what society teaches us about success and failure is wrong unfortunately.

Society tells us that successes and failures are all-defining events that will make or break us emotionally and financially. It tells us that these permanent events will define our identity in life as a winner or loser. It tells us our happiness is tied up in whether we succeed or fail. This simply isn't true.

The reason success and failure are so important is because we put all of our hopes into our goals. Our goals are what we believe will make us happy and give us the things we crave (like financial security, material possessions, and social standing).

But as we discussed earlier in this book, this false notion of success has made millions of people—including me—unhappy before. And this notion is what's kept millions of people unhappy OVER THE COURSE OF THEIR ENTIRE LIVES, particularly if they fail to achieve what they believe is permanent and all-defining external success. As a result, people have tied their happiness to the god of success and have been heartbroken because of it.

All of Us Experience Setbacks and Failures

The reality is every one of us will experience setbacks in our lives. And every one of us will experience failure.

In fact, we may even have season after season of setbacks and failures. We may even have seasons when we don't achieve all of our goals.

I know this is hard to hear, but it's the truth we should courageously accept.

Of course, we should never accept low expectations or expect failure, but we have to acknowledge that failure will come at times but we don't have to let unhappiness come with it. Here's what Neha from India said about dealing with failures and setbacks:

Neha's Story

I have always thought of myself as a confident, bright and studious girl. Then, there came a time when my failure broke me to the extent that I wanted to commit suicide. It overshadowed all the beautiful things in my life.

It was my final year of university and we were set for our first placement drive. The drive was for a multinational corporation which always recruited in bulk. I was confident about getting placed in this company, but life is never predictable. Surprisingly, I wasn't even able to crack the first round of interviews. On the contrary, almost all my friends got placed in that company. Even those people who weren't serious enough for studies and who I used to teach, cracked all the rounds of interviews and were celebrating their success.

I began blaming myself, my destiny, my luck and even my-then boyfriend who is now my husband. I believed that dating him diverted me from studies. My friends tried to console me but I used to scream at them that they could never understand me as they were not in my shoes. I isolated myself, crying for whole days. Getting placed in a company was the only thought that occupied my mind. Sometimes I even felt that I was useless and wanted to kill myself.

For the next company that came to recruit, I hid on the terrace—I didn't want to face the pain of failure again. That day when my mother called me, I broke down telling her that I didn't want to live anymore and that I was a bad daughter. She then reminded me of the incidence that in grade school I didn't score the best in my math class and I behaved the same way. She told me that I didn't want to go back to school then, that I used to cry and that I used to be so embarrassed. But she also told me that I didn't quit math class and that, instead, I practiced my math daily so I could get better.

That chat with my mother changed my whole perspective.

Today when I look back on my life, I feel it's not failure that makes us a loser but it's our way of dealing with it. Whether we are experiencing a good or bad time in life, it passes away. Either we can let our failure dominate our thoughts and actions or we can fight it and become a stronger version of ourselves when we do it.

Overcoming Failure and Setbacks

Millions of people have experienced similar emotions as Neha when they personally dealt with failure. But when you look at most of their stories, you will see common themes that emerge.[1] In fact, you will see that there are routine setbacks that most people regularly face that they have to learn to overcome:

1. **Losing motivation for a goal (which commonly creates setbacks and failures).**
2. **Self-sabotaging (when we deliberately limit or prevent our own progress).**
3. **Curveballs (when we face the unexpected and have to re-group fast).**

Recognizing that we will all experience these setbacks will allow us to learn one of our biggest lessons in life: to not panic or give up if failure comes. If we learn that this failure will eventually go away (and that we will experience success again in the future) we will begin to treat these setback moments simply as pieces of data, not as all important and all-defining propositions. That is, when we learn to do this we will stop tying our happiness to whether we have succeeded at our goals or in our lives.

Review:

Point to Ponder: Happy People Quit Thinking Their Success or Failure Define Them

Law to Remember: The Law of Good Success

Affirmation to Declare: "I have allowed my successes and failures to define too much of my identity up until today. Success and failure are merely data points in my life, not who I am. I will learn to be adaptable in all of the seasons of my life so I can quickly exit my low moments and keep the happiness I've been working so hard for. This is my declaration of happiness."

For more free resources on this topic, go to www.DrRob.TV/happiness/Chapter40

CHAPTER 41

HAPPY PEOPLE PLAY FOR A WHOLE SEASON, NOT JUST A SINGLE GAME

The Law of 2020 Vision

"If you are going through hell, keep going."

– Winston Churchill[1]

Our lives are a collection of experiences.

We will experience many good things. But we will also experience some bad things.

We will experience things that make us happy. We will experience things that make us sad.

And some of these experiences we will expect while others we won't.

The challenge that most people face when experiencing things—especially difficult things—is that they don't believe the difficult things will ever end. They don't think that their sad or negative experience will be replaced by a happy or positive experience. So they often tend to overreact to the negative.

This happens because of a false assumption of the mind. Most people overestimate their difficult experiences and underestimate their ability to cope with or overcome them. But the happiest people in the world understand that no matter what their negative experience or circumstance, it too will eventually pass.

Here's what Margo from Canada said about her experience dealing with negative circumstances:

Margo's Story

I decided at a young age to become a funeral director. I was fascinated with death and the funeral process. People think it must be hard to work as a funeral director because of all the death, gore, and grief. Those things can be hard to process, but the hardest part of the job for me was coping with my abusive coworkers.

I entered the funeral industry eager and excited to help broken people through their loss, only to leave as one of those broken people. At the time, I didn't know how to deal with my bitter feelings toward my coworkers. My coping mechanisms were unhealthy to say the least.

I experimented with drugs, I self-harmed, and seriously considered taking my own life. When I looked into the mirror, I didn't recognize myself anymore.

But before I could continue down my dark path, something else happened that was even worse than me taking my own life: my younger brother took his.

I saw the grief his death caused my parents and siblings; I felt it. Losing someone close to you results in a special kind of grief. It haunts you. It infects your body like a latent disease, spiking uncontrollably from time to time.

To cope with the onslaught of anxiety and depression that had been stewing in me for years, I attended therapy sessions. I learned how my pain manifested. I learned that I would lash out at others, as well as myself, out of defensiveness. I learned that it is important to understand the temporary nature of emotions. And I learned that it was ok to admit that I needed help. By opening up to others and allowing myself to feel, I was able to cope with and overcome my negative circumstances.

Margo's story is a testament to her strength and to the capacity of the human soul to make it through some of its most trying circumstances. Even if we never face what Margo has—I hope none of us ever has had to go through what she did—we can overcome enormous difficulties and experience healing. Here are just a few things you and I have probably already overcome as proof of this statement:

Negative Experiences We've Already Successfully Overcome

1. Cuts, bruises, and injuries as a child that seemed major but that we now never think about
2. Breaking up with somebody we cared about
3. Losing a friendship that we thought would be there for life
4. Gossip, ridicule, and bullying at different points in our lives

5. Being rejected

6. Being looked down on, overlooked, and underappreciated

7. And so much more

Putting Things in Perspective

Almost all of the things on this list seemed incredibly major to us at the time. Maybe you're even experiencing some of these things now. But if we think back on some of our negative experiences—especially if we had them growing up—we now realize that they all eventually passed.

We now realize they all ended.

The heartache, disappointment, tragedy, and struggle of the time slowly (or maybe even quickly) disappeared. Now, this in no way diminishes how hard these things were or their importance in our lives, but it helps put them into perspective for us.

Any negative life experience you might be going through right now—or that you will go through—will pass just like the experiences above passed as you were growing up. The deeper you and I let this truth sink in the more we will understand just how resilient we actually are. The deeper we let this truth sink in the more quickly you will be able to regain (or stay in) your own happiness.

Review:

Point to Ponder: Happy People Play for a Whole Season, Not Just a Single Game

Law to Remember: The Law of 2020 Vision

Affirmation to Declare: "I'm stronger than I think. I've had many negative experiences, but I've overcome most of them. I thought that they were going to be permanent but they were only temporary. Any negative experiences I'm going through now—or will go through in the future—will eventually pass. I just have to be patient and play the entire season, not just one game. This is my declaration of happiness."

For more free resources on this topic, go to www.DrRob.TV/happiness/Chapter41

CHAPTER 42

HAPPY PEOPLE RECOGNIZE MORE MONEY MEANS MORE PROBLEMS

The Law of Modesty

"Money won't make you happy...but everybody wants to find out for themselves"

- Zig Ziglar[1]

The wealthier you are, the more unhappy you are likely to be.[2]

Although we covered this partly in Chapters 30 and 31, I'd take us a little deeper here.

Numerous studies over several decades have revealed the simple fact that neither wealth nor possessions increase our happiness. In fact, emotional well-being doesn't rise after a $75,000 annual salary. In most cases, it does the opposite: It increases people's odds of becoming anxious, depressed, and unhappy.[3]

If one is a CEO, the chances of being depressed increases by over 200% compared to an average person, for example.[4] If one is a rich child, the probability that they will be anxious and depressed is higher than if they were a poor child (or middle-class one).[5]

The same is true with respect to fame and beauty. If people attain notoriety and glamour, they will reach "psychological dead ends" according to studies. These dead ends often drive them to very dark places and moments of unhappiness.

But the real question is why?

Why Too Much Wealth Decreases Happiness

There are myriad reasons, but a few major ones stand out:[6]

Wealthier people are far less generous.[7] When people have attained a certain level of wealth, they give less money to charity as a percentage of their income than poor and middle-class people. In addition, they are less generous in terms of how they treat others. When people drive a luxury car, for example, they are more likely to run over a pedestrian than if they drive an economy car. They are also more likely to demand their rights and be stingy with tips. As numerous studies have shown, the less generous one is, the more unhappy they usually are.

Wealthier people are more isolated.[8] As people acquire more and more things through competition and success, they want to distance themselves from others. They value indepen-dence more and social connectedness less, and prefer to erect boundaries and communities for themselves. Because human beings are built to connect with each other—they are not built to be superior to each other (or inferior) —developing meaning-ful relationships with regular people is harder and in some cases non-existent. When one is more isolated, they tend to become more unhappy.

Wealthier people experience more envy.[9] If people are wealthy, they are constantly looking to see who is better and how they can get more to impress and best others. Their envy is a root for major unhappiness. (Of course, poor and middle-class people have envy too, but it is especially heightened in wealthier individuals according to studies.)

Wealthier people are less resilient to setbacks.[10] Even if they have money to absorb losses, wealthy people develop less psychological resilience when turbulent times hit. Just look at all of the headlines when a rich guy on Wall Street jumps to his death because he's had a bad financial season. He has little resilience.

The Notorious B.I.G. summed this up so well in his hit song "Mo Money, Mo Problems": "It's like the more money we come across, the more problems we see."[11] In other words, too much comfort kills.

Of course, I don't believe wealth is inherently bad or that having nice things is bad. I think wealth can be a tool used to fuel dreams and help others. But if wealth isn't used in this way or if it is just a tool to be selfish, it is pointless. And it is a one-way ticket to unhappiness.

Average Wealth

But being consumed with vast wealth is not the only thing that tends to cause most people unhappiness when it comes to money. So is being consumed with average wealth or, put differently, average circumstances. When people face what they consider a ho-hum financial existence, this can often lead to unhappiness too. Here's what Tim from Britain had to say about dealing with "being average":

Tim's Story

Who wants to be average? Not me that's for sure.

But even though I don't want to be average, I am. And realizing this began to make me miserable.

I started to become more and more dissatisfied with all this average. I wanted to be exceptional, exciting, dynamic, inspiring, clever, witty, charming. I wanted to be rich. I wanted a second car. I wanted a second home.

I became even more dissatisfied not only because I wasn't getting these things, but because I saw that my old college friend was posting pics of yet another glamorous holiday with yet another pretty girl. Why couldn't I live that life?

I wanted to be more successful in work. I wanted to beat my friends who were winning bigger bonuses than me. I wanted to be better than I was. Yet I wasn't. I was just living this average, boring, unexceptional life.

In meditating on how normal my life was, the one thing I knew for sure was that everyone was doing much better than me. That is until I no longer knew this for sure. When I heard about the hard times of an old friend—who was a leader, adventurous, confident, and surrounded by friends when I knew him—I realized my life wasn't unexceptional any more.

I had heard my old friend was living on the streets. He had no place to live after being kicked out of the service and became addicted to drugs and alcohol. But realizing that I was doing so much better than him gave me no joy at all. In fact, it did the opposite: It made me think that I hadn't done too badly. Maybe I wasn't doing great, but I was at least doing ok. Just average, I guess.

In my desperate hunger for more wealth and success, I realized I had never learned to be happy with the average. Like most people. But this is a mistake. While we may not have private jets or private islands, most of us do have a place to stay, food to eat, entertainment to consume, and friends and family who love us. And if that's average, I'm ok with it—most of the time.

Review:

Point to Ponder: Happy People Recognize More Money Means More Problems

Law to Remember: The Law of Modesty

Affirmation to Declare: "I know I need a certain amount of wealth to pay my bills, fuel my dreams, and help others, but I will be realistic in terms of how much wealth I need to be happy. I will also be careful not to dismiss any area in my life that may seem average right now because my average isn't too bad. This is my declaration of happiness."

For more free resources on this topic, go to www.DrRob.TV/happiness/Chapter42

PART SEVEN

MASTERING HAPPINESS IN THE UNIVERSE

MASTERING HAPPINESS IN THE UNIVERSE:
Introduction

Finally, we have made it to the last section of our journey and we're going to talk about the "world out there." We're going to talk about it because the happiest people in the world are the ones who are most connected to the universe.

And by universe, I mean the collection of people, ideas, and spirituality beyond ourselves that give lives deep meaning. Deep joy. Deep happiness.

Yet, there are many traps set up preventing us from being as fully connected as possible to our universe. The social, economic, and political structures created by society, for example, have failed to create the conditions necessary to personally bring us to the top of our Happiness Spectrums.

Inexcusable poverty; mindless political debates; unending conflict; the danger of nuclear, chemical, and biological weapons; terrorism; economic exploitation and inequality; and so many other weapons of mass destruction (and distraction) are enough to leave us with deep anxiety and fear about our lives and the future.

But despite this, we can still learn to be happy in a world—in a universe—that wreaks of pain, unfairness, and injustice. We can still learn to be happy in a world that can be cold to us and our concerns. And we can still learn to be happy regardless of how the economy is doing, who is in or out of office, and what might happen from hostile nations or groups.

This happiness will not be as a result of turning a blind eye to any of these problems or ignoring that they exist. It will come as a consequence of learning how to engage with these issues with a sense of passion and conviction on the one hand, and a sense of deep love and compassion on the other. Our happiness in our own universe will come as we learn to better understand and engage with the people, ideas, and spiritual systems driving much of what is going on in the world.

In Part 7, we will discuss how to overcome the obstacles preventing us from finding happiness in the world so that we can be happy no matter what is going on all around us.

CHAPTER 43

HAPPY PEOPLE GIVE UP THEIR RIGHT TO BEING SELF-CENTERED

The Law of Generosity

"As we lose ourselves in the service of others we discover our own lives and our own happiness."

Dieter F. Uchtdorf[1]

E ven though you and I are BEAUTIFUL MASTERPIECES, other people matter just as much as we do. Their struggles matter. Their dreams matter. And their lives matter.

But right now, there are millions who will go to bed hungry tonight.[2] Millions who will wake up to domestic abuse.[3] Millions who will be sexually trafficked today.[4] And millions who are struggling in literally thousands of other ways.

We should help them.

I know this might be difficult to do, especially with our own challenges in life (you could be facing possible horrible circumstances yourself, for example). But the benefits other people will receive (and that we will personally receive) will be tremendous if we decide to reach out and help more people.

Showing Compassion to Others Is More Pleasurable Than Spending on Ourselves

The reality is the more we focus on helping and supporting others, the better we will feel about ourselves and the statistically happier we will become.[5] Research shows that when we show compassion to others, our pleasure centers in the brain are activated.[6] Our happiness emotions increase.[7] And health improves.[8]

On the other hand, studies show that if we are living selfishly (by not helping others), we experience higher anxiety and depression; have worse personal and professional relationships; experience more social isolation; make less money; and perform worse on a variety of tasks.[9]

What this means is that focusing on others is better emotionally, relationally, financially, and physically than only focusing on ourselves.

When we find ways to make life about more than just ourselves, our lives change.

When we find ways to make life about more than just our family and our friends, our world transforms.

And when we find ways to truly be of service to our community and to humanity, somebody else's world improves for the better.

Here's what Sanda from New York City wrote about spending a life dedicated to helping others.

Sanda's Story

"Guilt is garbage, awareness is everything," I used to say. Yet, as a Jew growing up in an affluent and safe suburb during a time of relative peace and prosperity, I felt no small amount of guilt about things large and small. I even felt guilty about my good spirits. How could I possibly be happy in a world rife with unhappiness and injustice? How could I "justify" being upbeat or an optimist if I was at all woke to the woes of the world? Sure, it's not hard to be happy when you've won a genetic lottery ticket but how could I reconcile that with recognition of the plight of those with less advantages? How could I overcome my white middle-class guilt?

What really made the difference for me was when I read a short story called "The Ones Who Walk Away From Omelas" that I knew I needed to do more than vacillate between feeling guilty on the one hand and thinking of myself as a "good person" on the other.

The short story describes a utopian community, "Omelas," where everyone seems to be happy and prosperous and carefree. Well, everyone except a little child in a windowless basement who is ruthlessly abused, neglected, and left to stay in his own excrement. The citizens of Omelas all know this, and accept it. Or at least most do. There are a few who can't stand this community's dirty little secret who decide to leave so they can clear their consciences, but it's only a handful of people.

As I read this, I felt I was living in my own Omelas but that I could no longer just ignore it and clear my conscience by telling myself that I was a good person. Would a good person really ignore all of the injustice in their own community like I was? Would they really?

I've come to realize that for me, the opposite of happiness isn't unhappiness. The opposite of happiness is injustice. And working to dismantle it is what makes me happy.

We Do Not Have to Become Mother Teresa to Be Happy

What a powerful story from Sanda. We should all work to do more in the world and to help right its wrongs. We should all be on the frontlines to make other people's lives better.

But doing this will not require of us what many assume it will. That is, how we serve and help others doesn't have to only look "one" way.

It doesn't mean we have to change our professions, for example, or sell all of our possessions, move to a foreign country, or things of that nature. We can actually serve others exactly where we are planted right now.

The main key is not how we serve but why we serve.

It is not where we serve, but that we serve.

In other words, the main key is finding people and issues that we care about so we can serve without growing weary or tired of serving.

If you're wondering how you can do this, here are a few simple steps:

1. Write down the top three injustices you hate the most in the world (homelessness, human trafficking, world hunger, etc.).

2. Identify local organizations that address these injustices and offer to volunteer two to three times per month (you might have to adjust your schedule and give up some things).

3. Budget a part of your discretionary income to donate to these organizations.

4. And as importantly, talk about your charitable work with others and tell them why they should be doing the same.

Doing these things will be a good way to help others and boost your own happiness. But that said, please do not think that serving others is only limited to non-profits or social causes.

Serving and helping others should also be a lifestyle we employ in our households, at our workplaces, in the grocery store, and everywhere we go.

The more we look to help others—even with just a smile—the happier we will be. Not everyone will be impressed or reciprocate our caring approach but many will.

Here are a few ways we can serve people in our daily lives:

1. Smile at everyone you greet (you have heard this before in this book, but this is truly an effective practice and literally releases chemicals in your brain to boost your happiness).

2. Make eye contact with those around you (by creating a meaningful connection with everyone you encounter), which will increase your oxytocin (i.e., bonding) chemicals.[10]

3. Give others the benefit of the doubt (hold doors for others, do not cut them off in traffic, try to find ways to make their

life a little easier in the brief moments you encounter with them).

4. Try to be fun and funny with those around you (it will bring great joy to your life and to theirs if you let loose a little).

5. Try to send one text, email, or note of encouragement a day to the people in your life (this can be to family and friends, but also coworkers, customers, and regular acquaintances).

In short, if you and I act like real and genuine people we can serve others so that they can live better lives and so that we can be happier—and so the world can be just a little bit better.

Review:

Point to Ponder: Happy People Give Up Their Right to Being Self-Centered

Law to Remember: The Law of Generosity

Affirmation to Declare: "I choose to not just look out for myself, but to look out for others. I choose to live a life of service in ways that best fit my lifestyle. And I choose to increase my happiness by helping others increase theirs. This is my declaration of happiness."

For more free resources on this topic, go to www.DrRob.TV/happiness/Chapter43

CHAPTER 44

HAPPY PEOPLE DON'T LET POLITICAL IDEOLOGIES THINK FOR THEM

The Law of Understanding

"You don't begin by dehumanizing those who are dehumanizing you, because it contributes to the cycle of dehumanization in the world."

- Cornel West[1]

Ideology isn't everything.

But regardless of who we are, we often buy into it unfortunately. And, in itself, it's not usually a bad thing.

Ideology is simply believing a certain set of facts and principles that help define our worldviews.

We can be liberal or conservative; a communist or a capitalist; a believer or an atheist; and so on, for example. Even if we say we are "practical" and not an "ideologue" we fall into the ideology of being "practical," which is a worldview in itself.

Ideology can be a double-edged sword, however.[2] On the one hand, it can help simplify what matters most to us, what information we choose to absorb, and what we choose to ignore. It can help us connect with other like-minded people. And it can help us accomplish many of our goals in the world.

On the other hand, ideology can blind us to facts that do not fit neatly within our worldview.[3] It can cause us to ignore or discard information that doesn't line up with our thinking. At its worst, it can cause us to distrust others who do not agree with us and in many cases, dehumanize them. It can even cause us to think others are crazy, stupid, or evil.

The fact is, ideology can be making us happy or unhappy depending on its role in our lives. If we have a healthy understanding of our own ideology, it can be a wonderful thing that helps give our lives more meaning.

If we don't have a healthy view of ideology's role in our lives, though, it can make us suspicious of those around us and cause us to become insular, critical, and even hateful. And if we're experiencing any of the downsides of ideology, we cannot be as happy as we could be.

Here are a few ideologies that are the most common in today's age. Think about the role each of them play in our lives and whether their worldviews are bringing you happiness, unhappiness, or indifference.

Common Ideologies

Social ideology. You identify with your social or educational class. You see the world through your social group, and life is all about the affiliations you carry.

Economic ideology. You belong to the group of people whose finances most closely match your own. Your friends are from your economic background, and everything hinges on money for you. It's all about the Benjamins.

Political ideology. You believe life is a political cause, and see every action taken through this lens. You don't understand how your political opponents could possibly disagree with you.

Gender ideology. You strongly identify with your gender and make this your dominant worldview. All or most issues in life are gender-based, and you believe the world is set up for or against your gender.

Racial ideology. You strongly identify with your race and make this your dominant worldview. You see the world through ethnic lenses, and your understanding of people's behavior is based on their racial motives and circumstances.

Religious ideology. Life is all about God, and you see the world in spiritual terms. You want to see others' come to know God the way you do.

The more strongly we identify with one (or more) of these ideologies, the less open minded we usually tend to be of people who do not subscribe to our ideology.

For example, if we are a strong liberal and we are in a workplace of strong conservatives we might feel uncomfortable because nobody agrees with us. We may not see our colleagues for who they are, but instead for what they believe. They do not just represent themselves, they represent what we disagree with and possibly hate. This could be bringing us frustration, anger, and stress. And anything that brings us anger or stress is bringing us unhappiness.

The point is, our ideology could be making us happy or unhappy depending on our relationship with it. If we see the world through a political lens but are ok with people disagreeing with us it is going to be easier to be happy in life. But if it is not ok that they disagree with us, it is going to be a lot more difficult for us to be happy.

Here's what Chris from the United Kingdom said about the role ideology played in his life and relationships, and how it impacted his happiness.

Chris's Story

Dan is one of my oldest and closest friends. We live in the same neighborhood and have the same interests. We even went to each other's weddings. But there was a time, not long ago, when this friendship could have been lost forever. All because of ideology.

You see, when the United Kingdom voted to leave the European Union, the process we call Brexit, the country was split down the middle. But Dan and I soon realized we were on opposite sides of the debate. We would hang out regularly but began finding ourselves in heated, often unfriendly, discussions over the issue. 1 would leave our meetups feeling very angry and frustrated that Dan didn't get it.

As I started to cling more and more to my side of the Brexit debate, I started to dismiss those who held the

opposite view. I dubbed the others as idiots, unpatri-
otic, and as traitors. To me, they were no longer people with different views, they were evil. And because
I saw them as evil unthinking traitors, I found it easy
to dismiss their very existence. They lacked the basic
capabilities to understand the simple notion that their
opinion was not only wrong, but damaging and evil.

I believed—to the very essence of my core—that they
were my enemy. They were no longer people; they
were simply a collection of hateful opinions and idi-
ocy. They were barely human. And I hated them.

I found hate to be a powerful emotion. I was right,
they were wrong, and as far as I was concerned they
could all go to hell. It even became normal for me
to want to see harm come to them. I began to think
we would be better off if all those others just died.

When it came to Dan, I couldn't even bear to spend
time with him anymore. He was one of "them": the
enemy. My enemy.

But it is when I started viewing my friend as my
enemy that I realized I had to stop. My constant
demonization of the other had made me into a hate-
filled monster to the extent I was learning to hate one
of my oldest friends. I realized how sad this was for
me personally. To hate so strongly, to want so many
others to suffer; I was consumed by negativity—and
frankly, I was consumed by the dark side of ideology.

Deep down, I felt there had to be a way back from the
darkness. So I decided to meet Dan again and when

he told me his views I actually made an effort to stay calm and listen. Instead of taking a hostile position toward him I began to relax, and I started to think more about the things he shared.

I began to realize that we really did have a lot in common. I began to realize we all just want food and shelter and happiness. I began to realize we all just want to feel valued.

Dan and I still talk about what divides us, but I now know it is relatively very little. There is so much more that unites us—as people and as friends. And knowing this has made me more relaxed and much happier.

Ideology Doesn't Have to Hold Us Back

It's not easy to admit when we've fallen into the trap of dark ideology, but Dan does so with strength and courage. Especially in today's age it is easy for all of us to do the same. Here are a few ways we can resist being critical of those who share different viewpoints than we do.

1. **Embrace humility.** When we acknowledge that our opinion and ideology are not the only ones that matters, we set ourselves up to not be so hostile to others.4 We can still believe we have the best opinion about something, but we should recognize they have valid opinions too that are just as worthy as ours.

2. **Recognize everyone makes up their own mind.** We cannot control what others think, and instead of thinking they are crazy, stupid, evil, or unthoughtful if they don't agree with us, we should just let them be. Most people are

just trying to love their crooked neighbors with their own crooked hearts. So are we.

3. **Understand we can be happy around those who disagree with us.** Ultimately, this is the big one. So many people judge the "other" and cannot believe they can be happy around them. We shouldn't waste our time letting our worldview prevent us from being happy until everyone agrees with our opinions.

Review:

Point to Ponder: Happy People Stop Letting Political Movements Think for Them

Law to Remember: The Law of Understanding

Affirmation to Declare: "I embrace my ideology, but I recognize that other people have different beliefs than my own. I cannot think they are all crazy, stupid, or evil. And I cannot let those with different beliefs cause me anger, frustration, or unhappiness. I will be humble and learn how to understand and be happy around all kinds of people regardless of if they agree with me or not. This is my declaration of happiness."

For more free resources on this topic, go to www.DrRob.TV/happiness/Chapter44

CHAPTER 45

HAPPY PEOPLE RECOGNIZE THE BENEFITS OF DIVERSITY

The Law of Diversity

"There's so many different worlds, so many different suns. And we have just one world, but we live in different ones."

- Mark Knopfler[1]

Diversity makes life better.

But in a poll conducted by Reuters, over 75% of white people responded they do not have a single friend of color.[2] For people of color, 25% responded they do not have a single white friend.[3] In total, over 30% of all people have reported that they do not interact with people of a different racial background.[4]

In terms of political affiliations, approximately 81% of people indicate they have an unfavorable opinion of people of the opposite political party.[5]

And in terms of relationships, over 80% of people indicate they do not date or marry interracially.[6]

The statistics go on and on and it's no wonder why we don't understand each other—and why we have so much conflict in the world.

Different Diversity We Need In Our Lives

Although the world is getting more and more diverse, it seems as though people are still choosing not to take advantage of this diversity. People who don't have friends of different ethnic or gender backgrounds; different political affiliations; different religious traditions; different nationalities; and in other areas, are cutting themselves off from the richness of the world.

Not engaging with a diverse group of people—people who look, think, and act differently—is very limiting. It skews and biases how we think about ourselves, about others, and about the world. It contributes to hostile and biased impressions of people with different political and religious backgrounds. And it helps fuel unnecessary misunderstandings.

In short, not having diversity in our lives increases our fears (consciously or subconsciously) of people different from us. And anything that increases our fears creates stress, and anything that creates stress causes unhappiness. It doesn't matter if we are liberal or conservative; black or white; male or female; or of other backgrounds, if we are not around people different from ourselves we are short-circuiting our own happiness.

Now, I'm not saying that we should voluntarily be around people that drive us nuts. Or that we should be around people who we think are evil or dishonest. But what I am saying is that, when we adjust our assumptions about ourselves and others, we will experience dramatically different (and happier) lives. But this isn't always easy.

Here's what Peter from Europe had to say about his lack of diverse acquaintances in his life:

Peter's Story

In a time where diversity is at the top of the political agenda I couldn't help but think about diversity in my own life. And I had to conclude that I had none. My life was extremely non-diverse. My friends were all from the same socio-economic group. We all had similar education backgrounds. We all lived in similar neighborhoods. And we were all the same ethnicity.

I wished this wasn't so and knew I wanted to change this. But I didn't know how. I thought, would it be insensitive or offensive of me to approach someone outside of my background just for the purposes of trying to be friends with them? If I do this, am I reducing these people to whatever label I think they fit into?

I over-thought this and did nothing about it. And I don't know why. I thought back to how easy it was for me to make friends as a kid with other kids who were different from me. I thought back to the fact that I once said I would never deliberately reject a friendship from somebody who was different from me. But I still did nothing about the lack of diversity in my adult life.

If people didn't live in the same building or neighborhood as me—or share the same company—it was
highly unlikely that I would ever speak to them. Sure,
I'd run into people who were different from me at the
store or out and about but I didn't expect a friendship
or relationship out of our brief encounter—no matter how pleasant.

What changed for me is when I finally realized
that I had to make more of an effort in my spare
time just to learn about people different from me.
Just to let things organically fall into place with
others. And when I did this, I started to see more
diversity around me. And I started to embrace it.

It wasn't that I was off trying to force things to happen, it was just that I became more interested in how
I could see and embrace the diversity in my life that
I wasn't before. It was just by doing this small thing
about wanting to learn more about others that made
all the difference. And just doing this has added tremendous value to my life.

Benefits of Diversity

I appreciate how open Peter is about the struggles he faced with
diversity in his life—like so many millions of people. But I also
appreciate how he has recognized diversity's value too. He is
tapping into something we should discuss a bit further.[7]

Studies have shown, for example, that people with a lot of
diverse acquaintances are 400% more likely to have high
well-being than people who responded with few diverse

acquaintances.[8] And well-being in this case is defined as: higher rates of happiness; better coping abilities during difficult situations; improved physical health; more effective decision-making; closer relationships; and more of a sense of meaning and purpose in life.[9]

In terms of work, people and teams that are more diverse are also more effective. Diverse teams produce 60% better results, 2.5x faster decisions with 50% fewer meetings, and report less workplace discrimination for example.[10] And the benefits go on and on.

If your life isn't as diverse as you would like it to be, you can make it so by starting to take genuine interest in people who are different from you. If you simply learn more about others, show up, and offer yourself as a true friend your new relationships will grow organically over time into something very special.

Review:

Point to Ponder: Happy People Recognize the Benefits of Diversity

Law to Remember: The Law of Diversity

Affirmation to Declare: "I know it's easier to be around people that are just like me. But I now recognize the enormous benefits of diversity to myself and those around me. I'm going to make more of an effort to be inclusive in my life so that I can be happier. And so that others can too. This is my declaration of happiness."

For more free resources on this topic, go to www.DrRob.TV/happiness/Chapter45

HAPPY PEOPLE DO NOT RELY ON TEMPORARY POP CULTURE TRENDS TO SATISFY THEIR SOUL'S DEEPEST NEEDS

The Law of Valuing the Right Things

"Popular culture is a place where pity is called compassion, flattery is called love, propaganda is called knowledge, tension is called peace, gossip is called news, and auto-tune is called singing."

- Criss Jam[1]

Unfortunately, pop culture cannot make us happy.

But we live in a culture that worships trends, fads, and the latest and greatest. A celebrity is up one day and down the next. The must-have product of today becomes the old and unwanted product of tomorrow. Diet fads come and they go. The have-to-experience event, movie, concert, or hashtag quickly exits our minds as quickly as they entered them.

Simply put, the over-hyped consumer culture we live in tells us we must have or experience something to get the high we need.

To have fun. To make us happy. And don't get me wrong: I am not arguing against getting new items or experiencing fun, new things. I get new items and experience fun things myself, and quite frequently. I enjoy them and I enjoy having fun—I'm actually a huge advocate for having as much fun as possible!

But the real danger for you and me in this is when we subconsciously think these new items or experiences are the only things—or the primary things—that should drive our happiness.

When trendy products or pop culture experiences become our go-to substitute for happiness—rather than doing the hard work of rewiring our thoughts and emotions to experience internal happiness—we have a problem. We end up making these things or experiences our "happiness gods," and we subconsciously stop striving to be happy on our own without these things.

Now don't get me wrong: Trendy products, pop culture, and new experiences can bring us happiness—temporarily. Study after study shows our happiness hormones will peak for a moment by getting something new or going to an event or party we're looking forward to.[2] But then these same happiness hormones will come crashing back down—and quickly—and bring us many physiological and emotional hangovers according to science.[3]

What's Wrong with Being Happy with Pop Culture?

Again, I'm not saying not to go to our favorite events or get a fun new item. But what happens for millions of people—and perhaps it's happened to you or people you know—is that people begin to live for these things without even knowing or realizing it. They put all of their hope and excitement into a big concert that they want to see or a party or night club they want to attend or a trendy new product they want to get. But they fail to think about how they'll be happy on the days they're not engaging with these things.

Even if we go to twenty or even fifty big concerts in our lifetimes—or to hundreds of parties or get all the trendy things in the world that bring us momentary happiness—what happens to our happiness on the other 27,350 days we are alive (this is the average life span most people have) and not experiencing these exciting new things?[4] Are we thinking about how we'll be happy during these days? Are we thinking about how we'll be happy during the 99% of time where we spend real life and not the 1% of life we're experiencing a new pop culture product or experience?

The point I'm trying to get us to see is that while pop culture does have some good things for us to escape into, allowing them to be our substitutes for happiness often can become our default if we're not careful. It's ok to look forward to these things, but they shouldn't distract us from being happy where we are right now—in the mundane and everyday moments of life.

Here's what Lauren from Corona, California said about her crazy experience making pop culture her substitute for happiness:

Lauren's Story

I had a strong fear of missing out (FOMA). It all started when I was eleven and would watch my eighteen-year-old cousin getting ready for wild nights of dancing at the hottest clubs. I couldn't wait for the day when it was my turn to have all the fun, and boy did I when I was of age. I became a pinup model, knew I was hot, and was determined to do whatever I needed to do to live the fast life I believed would make me happy.

From nightclubs to concerts, from raves to concerts and art festivals, I had to be there. I went to the biggest events and partied with the biggest celebrities and "it people." I had all the latest fashion and was a walking, talking pop culture dictionary. I was one of the "cool people," one of the "chosen ones." And I met some truly amazing people.

But I also met…well, some not so amazing people. I put myself not only in a very superficial scene that was not only undermining my happiness, but I put myself in a lot of dangerous situations that resulted in drugs and sexually transmitted diseases (even though I was taking "precautions" and being "careful").

It is only by the grace of God that I literally survived being a "wild child" during my twenties and early thirties—and didn't end up overdosing or committing suicide.

Now I'm not a prude—I understand the thrill of it all; pop culture creates excitement and an escape from the mundane living and working a nine to five job year after year. I believe we are created to dance, sing, and enjoy the people that surround us—and I will never stop doing these things—but in a much healthier way than I was (or than most of the people around me were). I realized that the worst of pop culture was draining me financially, physically, emotionally, and even spiritually. And what did I have to show for it? A few social media pictures and likes? A few drugged-up and drunken experiences that I didn't remember? Was this really what I had reduced my life and happiness to? Really?

My lowest point is when I woke up in a hospital not knowing how I got there. I knew other people who had died and it was a wake-up call to change my reckless behavior that the party and concert and festival scene encouraged. So I did what all of my so-called friends warned me against: I looked into church. I started to seek God and surround myself with people who knew how to have fun without excessive drinking, drugs, or having the need to be "seen." Everyone was seen in my new circle, and they taught me it was ok to be my true self without having to fit in by being rude or crude or using endless cursing to express myself (my old friends didn't think it was cool to not do these things).

I still have many regrets. And most of them came from these so-called "festival seasons." But I learned there's much more to life than just living for pop culture. I learned there are more ways to have fun than the limited ways pop culture tells us we can have fun. And I learned that God can turn anyone's bad situation around for our good. Ultimately I learned that family and friends, helping other people, and educating myself—and not just being swept up in trends—is what life is all about.

If you're having trouble like I used to with thinking the fast life will make you happy I encourage you to ask God to open your eyes, ears, and heart to the healthy part of the world He created, and He will always answer you back and fill that void that you once thought you could only fill with pop culture.

Review:

Happy People Do Not Rely on Temporary Pop Culture Trends to Satisfy Their Souls' Deepest Needs

Law to Remember: The Law of Valuing the Right Things

Affirmation to Declare: "I love new products and movies and adventures. And I'm looking forward to having and experiencing more of them. But I will not just live my life for these things. I will not live my life for just the big moments and overlook all of the small moments of everyday happiness that I could be experiencing. I will learn to enjoy the 99% of time I live where I'm not experiencing the best and worst of pop culture. This is my declaration of happiness."

For more free resources on this topic, go to www.DrRob.TV/happiness/Chapter46

CHAPTER 47

HAPPY PEOPLE SURROUND THEMSELVES WITH A POSITIVE TRIBE

The Law of the Tribe

"Surround yourself with people that reflect who you want to be and how you want to feel."

- *Anonymous*

Our personal growth directly affects our happiness.

For those with growth mindsets, the world is big and shiny and a huge playground to grow and experiment within. For those with fixed mindsets, the world is just the opposite.

Yet research shows us that those with growth mindsets—those committed to making personal and professional progress—experience more happiness.[1]

But regardless of if we start with growth or fixed mindsets, it doesn't matter where we currently are to be happier. Whether we start with a lot of happiness—or just a little or none at all—all that matters is that we're growing and making progress. And whenever we're making progress, we're making happiness.

Because you've picked up this book, you have intentionally invested in your own progress and in your own happiness. But you'll want to continue the momentum you've built. The best way to do this is to invest in surrounding yourself with more mentors who can help you on your personal growth path.

Another way to keep up the momentum is to become a mentor yourself to others. Because you have invested so heavily in your own happiness, you will be rubbing off on others so that they can be inspired and happier too. After all, 89% of learned behavior comes when people observe those around them to things.[2]

Here's what La Verne from Hawaii told me about the powerful role of mentorship in her life, how it led her to how calling, and how it brought her the happiness she was searching for:

La Verne's Story

I got pregnant at sixteen. My guidance counselor told me not to bother finishing with school as I would surely have more children. He actually told me this. I took his negative words as a challenge to prove something to him—and to myself.

I chose to not only keep my child but to finish school. Back then, high schools didn't have the resources to support pregnant teens so I had to get my GED. I enrolled in the local community college in Hawaii thinking that I was going to show this guy AND make something of myself. What I didn't realize is that I would find my life's calling by doing this.

In college, I met other teen moms who were just like me. They were struggling with raising a child on their own and also finishing their education. They had good moments, but like me had many unhappy moments. These unhappy moments were from all of the emotional and financial struggles we had to face. They were also from the social struggles, as being a young single mom was definitely stigmatized by our community.

Despite our struggles, I recognized the ambition, the hunger, and the drive of these beautiful young women who wanted to make something of them-selves. Who wanted to create better, happier lives for their children. I admired their grit and so I tried to help them—not really knowing what I was doing. But what I found is that I was able to help one mom, then a second, and then a third get jobs. Get resources. And I found that I was really good at it.

I started to help as many people as I could. And when I did this, I realized that I could help people for a living, that I could help people just like me become better versions of themselves. So I hit the books even harder. I got my B.A. and then Master's degree and got my doctorate. I got work as a guidance counselor at a continuation school. And I started to use my own personal experience, education, and expanded resources to help kids who nobody wanted to help.

One of my kids got kicked out of school by her principal. They sent her to my school, and I told her that I would help her. I told her there would be days that she loves me and days that she hates me, but if she followed what I said she would be better off. She did. She applied herself, dropped her bad habits, and won a $100,000 scholarship to go off to college. The principal that kicked her out of her old school even asked her to come back to that school and talk to his students on how to be successful and overcome adversity.

I had another student who had a similar story. He was a Crips gang member but came to me and we got him out of that. Now he is on his way finishing college, making a better life for himself.

For me, happiness is helping others become the best of themselves. When I was in school, I wasn't connected to a community of people who could help me, so I had to build it for myself. And in building that community for myself, I inadvertently built it for others too. I just know that the communities I have helped build are making a great difference in people's lives and this brings me great happiness.

Three Ways to Continue Your Happiness Journey With Mentors and Allies

La Verne's mentorship journey is very inspiring. It shows that, even if you don't have good mentors to start off with, you can still find your happiness by mentoring others—and helping them become happy too. It also shows the importance of not relying on one mentor (who could possibly steer you wrong if they're not invested in your growth and success like La Verne's old counselor). Here's how you can continue to make progress on your own journey when it comes to mentorship and personal growth you'll need to continue getting happier.

1. ***Find many mentors.*** A mentor is somebody who has experienced pain so you don't have to.[3] A mentor is somebody who has been to where you want to be and who can help get you there. And a mentor is somebody who takes joy in seeing you succeed. A mentor could be writers of books or articles, makers of online videos, or just people from your own workplace of community. But the important thing is to search them out so that you can be empowered and keep growing. Now you don't need to have a formal relationship with them (mentors can be casual) or even meet all of them or talk to them in person, but you should become familiar with their work and let their life's teachings propel you forward. This will help you do life in smarter ways than by "trial-and-error."

2. **Get an accountability partner.** Find somebody who is willing to make the journey with you in terms of your own personal growth. Somebody who will commit to reading books, listening to audiotapes, and informally sending you things you need to encourage you and help grow you daily. Ideally this will be your spouse, but if not them can be a good friend.

3. ***Find a community of people committed to personal growth.*** If you surround yourself with people in book clubs, conferences, and other personal-development oriented events and activities you can accelerate your learning and growth— and happiness. The more you do this, the more you'll put

yourself in a position to make a new community of friends who will help propel you forward.

The reality is when you find the right mentors, the right accountability partner, and the right support group of growth-oriented friends, you will start to come alive in new and exciting ways. You will make progress and your growth and happiness will spike as a result—as will theirs.

Review:

Point to Ponder: Happy People Surround Themselves with a Positive Tribe

Law to Remember: The Law of the Tribe

Affirmation to Declare: "I will commit myself to finding more mentors, to establishing a true accountability partner, and to surrounding myself with a community of people who are developing personally and who are helping me develop. This is my declaration of happiness."

For more free resources on this topic, go to www.DrRob.TV/happiness/Chapter47

CHAPTER 48

HAPPY PEOPLE EMBRACE THEIR SPIRITUAL SIDE

The Law of Spirituality

"I close my eyes in order to see."

- Paul Gaugin[1]

Happy people are often highly spiritual.

In study after study, people who describe themselves as spiritual are happier than those who do not.[2] In this context, spiritual is defined as those who have a curiosity about and an ongoing relationship with God. And by God I mean the God who is the Creator of the universe.

In addition to being happier, spiritual people are also less depressed and less anxious than non-spiritual people.[3]

They are better able to handle shock.[4]

They have higher levels of self-esteem and optimism.[5]

They are more likely to self-actualize, and they have a greater sense of meaning and purpose.[6]

And they are also more financially generous and productive.[7]

This is all according to the research, conducted by people who are both spiritual and non-spiritual.[8]

But the big question is why are spiritual people happier than non-spiritual people on average? Does happiness lead people to seek spirituality or does spirituality lead people to seek happiness?

While researchers haven't been able to answer these types of questions, the fact remains that happy people are usually (but definitely not always) more spiritual. What's interesting is that studies show participating in a spiritual activity is the only form of sustained long-term form of happiness in terms of community activities.[9] Volunteering for charity, participating in political and community organizations, and taking educational courses are all fantastic but they don't bring the kind of long-term happiness and joy that spirituality does.

Again, these are all great activities, but they are in a different league from spirituality as far as happiness is considered.

For you, you may or may not define yourself as a spiritual person. Usually people who don't define themselves as spiritual do so for one or more of the following reasons:

1. They choose not to because they had negative experiences in spiritual communities.
2. They saw hypocritical behaviors from people who claimed to be spiritual.

3. They see spirituality mocked in pop culture and believe it's unfashionable.

4. They have deep stereotypes about spiritual people.

5. They believe that spiritual people are not as intelligent as they are.

6. They saw bad examples of a few people in history claiming to do bad things in the name of religion and spirituality.

7. They see some ancient texts as out of step with their modern beliefs.

8. They believe their intelligence or beauty or success make them superior to spirituality.

9. Or they just simply don't believe.

Of course, there are other reasons people decline spirituality too. While I would never force my spirituality on anyone (I was very careful to include stories from people in this book of all faith and non-faith backgrounds), I am happy to share my beliefs and would encourage everyone to find answers for themselves so they can put themselves in the best possible position to experience the happiness benefits spirituality provides.

I, for the record, did not grow up spiritual or religious in any way, shape, or form. But after growing up in a secular environment in California, I became hungry to know more and studied all of the major religions on my own without anyone pressuring me to. And what I found was that spirituality brought me peace, comfort, and happiness.

In particular, when I discovered a man who modeled how to love our neighbors as ourselves and who died a brutal death for his love and beliefs when He could have protested I became hooked. I knew I wanted to spiritually believe in and follow Jesus. And as I did more objective research into Jesus, I found that others who believed deeply in him started the first schools and hospitals and Ivy League universities; led the anti-slavery, women's rights, and civil rights movements; and have given trillions of dollars to charity in every nation on earth.[10] [11] [12] [13] [14] Needless to say, I felt comfortable and inspired to become spiritual even though my upbringing wasn't spiritual and even though my friends weren't spiritual. For me, developing my spirituality exponentially multiplied my happiness and I'm so glad that I did.

I'm not sure where you are on your own spiritual walk, but here's what Eloise from Australia wrote about finding spirituality in her own way:

Eloise's Story

I felt so alone. Not physically alone—my family and friends were always close and ready to comfort me when I needed them to. But I was feeling mentally and emotionally alone. I had just come out of a long-term relationship and started a new job and it was a lot of change in such a short period of time. I could not help but be overwhelmed by negative emotions, feeling as if I was not good enough for relationships or my work.

There was a void in my life. A hole in my heart that could not be filled by material objects, or by the company of others. I was soon to find that it could only be filled by something else. I felt disconnected in my day-to-day life. I went about the motions—work, home, bed, repeat. When I was not alone I tried my best to smile and put on a happy face, but I could not shake that nagging sense that something was missing.

That was when I started looking into the spiritual world. As a writer I am always learning new things, from DIY projects to informative scientific articles, but it was rare that I found something that truly spoke to me. But looking into spiritual things did.

I learned about how to take time for myself. To let go of negative feelings and be at peace, physically, emotionally, and mentally. It sounded so farfetched at first to be doing this, but I decided to try for myself—to go on a little spiritual journey.

I didn't know what I was doing, but I started by taking myself to the beach, laying out a towel, and closing my eyes. When I did, I could hear the sound of the waves crashing down before me. I could hear the birds whistling in the distance. I could feel the wind softly brushing against my very being. I could feel God Himself gently healing my soul.

In that moment, I let go of what was causing me angst. I let go of the stress of work and feeling that I wasn't enough. I somehow felt a connection not only to myself but the world around me. It was truly the first time in my life that I felt a deep inner happiness.

After experiencing this, I yearned to feel that way again and vowed to myself that I would always seek out this spiritual connection, no matter what turmoil was erupting around me. If you're wanting to be at peace with yourself and the world, I would encourage you to do the same. If God does for you what He's done for me, it'll make all the difference in your life.

Review:

Point to Ponder: Happy People Embrace Their Spiritual Side

Law to Remember: The Law of Spirituality

Affirmation to Declare: "I know all of the research shows that the more spiritual I am, the happier I will be. I'm going to make efforts to seek answers for myself, and I'm going to voluntarily invite God more into my life so that I can become the happiest possible version of me. This is my declaration of happiness."

For more free resources on this topic, go to www.DrRob.TV/happiness/Chapter48

CONCLUSION AND NEXT STEPS

Congratulations! You have made it to the end of this book (which is a huge accomplishment since most people don't usually read books past the second chapter!).

But even though this is the end of the book, I hope it is not the end of your happiness journey. The last forty-eight days we've taken together have been a process for you to not only reflect on every area of your life—your mind, emotions, relationships, health, career, circumstances, and the world—but to gain proven tools (and hidden secrets) so that you can know exactly how to be happier in each.

You've learned the common traps people encounter from not feeling good enough about themselves to body image issues to beliefs about money and mindsets about relating to the world and more. And you've learned that most of the assumptions and things we've been taught about happiness are just not true.

I hope the forty-eight inspirational stories of people from around the world who have overcome their happiness traps have inspired you. And I hope they've shown that, no matter what's going on in your life, that you too can be happy regardless of whatever circumstances you're in.

I encourage you to re-read this book every year just to stay refreshed as these traps can try to rear their ugly heads every so often. I also encourage you to give a copy to your friends and family if you've found any value in this book. Nothing—and absolutely nothing—could be more important than your loved ones happiness.

If you would like to continue your journey, I invite you to consider enrolling in my School of Happiness at www.DrRob.TV/SchoolofHappiness. It is a virtual school designed to allow you to go deeper on the issues you've read about in the book. You can go at your own pace and find community with other people who are also focused on being the happiest possible versions of themselves.

I would also be honored if you considered signing up for my free mailing list at www.DrRob.TV. You'll get a free gift if you do and I promise I will never, ever spam you or sell your information.

And finally, if you would like to learn other tips for personal and professional empowerment, please feel free to check out my podcast, The Dr. Rob Show, where I interview world-class performers like celebrities, pro athletes, business titans, visionary thinkers, and more. In the podcast I focus on one important question for these amazing individuals: What's the most important thing you have ever learned in your life?

Thank you again for trusting me to be your guide and for reading this book. I wrote it just for you and it honors me that you have invested your valuable time and resources.

Keep being special, unique, and amazing, and keep chasing your dreams and pursuing your heart's desires. You are a **BEAUTIFUL MASTERPIECE** and no one can ever take that away from you. So from the bottom of my heart, I sincerely wish you all of the happiness in the world!

Natural Ways to Increase Your Body's Happiness Hormones

5 Happiness Hormones

- **Endorphins** (Your "pain-killing" and "relaxation" hormone)
- **Dopamine** (Your "pleasure" and "reward" hormone)
- **Oxytocin** (Your "bonding" and "love" hormone)
- **Serotonin** (Your "confidence" and "well-being" hormone)
- **Gaba** (Your "anti-anxiety" hormone)

Ways to Boost Your Pain-Killing and Relaxation Hormone (Endorphins)

1. Exercise at high intensity
2. Eat spicy foods
3. Eat dark chocolate
4. Watch or listen to something funny
5. Put the smell of vanilla and lavender in your home, car, or workplace

Ways to Boost Your Confidence and Well-Being Hormone (Serotonin)

1. Choose gratitude. Every time a negative thought comes in, remind yourself what you're grateful for. This will increase your positive thoughts and secrete serotonin throughout your system.

2. Get sunlight. When you get Vitamin D from sunlight your body naturally produces serotonin (be sure to expose yourself to twenty minutes a day).

3. Exercise at low intensity. Serotonin will stay in your system for much longer.

4. Eat carbs with tryptophan (i.e., milk and corn).

Ways to Boost Your Bonding and Love Hormone (Oxytocin)

1. Get a massage

2. Give eight hugs per day

3. Give a simple, thoughtful gift to others regularly

Ways to Boost Your Pleasure and Reward Hormone (Dopamine)

1. Set specific, measurable goals daily and monthly

2. Set specific goals when you exercise

Ways to Boost Your Anti-Anxiety Hormone (GABA)

1. Practice stretching

2. Practice meditation

Fifteen Steps to Building a Happy Day

1. **Anticipate the day the night before.** Plan good deeds you will do before you go to bed, set three to five daily goals, and break each of your goals into manageable steps.

2. **Stick to a routine.** The fewer decisions you have to make the less stressed you'll be.

3. **Place flowers next to your bed.** When you wake up, you will feel happier and less anxious.

4. **Drink water right away.**

5. **Pray, meditate, or say your affirmations** as soon as you get up; read a positive quote; and mentally list three things you're grateful for.

6. **Read for 6 minutes.** It can reduce your stress levels by almost 70%.

7. **Exercise in your yard/outside for just five minutes**

8. **Do something that makes you happy right away**

9. **Give yourself the feeling of control.** This gives you the perception of control, which reduces your stress levels (i.e., make your bed right away or do something positive you can control in the morning).

10. **Don't check email, news, or texts right away**. These things stress you out quickly.

11. **Eat and savor your breakfast.** This puts you in a better mood and increases your willpower (believe it or not, this is what separates the happiest people from everybody else).

12. **Do what you dread first**. You have the most willpower in the morning and afterward the rest of the day will look comparatively easy.

13. **Send a thank you email or text to someone**. Doing this every day can dramatically boost your happiness.

14. **Ask yourself what's the worst that can happen today?** Prepare yourself.

15. **Hug or kiss somebody you love.** If you give five to eight hugs a day you'll be a lot happier.

What to Wear to Feel Happier According to Science

The colors of our clothing carry symbolic and psychological meaning. In fact, our clothing can trigger chemicals in our brains so we can dress ourselves happier. Here's what to wear if you want to be more intentional about using your wardrobe to boost your happiness.

1. **Choose clothing that radiates color and positivity**. This often means brighter colors than blacks, grays, and navy blues. Instead think yellows, oranges, greens, lighter blues, etc.

2. **Choose clothing that is fun and makes you smile**. This could be because of a unique or over the top design—or clothing that triggers happy memories. Either way, when you put on clothing that puts a smile on your face you'll boost your mood.

3. **Choose clothes that make you feel powerful.** When you wear reds you can boost your confidence, energy, and strength, all of which increase your happiness because you feel comfortable and like you can take on the world.

APPENDIX D

Twenty-Five Foods to Eat to Boost Your Happiness According to Science

The foods we eat do not just determine our physical health. They also help determine our mental health. The foods below have complex nutrients that interact with the body and trigger the release of mood-boosting chemicals into your system.

1. **Dark chocolate** (elevates your mood and energy)
2. **Honey** (fights depression)
3. **Avocados** (reduce anxiety)
4. **Seaweed** (fights depression)
5. **Beets** (elevates your mood)
6. **Chia seeds** (fights depression)
7. **Whole grain bread** (elevates your mood)
8. **Cherry tomatoes** (fights depression)
9. **Lemons** (elevates your mood)
10. **Bananas** (fights depression and stress)
11. **Salmon** (elevates your mood)
12. **Blueberry juice** (fights depression)
13. **Brussel sprouts** (elevates your mood)

14. **Red wine** (fights depression)

15. **Eggs** (elevates your mood)

16. **Red peppers** (elevates your mood)

17. **Coconuts/coconut creams** (elevates your mood)

18. **Greek yogurt** (elevates your mood, fights depression, fights anxiety)

19. **Asparagus** (fights depression)

20. **Green tea** (elevates your mood)

21. **Crab** (fights depression)

22. **Peas** (fights depression and exhaustion)

23. **Chicken** (fights depression and improves self-esteem)

24. **Apricots** (fights depression)

25. **Broccoli** (elevates your mood)

APPENDIX E

How to Decorate Your Home to Boost Your Happiness

1. **Add lots of bright colors throughout your room, home, or apartment.** This will trigger the happiness hormones associated with these colors and release them into your body.

2. **Let in the light.** Natural sunlight will bring in more Vitamin D in your environment and positivity.

3. **Fill your home with plants.** Plants decrease your stress and elevate your mood.

4. **Release "happiness scents" into your home.** Candles, oils, and diffusers can fill your space with mood-boosting smells.

5. **Personalize your space.** You don't have to go with cookie-cutter or designer furniture or decorations to impress others; instead, fill your place with things that are fun and completely expressive of you.

6. **Keep organized.** The more tidy you keep your space the more relaxed you'll feel.

Ten Songs That Make You Happy According to Science

M usic can heavily influence our moods. Below are a few songs researchers have determined release dopamine into our bodies that make us happy.

10. Beethoven – Moonlight Sonata (classic)

9. Cannonball Adderly – Work Song (jazz)

8. Led Zeppelin – Moby Dick (rock)

7. DJ Tiesto – Adagio for Strings (techno)

6. Shore – Concerning Hobbits (film score from *The Fellowship of the Ring*)

5. Don't Stop Me Now (1978) – Queen

4. Dancing Queen (1976) – Abba

3. Good Vibrations (1966) – The Beach Boys

2. Uptown Girl (1983) – Billy Joel

1. Eye of the Tiger (1982) – Survivor

Forty-Seven Things That Make Most People Happy

1. Sleeping in a freshly made bed
2. Feeling the sun on your face
3. People saying thank you or random act of kindness from a stranger
4. Finding money in unexpected places
5. Having "me time"
6. Laughing so hard it hurts
7. Snuggling on the sofa with a loved one
8. Freshly made bread
9. Doing something for others
10. The clean feeling after a shower
11. When your favorite song comes on the radio
12. Finding a bargain in the sales
13. Listening to rainfall when you're inside
14. Freshly brewed tea/coffee
15. The thrill of personal achievement
16. Having a long hot bath

17. Seeing a fresh coating of snow

18. Freshly cut grass

19. Doing something active outdoors

20. Bacon cooking in the morning (sorry, vegans)

21. Talking to or playing with your pet

22. A soothing massage

23. A perfectly cooked steak

24. Waking up before the alarm and realizing there's more time to sleep

25. Doing exercise

26. Rainbows

27. Remembering the name of something/someone you've forgotten

28. Making a perfectly baked cake/pie

29. Stepping on crunchy autumn leaves

30. Swimming in the sea/lake

31. New car smell

32. Dancing like nobody is watching

33. The smell of new books/magazines

34. Smell of a fine wine

35. Putting your "out of office on" before a vacation

36. Putting on a brand new pair of socks

37. Watching your breath float away in cold air

38. Getting new stationary

39. Singing in the shower

40. Getting a seat on the bus/train/subway

41. Picking an easy peel orange from a fruit bowl

42. Loosening your jeans after you've eaten

43. The pop when you open a new jar of jam

44. Squeezing a pimple

45. Cleaning the wax from your ears

46. Cleaning the bathroom

47. The royal family

APPENDIX H

Scientific Studies on Happiness

In addition to the research you read earlier in the book, here are a few more findings from studies on happiness I thought you'd find interesting and useful.

1. Close relationships, not money or fame, keep you happy over a lifetime- Harvard University

2. Expressing gratitude three times per day dramatically increases happiness - University of Pennsylvania

3. Being surrounded by happy people dramatically increases your own happiness - University of California, San Diego

4. Exercising on work days significantly increases your happiness - University of Bristol

5. Spending money on others increases happiness more than spending money on yourself- University of California, Berkeley

6. Those with a good sense of humor raise their positivity/happiness by 33%

APPENDIX I

The 48 Laws of Happiness

1. The Law of Acceptance
2. The Law of Realization
3. The Law of Comparison
4. The Law of Abundant Thinking
5. The Law of the Moment
6. The Law of Recognition
7. The Law of Positive Thinking
8. The Law of Fun
9. The Law of Fearlessness
10. The Law of Chill
11. The Law of Patience
12. The Law of Zen
13. The Law of Encouragement
14. The Law of Independence
15. The Law of Resilience
16. The Law of Contentment
17. The Law of Living Your Own Life
18. The Law of Relinquishing Control

19. The Law of Personal Responsibility
20. The Law of the Deep Cleanse
21. The Law of Interdependence
22. The Law of Communication
23. The Law of Positivity
24. The Law of Haters
25. The Law of The Assignment
26. The Law of Commitment
27. The Law of the Potter's Wheel
28. The Law of Grace
29. The Law of Balance
30. The Law of Fulfillment
31. The Law of Superiority
32. The Law Relative Beauty
33. The Law of Consecration
34. The Law of Overcoming
35. The Law of Body Language
36. The Law of the Filter
37. The Law of Perceptions & Reactions
38. The Law of Embracing The Unknown
39. The Law of Testing
40. The Law of Good Success
41. The Law of 2020 Vision
42. The Law of Modesty
43. The Law of Generosity
44. The Law of Understanding

ACKNOWLEDGEMENTS

I wanted to sincerely thank everyone who has contributed to the writing of this book. To the contributors around the world who shared their amazing stories with me, thank you from the bottom of my heart—you know who you are and I deeply value you. Your words and experiences have helped bring healing, transformation, and happiness to many throughout the globe and this is no small thing. To my amazing publishing and editing team led by Keri-Rae Barnum and Melanie Zimmerman, I could not have done this without you. Your insights, kindness, and leadership helped make this book a reality. To my Mom and Dad, family, friends, and teachers thank you for your continued support and belief in me, this project, and my journey. To my best friend Arienne Gachupin, thank you for always being there for me. And finally to God, thank you for loving me and empowering me to write this book and to share it to help bless and empower so many people in the world!

WORKS CITED

Introduction

1. Miller, K. 2020. Is Happiness Genetic and What Causes It? Accessed from: https://positivepsychology.com/is-happiness-genetic/

2. Legg, T. 2019. Happiness Hormones: What They Are and How to Boost Them. Accessed from: https://www.healthline.com/health/happy-hormone#exercise

3. Bhattacharya, S. 2015. Happiness Helps People Stay healthy. Accessed from: https://www.newscientist.com/article/dn7282-happiness-helps-people-stay-healthy/#:~:text=%E2%80%9CThe%20happier%20you%20were%2C%20the,type%20II%20diabetes%20and%20hypertension.

4. Mead, E. 2005. 6 Benefits of Happiness According to the Research. Accessed from: https://positivepsychology.com/benefits-of-happiness/

5. Ibid.

6. Oppong, T. 2019. Good Social Relationships Are the Most Consistent Predictor of a Happy Life. Accessed from: https://thriveglobal.com/stories/relationships-happiness-well-being-life-lessons/

7. Mead, E. 2005. 6 Benefits of Happiness According to the Research. Accessed from: https://positivepsychology.com/benefits-of-happiness/

8. Ibid.

9. Newman, K. 2020. How Much of Your Happiness Is Under Your Control? Accessed from: https://greatergood.berkeley.edu/article/item/how_much_of_your_happiness_is_under_your_control

Chapter 1

1. Shannon Ables Quotes. Accessed from: https://positivepsychology.com/self-acceptance-quotes/#:~:text=%E2%80%9CWhat%20self%2Dacceptance%20does%20is,fighting%20yourself%20along%20the%20way.%E2%80%9D&text=%E2%80%9CSo%20we%20scramble%20to%20fill,ourselves%20in%20mindless%20small%20talk.

2. Dominguez, T. 2014. How Much Are Your Body Parts Worth? Accessed from: https://www.seeker.com/how-much-are-your-body-parts-worth-1792475763.html

3. Guttman, Jennifer. 2019. The Relationship with Yourself. *Psychology Today*. July 27, 2019. Accessed from: https://www.psychologytoday.com/us/blog/sustainable-life-satisfaction/201906/the-relationship-yourself

4. Ross, Valerie. 2020. Six Scientific Reasons Why Your Friends Really Do Make You Happier. Accessed from: https://www.birchbox.com/magazine/article/6-scientific-reasons-why-your-friends-really-do-make-you-happier

5. Carpenter, S. 2001. A New Reason for Keeping a Diary. September 2001. Accessed from: https://www.apa.org/monitor/sep01/keepdiary

6. Browdin, E. 2019. 24 Easy Habits That Psychologists Have Linked with Health and Happiness. Accessed from: https://www.businessinsider.com/science-backed-things-that-make-you-happier-2015-6#volunteer-14

Chapter 2

1. Mandy Hale Quotes. 2020. Accessed from: https://www.goodreads.com/quotes/861928-so-you-re-a-little-weird-work-it-a-little-different

2. Abrams, A. 2018. Yes, Imposter Syndrome Is Real. Here's How to Deal with It. Accessed from: https://time.com/5312483/how-to-deal-with-impostor-syndrome/

3. Croteau, J. 2014. Imposter Syndrome - Why It's Harder Today Than Ever. Accessed from: https://www.forbes.com/sites/jeannecroteau/2019/04/04/imposter-syndrome-why-its-harder-today-than-ever/?sh=2b120fd09ac5

Chapter 3

1. Henri Frederic Amiel Quotes. 2020. Accessed from: https://www.brainyquote.com/quotes/henri_frederic_amiel_104285

2. Love, S. 2018. There's a Chemical in Your Brain That Makes You Want More. Accessed from: https://www.vice.com/en/article/d3e53w/theres-a-chemical-in-your-brain-that-makes-you-want-more

Chapter 4

1. Paula Maier Quotes. 2020. Accessed from:

2. https://www.pinterest.ca/pin/814166438881679308/

3. Marano, H. 2003. Our Brain's Negativity Bias. Accessed from: https://www.psychologytoday.com/us/articles/200306/our-brains-negative-bias

4. Ciotti, G. 5 2013. Scientific Ways to Build Habits That Stick. Accessed from: https://99u.adobe.com/articles/17123/5-scientific-ways-to-build-habits-that-stick

5. Pryor, K. 2004. Making the Connection: Behavior Chains. Accessed from: https://www.clickertraining.com/node/111#:~:text=A%20behavior%20chain%20is%20an,next%2C%20is%20a%20training%20technique.

6. Thorp, J. 2013. Visualization As Process, Not Output. Accessed from: https://hbr.org/2013/04/visualization-as-process?ab=at_articlepage_whattoreadnext

7. Tsaousides, T. 2018. Is It Time to Give Up on Your Dreams? Accessed from: https://www.psychologytoday.com/us/blog/smashing-the-brainblocks/201805/is-it-time-give-your-dreams

Chapter 5

1. Emily Dickinson quotes. 2020. Accessed from: https://www.pinterest.ca/pin/AeeaJ-hc9RdStbjhJIA-j91FkeD81JSdaK-lk0nrGY1wQeZzfBvnYJmo/

2. Bradt, S. 2010. Wandering Mind Not a Happy Mind. Accessed from: https://news.harvard.edu/gazette/story/2010/11/wandering-mind-not-a-happy-mind/

3. Andrews, L. 2017. Overthinking? It Could Be Depressing You. Accessed from: https://www.everydayhealth.com/emotional-health/depression/overthinking-it-could-depressing-you/

4. Raghavan, S. 2018. 6 Health Problems Caused by Overthinking. Accessed from: https://www.thehealthsite.com/diseases-conditions/stress-diseases-conditions/health-problems-caused-by-over-thinking-k0118-553937/

5. Stanley, S. 2019. The Science of Savoring. Accessed from: https://www.livehappy.com/science/science-savoring

6. Bullock, B. 2019. What Focusing on the Breath Does to the Brain. Accessed from: https://greatergood.berkeley.edu/article/item/what_focusing_on_the_breath_does_to_your_brain

7. Oppland, M. 2020. 8 Ways to Create Flow According to Mihaly Csikszentmihalyi. Accessed from: https://positivepsychology.com/mihaly-csikszentmihalyi-father-of-flow/

8. Pillay, S. 2016. Greater Self-Acceptance Improves Emotional Well-Being. Accessed from: https://www.health.harvard.edu/blog/greater-self-acceptance-improves-emotional-well-201605169546

9. University of Miami. 2020. Find More Satisfaction by Changing Your Daily Routines, Study Says. Accessed from: https://news.miami.edu/stories/2020/05/find-more-satisfaction-by-changing-daily-routines-study-says.html

10. Lebowitz, S. 2013. The Scientific Reasons Why Being Creative Can Make You Happier. Accessed from: https://greatist.com/happiness/how-creativity-makes-us-happier#1

Chapter 6

1. Thomas Monson Quotes. 2020. Accessed from:https://quotefancy.com/quote/920246/Thomas-S-Monson-At-times-some-may-think-that-no-one-cares-but-someone-always-cares-Your

2. Miller, K. 2020. How to Cope When You Think Nobody Cares About You. Accessed from: https://www.wikihow.com/Cope-when-No-One-Cares-About-You

Chapter 7

1. Eddie Capparucci. 2020. Accessed from: https://www.goodreads.com/quotes/9577691-remember-what-you-feel-and-what-is-real-are-often

2. Goewey, D. 2015. 85 Percent of What We Worry About Never Happens. Accessed from: https://www.huffpost.com/entry/85-of-what-we-worry-about_b_8028368

3. Ibid.

4. Dogson, L. 2018. Constantly Imagining the Worst Case Scenario Is Called 'Catastrophising' - Here's How to Stop Your Mind from Doing It. Accessed from: https://www.businessinsider.com/what-catastrophising-means-and-how-to-stop-it-2018-3

5. WebMD. 2020. Accessed from: https://www.webmd.com/balance/guide/how-worrying-affects-your-body#1

6. Ibid.

7. Ibid.

8. Ibid.

Chapter 8

1. Dr. Rob Quotes. 2020. Accessed from: https://www.instagram.com/thedr.rob/

2. Hall, S. 2019. People Have the Least Fun When They Are 45, Survey Claims. Accessed from: https://www.independent.co.uk/news/uk/home-news/fun-age-older-people-responsibilities-energy-a9160286.html

3. Life in Half a Second. 2020. Accessed from: https://www.whatyouwilllearn.com/book/life-in-half-a-second/

4. Taylor, S. Why Hedonism Doesn't Lead to Happiness. Accessed from: https://www.psychologytoday.com/us/blog/out-the-darkness/201708/why-hedonism-doesnt-lead-happiness

5. Van Wilder Quotes. 2020. Accessed from: https://www.quotes.net/mquote/131236

6. Rucker, M. 2016. Why You Need to Have More Fun in Your Life, According to Science. Accessed from: https://michaelrucker.com/having-fun/why-you-need-more-fun-in-your-life/#:~:text=Research%20

shows%20that%20when%20we,to%20connect%20and%20be%20creative.

7. 2016. 8 Health Benefits of Having Fun. Accessed from: https://heelthatpain.com/8-health-benefits-of-having-fun/

8. Ibid.

9. Ibid.

10. Ibid.

11. Ibid.

12. Ibid.

13. Ibid.

14. Ibid.

15. Ibid.

16. Ibid.

Chapter 9

1. George Addair Quotes. 2020. 10 Motivational Quotes That'll Make You Fearless. Accessed from: https://www.themuse.com/advice/10-quotes-thatll-make-you-fearless

2. Mobbs, D., Adolphs, R., Fanselow, M., Barret, L., LeDoux, J., Ressler, K., Tye, K. 2019. On the Nature of Fear. Accessed from: https://www.scientificamerican.com/article/on-the-nature-of-fear/

3. Javanbakht, A. 2019. A Neuroscientist Explains How Politicians and Media Use Fear to Make Us Hate Without Thinking. Accessed from: https://www.marketwatch.com/story/a-neuroscientist-explains-how-politicians-and-the-media-use-fear-to-make-us-hate-without-thinking-2019-07-18

4. 2020. Coronavirus: Retailers Warned Not to 'Exploit' Consumer Fears. Accessed from: https://www.bbc.com/news/business-51750124

5. Politicians Can Use Fear to Manipulate the Public. Accessed from: https://phys.org/news/2009-03-politicians.html

6. Borum, R. 2004. Psychology of Terrorism. Accessed from: https://www.ncjrs.gov/pdffiles1/nij/grants/208552.pdf

7. EMC Corporation. 2013. Accessed from: https://www.prnewswire.com/news-releases/84-of-people-hold-onto-an-irrational-fear-213298101.html

8. Stockwell-Rose, T. 2017. Accessed from: https://medium.com/@tobiasrose/the-enemy-in-our-feeds-e86511488de

9. Serani, D. 2011. Accessed from: https://www.psychologytoday.com/us/blog/two-takes-depression/201106/if-it-bleeds-it-leads-understanding-fear-based-media

10. Gillihan, S. 2019. How Often Do Your Worries Come True? Accessed from: https://www.psychologytoday.com/us/blog/think-act-be/201907/how-often-do-your-worries-actually-come-true

11. Nauert, R. 2019. How Fear Is Learned. Accessed from: https://psychcentral.com/news/2017/03/16/how-fear-is-learned/691.html

12. 2003. Scientists Find More Efficient Way to "Unlearn" Fear, Which Could Improve Treatment Of Anxiety. Accessed from:https://www.apa.org/news/press/releases/2003/10/conditional-fear

13. Josselyn, S., Frankland, P. 2018. Facing Your Fears. Accessed from: https://science.sciencemag.org/content/360/6394/1186.summary

Chapter 10

1. Swedish Proverb. 2020. Accessed from: https://philosiblog.com/2016/03/03/worry-often-gives-a-small-thing-a-big-shadow/

2. Chronic Stress Puts Your Health at Risk. 2020. Accessed from: https://www.mayoclinic.org/healthy-lifestyle/stress-management/in-depth/stress/art-20046037

3. Beware High Levels of Cortisol. 2020. Accessed from: https://www.premierhealth.com/your-health/articles/women-wisdom-wellness-/beware-high-levels-of-cortisol-the-stress-hormone

4. Ibid.

5. Anxiety Disorders and Panic Attacks. 2020. Accessed from: https://uhs.umich.edu/anxietypanic

6. Pesce, N. 2020. Google Searches for 'Panic Attack,' 'Anxiety Attack,' Hit All-Time Highs. Accessed from: https://nypost.com/2020/08/26/google-searches-for-panic-attack-anxiety-attack-hit-all-time-high-amid-coronavirus/

7. Why 75% of Anxiety Sufferers Fail to Get Proper Care. 2018. Accessed from: https://www.psychology-today.com/us/blog/psychiatry-the-people/201808/why-75-percent-anxiety-sufferers-fail-get-proper-care

8. Britto, J. 2019. What's the Difference Between a Panic Attack and an Anxiety Attack? Accessed from: https://www.healthline.com/health/panic-attack-vs-anxiety-attack

9. Panic Disorder: When Fear Overwhelms. 2016. Accessed from: https://www.nimh.nih.gov/health/publications/panic-disorder-when-fear-overwhelms/index.shtml#:~:text=Physical%20symptoms%20during%20a%20panic,pain%2C%20stomach%20pain%2C%20and%20nausea

10. Brownstein, J. 2011. Planning 'Worry Time' May Help Ease Anxiety. Accessed from: https://www.livescience.com/15233-planning-worry-time-ease-anxiety.html

11. 10 Best Ways to Increase Dopamine Levels Naturally. Accessed from: https://www.healthline.com/nutrition/how-to-increase-dopamine#:~:text=However%2C%20one%20three%2Dmonth%20study,ability%20to%20control%20body%20movements.

12. Hampton, K. 2015. Psychological Stress and Social Media Use. Accessed from: https://www.pewresearch.org/internet/2015/01/15/psychological-stress-and-social-media-use-2/

13. Cirino, E. 2018. What Are the Benefits of Hugging? Accessed from: https://www.healthline.com/health/hugging-benefits

Chapter 11

1. Delayed Gratification Quotes. 2020. Accessed from: https://www.goodreads.com/quotes/tag/delayed-gratification

2. Thrasybule, L. 2019. Why Impatience May Hurt Your Heart. Accessed from: https://www.livescience.com/25085-impatience-may-hurt-heart.html

3. Cohen, I. 2017. The Benefits of Delaying Gratification. Accessed from: https://www.psychologytoday.com/us/blog/your-emotional-meter/201712/the-benefits-delaying-gratification

4. Ibid.

5. Hawton, K. Slow Down: Behavioral and Physiological Effects of Reduced Eating Rate. Accessed from: https://www.ncbi.nlm.nih.gov/pmc/articles/PMC6357517/

6. Fabrega, M. 2020. 16 Hobbies That Will Improve Your Quality of Life. Accessed from: https://daringtolivefully.com/hobbies-to-improve-your-life

Chapter 12

1. Ambrose Bierce Quotes. 2020. Accessed from: https://www.goodreads.com/quotes/9909-speak-when-you-are-angry-and-you-will-make-the

2. Dougherty, E. 2020. The Science of Emotion: Anger Management. Accessed from: https://hms.harvard.edu/magazine/science-emotion/anger-management

3. 2020. Anger Management: 10 Tips to Tame Your Temper. Accessed from: https://www.mayoclinic.org/healthy-lifestyle/adult-health/in-depth/anger-management/art-20045434

Chapter 13

1. Vincent Van Gough Quotes. 2020. Accessed from: https://www.goodreads.com/quotes/158481-in-spite-of-every-thing-i-shall-rise-again-i-will#:~:text=Quotes%20%3E%20Quotable%20Quote-,%E2%80%9CIn%20spite%20of%20everything%2C%20I%20shall%20rise%20again%3B%20I,go%20on%20with%20my%20drawing.%E2%80%9D

2. National Network of Depression Centers. 2020. Accessed from: https://nndc.org/facts/?gclid=Cj0KCQiAhZT9BRDmARIsAN2E-J3BzR_OihucPmb2WtWMaPy9GNHdPee-N0r4ri6_B31MbBdHdwJ_oR0aApMzEALw_wcB

3. Albert, P. 2015. Why Is Depression More Prevalent in Women? Accessed from: https://www.ncbi.nlm.nih.gov/pmc/articles/PMC4478054/

4. Ibid.

5. Suttie, J. 2017. How Does Valuing Money Affect Your Happiness? Accessed from: https://greatergood.berkeley.edu/article/item/how_does_valuing_money_affect_your_happiness

6. Mufson, L. 2016. Overcoming Depression: How Psychologists Help with Depressive Orders. Accessed from: https://www.apa.org/topics/overcoming-depression

7. Bushman, B. 2017. 7 Ways to Overcome Depression Without Medication. Accessed from: https://intermountainhealthcare.org/blogs/topics/live-well/2017/05/7-ways-to-overcome-depression-without-medication/

Chapter 14

1. Joseph Conrad Quotes. 2020. Accessed from: https://www.goodreads.com/quotes/495717-we-live-as-we-dream---alone-while-the-dream

2. The Loneliness Epidemic. 2019. Accessed from: https://www.hrsa.gov/enews/past-issues/2019/january-17/loneliness-epidemic

3. Bryner, J. 2011. Close Friends Less Common Today, Study Finds. Accessed from: https://www.livescience.com/16879-close-friends-decrease-today.html

4. Perry, S. 2020. Loneliness in American Adults Report Feeling Lonely, and Younger Adults Feel It Most, Survey Finds. Accessed from: https://www.minnpost.com/second-opinion/2020/01/3-in-5-american-adults-report-feeling-lonely-and-younger-adults-feel-it-the-most-survey-finds/

5. Goossens, L. 2015. The Genetics of Loneliness. Accessed from: https://pubmed.ncbi.nlm.nih.gov/25910391/#:~:text=Studies%20in%20behavioral%20genetics%20indicate,neurotransmitters%20and%20the%20immune%20system.&text=Such%20studies%20would%20allow%20researchers,genes%20that%20contribute%20to%20loneliness.

6. 2020. Loneliness and Social Isolation Linked to Serious Health Conditions. Accessed from: https://www.cdc.gov/aging/publications/features/lonely-older-adults.html

7. Ibid.

8. Ibid.

9. Ibid.

10. 2009. Loneliness May Be Contagious. Accessed from: https://www.wired.com/2009/12/loneliness-may-be-contagious/

11. 2020. Loneliness and Social Isolation Linked to Serious Health Conditions. Accessed from: https://www.cdc.gov/aging/publications/features/lonely-older-adults.html

12. Ibid.

13. Ibid.

14. Ibid.

15. Ibid.

16. Ibid.

17. Ibid.

18. Ibid.

19. Ibid.

20. Jauwea, G. 2019. 4 Ways to Tackle Loneliness. Accessed from: https://lifeandhealth.org/mindfulness/4-ways-to-tackle-loneliness/1515777.html?gclid=Cj0KCQiAhZT9BRDmARIsAN2E-J19UQQqJ4DuGnLphiazw7F5DBqVOFhLm-5RBzX0fG0-Cb94hMzxMdLAaAl1fEALw_wcB

Chapter 15

1. Quotes. Accessed from: notsalmon.com

2. Moore, C. Resilience Theory: What Research Articles in Psychology Teach Us. Accessed from: https://positivepsychology.com/resilience-theory/

3. Mayo Clinic. 2020. Shock: First Aid. Accessed from: https://www.mayoclinic.org/first-aid/first-aid-shock/basics/art-20056620

4. Zimbardo, P., Sword, R. 2019. The Ripple Effect. Accessed from: https://www.psychologytoday.com/us/blog/the-time-cure/201911/the-ripple-effect

5. Palmiter, D. Building Your Resilience. 2020. Accessed from: https://www.apa.org/topics/resilience

6. Mayo Clinic. 2020. Shock: First Aid. Accessed from: https://www.mayoclinic.org/first-aid/first-aid-shock/basics/art-20056620

7. Ibid.

Chapter 16

1. Khloe Kardashian Quotes. 2020. Accessed from: https://quotecatalog.com/quote/khloe-kardashian-if-i-am-always-ga46LA7

2. 2020. Jealousy. Accessed from: https://www.psychologytoday.com/us/basics/jealousy

3. Sanoff, R. 2016. The Science Behind Jealousy and How to Overcome It. Accessed from: https://www.bustle.com/articles/139916-heres-the-science-behind-jealousy-and-how-to-overcome-it

Chapter 17

1. Steve Job Quotes. 2020. Accessed from: https://www.goodreads.com/quotes/374630-your-time-is-limited-so-don-t-waste-it-living-someone

2. Morin, M. 2017. 10 Signs You're a People Pleaser. Accessed from: https://www.psychologytoday.com/us/blog/what-mentally-strong-people-dont-do/201708/10-signs-youre-people-pleaser

3. Van Edwards, V. 2020. The Science of People. Accessed from: https://www.scienceofpeople.com/people-pleaser/

Chapter 18

1. Celestine Chua Quotes. 2020. Accessed from: https://www.pinterest.ca/pin/376965431311349914/

2. Carter, C. 2018. How to Stop Being a Control Freak. Accessed from: https://greatergood.berkeley.edu/article/item/how_to_stop_being_a_control_freak

3. Raghunathan, R. 2016. Is Being a Control Freak Ruining Your Happiness? Accessed from: https://www.psychologytoday.com/us/blog/sapient-nature/201604/is-being-control-freak-ruining-your-happiness

4. Hendriksen, E. 2017. 5 Ways to Stop Being a Control Freak. Accessed from: https://www.scientificamerican.com/article/5-ways-to-stop-being-a-control-freak/

5. Bergland, C. 2015. Holding a Grudge Produces Cortisol and Diminishes Oxytocin. Accessed from: https://www.psychologytoday.com/us/blog/the-athletes-way/201504/holding-grudge-produces-cortisol-and-diminishes-oxytocin

Chapter 19

1. Deepak Chopra Quotes. 2020. Accessed from: https://www.pinterest.ca/pin/48695239706081640/

2. Breener, G. 2017. Research Shows How We Decide Whether to Blame. Accessed from: https://www.psychologytoday.com/us/blog/experimentations/201703/research-shows-how-we-decide-whether-blame

3. Bergland, C. 2015. Holding a Grudge Produces Cortisol and Diminishes Oxytocin. Accessed from: https://www.psychologytoday.com/us/blog/the-athletes-way/201504/holding-grudge-produces-cortisol-and-diminishes-oxytocin

4. USC Marshall School of Business. 2009. Shifting Blame Is Socially Contagious. Accessed from: https://www.sciencedaily.com/releases/2009/11/091119194124.htm

5. Colier, N. 2018. Are You Ready to Stop Feeling Like a Victim? Accessed from: https://www.psychologytoday.com/us/blog/inviting-monkey-tea/201801/are-you-ready-stop-feeling-victim

Chapter 20

1. Carroll Bryant Quotes. 2020. Accessed from: https://www.goodreads.com/quotes/477644-the-shattering-of-a-heart-when-being-broken-is-the

2. Suval, L. 2019. The Psychology Behind Remaining in Toxic Relationships. Accessed from: https://psychcentral.com/blog/the-psychology-behind-remaining-in-toxic-relationships/

3. Forbes. 2018. Research Shows Bad Relationships Can Also Mean Bad Health. Accessed from: https://www.forbes.com/sites/quora/2018/05/03/research-shows-bad-relationships-can-also-mean-bad-health/?sh=e1da0f21d5e1

4. Sword, R., Zimbardo, P. 2013. Toxic Relationships. Accessed from: https://www.psychologytoday.com/us/blog/the-time-cure/201308/toxic-relationships

5. Bankschick, M. 2012. Who Wants to Be Needy? Six Solutions. Accessed from: https://www.psychology-today.com/us/blog/the-intelligent-divorce/201208/who-wants-be-needy-six-solutions

6. Broggard, D. 2016. Parental Attachment Problems. Accessed from: https://www.psychologytoday.com/us/blog/the-mysteries-love/201611/parental-attachment-problems

Chapter 21

1. Esposito, L. 2016. 6 Signs of a Codependent Relationship. Accessed from: https://www.psychologytoday.com/us/blog/anxiety-zen/201609/6-signs-codependent-relationship

2. Canevello, A., Crocker, J. Creating Good Relationships: Responsiveness, Relationship Quality, and Interpersonal Goals. Accessed from:

3. https://www.ncbi.nlm.nih.gov/pmc/articles/PMC2891543/

Chapter 22

1. George Bernard Shaw Quotes. 2020. Accessed from: https://www.pinterest.ca/pin/249668373071561013/

2. Goman, C. 2011. How Culture Controls Communication. Accessed from: https://www.forbes.com/sites/carolkinsey-goman/2011/11/28/how-culture-controls-communication/?sh=7f2d8e42263b

3. Ibid.

4. Willkomm, A. 2019. 8 Communication Bad Habits You Need to Break. Accessed from: https://drexel.

edu/goodwin/professional-studies-blog/overview/2019/
January/8-communication-bad-habits-you-need-to-break/

5. Ohlin, B. 2020. 7 Ways to Improve Communication in Relationships. Accessed from: https://positivepsychology.com/communication-in-relationships/#:~:text=Available%20on%20Amazon.-,Quotes%20on%20Communication%20in%20Relationships,don't%20listen%20to%20understand.

Chapter 23

1. Fearless Soul Quotes. Accessed from: https://iamfearlesssoul.com/stay-away-from-negative-people/

2. Brown, J. 2020. The Shocking Impact That Negative People Have on Your Brain, According to Science. Accessed from: https://ideapod.com/research-explains-impact-around-negative-people-brain/

3. Kaplan, E. 2016. Why Negative People Are Literally Killing You. Accessed from: https://medium.com/the-mission/why-negative-people-are-literally-killing-you-and-how-to-obliterate-pessimism-from-your-life-eb85fadced87

Chapter 24

1. Tiny Fey Quotes. 2020. Accessed from: https://www.goodreads.com/quotes/457709-do-your-thing-and-don-t-care-if-they-like-it

2. 2018. Only Half of Your Friends Actually Like You. Accessed from: https://www.sciencealert.com/you-have-half-as-many-real-friends-as-you-think-you-do-study-finds

3. Guerra, D. 2016. The Rule of 25%. Accessed from: https://daveguerra.com/2016/05/the-rule-of-25/

4. Ibid.

5. Ibid.

Chapter 25

1. Robin Sharma Quotes. 2020. Accessed from: https://www.brainyquote.com/quotes/robin_s_sharma_628769

2. Shontell, A. 2010. 80% of People Hate Their Jobs - But Should You Choose a Passion or a Paycheck? Accessed from: https://www.businessinsider.com/what-do-you-do-when-you-hate-your-job-2010-10

3. Lindzon, J. 2020. Hate Your Job? Being Unhappy at Work Might Have Long-Term Health Effects. Accessed from: https://www.fastcompany.com/90361554/being-unhappy-at-work-might-have-longterm-health-effects

4. Ibid.

5. Policy, Data, Oversight. 2020. Accessed from: https://www.opm.gov/policy-data-oversight/pay-leave/pay-administration/fact-sheets/computing-hourly-rates-of-pay-using-the-2087-hour-divisor/#:~:text=Thus%2C%20a%20calendar%20year%20may,work%20hours%20per%20calendar%20year.

6. Renner, B. 2018. American Families Spend Just 37 Minutes of Quality Time Together Per Day, Study Finds. Accessed from: https://www.studyfinds.org/american-families-spend-37-minutes-quality-time/

7. Ibid.

8. Lindzon, J. 2020. Hate Your Job? Being Unhappy at Work Might Have Long-Term Health Effects. Accessed from: https://www.fastcompany.com/90361554/being-unhappy-at-work-might-have-longterm-health-effects

9. Ibid.

10. Anderson, P. 2020. Doctors' Suicide Rate Highest of Any Profession. Accessed from: https://www.webmd.com/

mental-health/news/20180508/doctors-suicide-rate-highest
-of-any-profession#1

11.Carter, S. 2015. Why Lawyers Are Miserable. Accessed from:
https://www.chicagotribune.com/opinion/commentary/ct-
why-lawyers-are-miserable-20150907-story.html

12.Egan, M, Harrison, V. 2015. Wall Street Is a Miserable Place
to Work. Accessed from: https://www.chicagotribune.
com/opinion/commentary/ct-why-lawyers-are-miserable-
20150907-story.html

13.Riggio, R. 2012. There's Magic in Your Smile. Accessed from:
https://www.psychologytoday.com/us/blog/cutting-edge
-leadership/201206/there-s-magic-in-your-smile

Chapter 26

1. Imran Khan Quotes. 2020. Accessed from: https://quotefancy.
com/quote/1272278/Imran-Khan-Talent-or-intelligence-
doesn-t-matter-Its-your-dreams-that-will-decied-how-big

2. Maxwell, J. 2016. Destination Disease. Accessed from:
https://abdulquasimkhan.wordpress.com/2016/02/22/
destination-disease/

3. Parren, A. 2020. Research Shows 43% of People Expect to Give
up Their New Year's Resolutions by February. Accessed from:
https://www.sundried.com/blogs/training/research-shows-
43-of-people-expect-to-give-up-their-new-year-s-resolutions-
by-february:

Chapter 27

1. Mindy Kaling Quotes. 2020. Accessed from: https://www.pin-
terest.ca/pin/56717276536137971/

2. Johnson, R. 2020. Workplace Negativity Can Hurt Productivity. Accessed from: https://research.msu.edu/workplace-negativity-can-hurt-productivity/

3. Priesemuth, M. 2020. Time's Up for Toxic Workplaces. Accessed from: https://hbr.org/2020/06/times-up-for-toxic-workplaces

Chapter 28

1. Seppala, E., Cameron, K. 2015. Proof That Positive Work Cultures Are More Productive. Accessed from: https://hbr.org/2015/12/proof-that-positive-work-cultures-are-more-productive

2. Levin, M. 2018. Harvard Research Proves Toxic Employees Destroy Your Culture and Bottom Line. Accessed from: https://www.inc.com/marissa-levin/harvard-research-proves-toxic-employees-destroy-your-culture-your-bottom-line.html

3. Kline, D. 2013. Workplace Drama: Nearly Half of U.S. Workers Have Sought Revenge on a coworker. Accessed from: https://www.usatoday.com/story/money/careers/work-relationships/2018/04/23/nearly-half-of-us-workers-have-sought-revenge-on-a- coworker/34159383/

4. Bureau of Labor Statistics. 2020. American Time Use Survey - 2019 Results. Accessed from: https://www.bls.gov/news.release/pdf/atus.pdf

5. Morrison, R., Nolan, T. 2007. Negative Relationships in the Workplace: A Qualitative Study. Accessed from: https://www.researchgate.net/publication/227430136_Negative_relationships_in_the_workplace_A_qualitative_study

Chapter 29

1. Henry David Thoreau Quotes. 2020. Accessed from: https://www.goodreads.com/quotes/7273089-it-s-not-enough-to-be-busy-so-are-the-ants

2. Giang, V. 2016. How Busyness Affects Your Brain and Health. Accessed from: ' https://www.fastcompany.com/3061048/how-busyness-affects-your-brain-and-health

3. Murphy, K. 2014. No Time to Think. Accessed from: https://www.nytimes.com/2014/07/27/sunday-review/no-time-to-think.html

4. Gaskell, K. 2016. The Impact of Long Hours on Our Relationships. Accessed from: https://www.forbes.com/sites/adigaskell/2016/01/12/the-impact-of-long-hours-on-our-relationships/?sh=71df1bec3a04

5. Giang, V. 2016. How Busyness Affects Your Brain and Health. Accessed from: https://www.fastcompany.com/3061048/how-busyness-affects-your-brain-and-health

6. Ibid.

7. Ibid.

8. Ibid.

9. Ibid.

10. Gaskell, K. 2016. The Impact of Long Hours on Our Relationships. Accessed from: https://www.forbes.com/sites/adigaskell/2016/01/12/the-impact-of-long-hours-on-our-relationships/?sh=71df1bec3a04

11. Ibid.

12. Ibid.

13. Ibid.

14. Ibid.

15. Ibid.

16. Ibid.

17. Ibid.

18. White, P. 2018. Are You Too Busy to Learn to Overcome Busyness? Accessed from: https://www.appreciationatwork.com/blog/are-you-too-busy-to-learn-how-to-overcome-busyness/

19. 5 Benefits of Reading as Little as 20 Pages Per Day. 2019. Accessed from: https://www.sacap.edu.za/blog/applied-psychology/benefits-of-reading/

Chapter 30

1. Johnson, Z. 2015. Chris Hemsworth Opens Up on the Ugly Side of Fame. Accessed from: https://www.eonline.com/news/616398/chris-hemsworth-reflects-on-his-success-it-didn-t-actually-bring-me-the-happiness-i-thought-it-was-going-to

2. Tony Hawks Quotes. 2020. Accessed from: https://sites.google.com/site/famousquotations213/you-might-not-make-it-to-the-top-but-if-you-are-doing-what-you-love-there-is-much-more-happiness-there-than-being-rich-or-famous

3. Stilman, J. 2020. Why So Many Successful People Are Unhappy. Accessed from: https://www.inc.com/jessica-stillman/why-so-many-successful-people-are-still-unhappy.html

4. Kulraj. 2015. Are Famous People Happy? Accessed from: http://kulraj.org/2015/12/31/are-famous-people-happy-a-data-driven-answer/

5. Doheny, K. 2009. Looks, Money, Fame, Don't Bring Happiness. Accessed from: https://abcnews.go.com/Health/Healthday/story?id=7658253&page=1#:~:text=%22The%20

attainment%20of%20extrinsic%2C%20or,Edward%20
Deci%2C%20a%20psychology%20professor.

6. Achieving Fame, Wealth, and Beauty are Psychological Dead
Ends, Study Says. 2019. Accessed from: https://www.science-
daily.com/releases/2009/05/090514111402.htm

Chapter 31

1. Jebb, A. 2018. Happiness, Income Satiation and Turning Points Around the World. Accessed from: https://
www.nature.com/articles/s41562-017-0277-0?WT.
feed_name=subjects_economics

2. Chan, M. 2016. Here's How Winning the Lottery Makes
You Miserable. Accessed from: https://time.com/4176128/
powerball-jackpot-lottery-winners/

3. Cohan, P. 2020. This Harvard Study of 4,000 Millionaires
Revealed Something Surprising About Money and Happiness.
Accessed from: https://www.inc.com/peter-cohan/will-10-mil-
lion-make-you-happier-harvard-says-yes-if-you-make-it-your-
self-give-it-away.html

4. Oppong, T. 2019. The Arrival Fallacy: A Psychologist Explains
Why Reaching Your Goals Won't Make You Happy. Accessed
from: https://medium.com/better-marketing/the-arrival-
fallacy-a-psychologist-explains-why-reaching-your-goals-wont-
make-you-happy-b2cd359b07

5. Cohan, P. 2020. This Harvard Study of 4,000 Millionaires
Revealed Something Surprising About Money and Happiness.
Accessed from: https://www.inc.com/peter-cohan/will-10-mil-
lion-make-you-happier-harvard-says-yes-if-you-make-it-your-
self-give-it-away.html

6. Oppong, T. 2019. The Arrival Fallacy: A Psychologist Explains Why Reaching Your Goals Won't Make You Happy. Accessed from: https://medium.com/better-marketing/the-arrival-fallacy-a-psychologist-explains-why-reaching-your-goals-wont-make-you-happy-b2cd359b07

7. Facebook Likes Don't Make You Feel Better. 2017. Accessed from: https://www.sciencedaily.com/releases/2017/05/170502204548.htm

Chapter 32

1. Louise Hay Quotes. 2020. Accessed from: https://www.goodreads.com/quotes/9650-remember-you-have-been-criticizing-yourself-for-years-and-it

2. Linardon, J. 2020. The Ultimate List of Body Image Statistics. Accessed from: https://breakbingeeating.com/body-image-statistics/

3. Fox, K. 1997. Mirror, Mirror. Accessed from: http://www.sirc.org/publik/mirror.html

4. Magrath, A. 2015. Watch What Happens When Women Are Forced to Choose Between Walking Through Doors Marked 'Average' or 'Beautiful'... As It Is Revealed That 96 PER CENT of Women Rate Themselves as Average Looking. Accessed from: https://www.dailymail.co.uk/femail/article-3029777/Dove-survey-reveals-96-CENT-women-rate-average-looking.html

5. Linardon, J. 2020. The Ultimate List of Body Image Statistics. Accessed from: https://breakbingeeating.com/body-image-statistics/

6. Pergament, D. 2016. Exactly How Much Appearance Matters, According to Our National Judgment Survey. Accessed from:

https://www.allure.com/story/national-judgement-survey-statistics#:~:text=A%20whopping%2080%20percent%20of,judgmental%20(thanks%2C%20guys!).

7. Ibid.

8. Pergament, D. 2016. Exactly how much appearance matters, according to our National Judgment Survey. Accessed from: https://www.allure.com/story/national-judgement-survey-statistics

9. 2019. Plastic Surgery Statistics. Accessed from: https://www.plasticsurgery.org/news/plastic-surgery-statistics

10. Scheel, J. 2014. Culture Dictates the Standard of Beauty. Accessed from: https://www.psychologytoday.com/us/blog/when-food-is-family/201404/culture-dictates-the-standard-beauty

11. Davis, C. 2016. Media Today: Unattainable Beauty Standards. Accessed from: https://www.girlsempowermentnetwork.org/blog/media-today-unattainable-beauty-standards

12. 2019. Slim and Skinny: How Access to TV Is Changing Beauty Ideals in Rural Nicaragua. Accessed from: https://theconversation.com/slim-and-skinny-how-access-to-tv-is-changing-beauty-ideals-in-rural-nicaragua-128717

13. Carr, S. 2020. How Many Ads Do We See in a Day In 2020? Accessed from: https://ppcprotect.com/how-many-ads-do-we-see-a-day/

14. Weber, J. 2016. 5 Ways to Become More Attractive to Others. Accessed from: https://www.psychologytoday.com/us/blog/having-sex-wanting-intimacy/201612/5-ways-become-more-attractive-others

15. Gruys, K. 2019. How Does Appearance Affect Our Success? Accessed from: https://www.unr.edu/nevada-today/news/2019/atp-appearance-success

Chapter 33

1. Audre Lorde Quotes. 2020. Accessed from: https://www. goodreads.com/quotes/3203941-i-have-come-to-believe-that-caring-for-myself-is

2. 2020. Obesity Among U.S. Adults Hits All-Time Highs. Accessed from: https://www.wtvm.com/2020/09/18/obesity-among-us-adults-hits-all-time-high-report-says/#:~:text=(CNN)%20 %2D%20According%20to%20a,has%20hit%20a%20new%20 record.&text=The%20latest%20data%20shows%2019.3,19%20 years%20old%20are%20obese.

3. National Institute on Drug Abuse. 2020. Accessed from: https:// www.drugabuse.gov/drug-topics/trends-statistics

4. Weir, K. 2013. Is Pornography Addictive? Accessed from: https://www.apa.org/monitor/2014/04/pornography

5. America's Drug Overdose Epidemic. 2020. Accessed from: https://www.cdc.gov/injury/features/prescription-drug-over-dose/index.html

6. Domonoske, C. 2017. Drinking on the Rise in U.S., Especially for Women, Minorities, and Older Adults. Accessed from: https:// www.npr.org/sections/thetwo-way/2017/08/10/542409957/ drinking-on-the-rise-in-u-s-especially-for-women-minorities-older-adults

7. Dickson, S. 2020. How Diet Affects Mental Health. Accessed from: https://neurosciencenews.com/diet-mental-health-15384/#:~:text=Poor%20diets%2C%20researchers%20 say%2C%20play,symptoms%20of%20depression%20and%20 anxiety.

8. 2020. This Is How Sleep Deprivation Hurts Mental Health. Accessed from: https://www.ehe.health/blog/

sleep-deprivation#:~:text=While%20causation%20is%20 often%20tricky,to%20develop%20a%20panic%20disorder.

9. Alcohol and Mental Health. 2020. Accessed from: https:// www.drinkaware.co.uk/facts/health-effects-of-alcohol/ m e n t a l - h e a l t h / a l c o h o l - a n d - m e n t a l - health#:~:text=Alcohol%20is%20a%20depressant%2C%20 which,in%20the%20brain%20to%20another.

10. Kohut, T. 2018. Is Pornography Use a Risk for Adolescent Well-Being? An Examination of Temporal Relationships in Two Independent Panel Samples. Accessed from: https:// www.ncbi.nlm.nih.gov/pmc/articles/PMC6088458/#:~:tex t=Furthermore%2C%20cross%2Dsectional%20surveys%20 have,12%2C26%E2%80%9328%5D.

11. 2013. Casual Sex Linked to Depression and Anxiety. Accessed from: https://www.nhs.uk/news/mental-health/casual-sex- linked-to-depression-and-anxiety/#:~:text=Researchers%20 found%20that%20having%20casual,one%20particular%20 point%20in%20time.

12. 2020.Part I: The Connection Between Substance Use Disorders and Mental Illness. Accessed from: https://www.drugabuse.gov/ publications/research-reports/common-comorbidities-sub- stance-use-disorders/part-1-connection-between-substance- use-disorders-mental-illness

Chapter 34

1. Tim Fargo Quotes. 2020. Accessed from: https://quotlr.com/ image/4471

2. Stress Symptoms. 2020. Accessed from: https://www. webmd.com/balance/stress-management/stress-symptoms -effects_of-stress-on-the-body#1

3. 2014. 90% of Illness Is Caused by Stress According to U.S. Center for Disease Control. Accessed from: https://www.kari-nagrant.co.uk/blog/90-of-illness-is-caused-by-stress-according-to-the-us-centre-of-disease-control/

4. Griffin, M. 2020. 10 Health Problems Related to Stress That You Can Fix. Accessed from: https://www.webmd.com/balance/stress-management/features/10-fixable-stress-related-health-problems#1

5. Jennings, K. 2018. 16 Simple Ways to Relieve Stress and Anxiety. Accessed from: https://www.healthline.com/nutrition/16-ways-relieve-stress-anxiety

6. Ibid.

7. Ibid.

8. Ibid.

Chapter 35

1. Ludwig Wittgenstein Quotes. 2020. Accessed from: https://www.brainyquote.com/quotes/ludwig_wittgenstein_139240

2. Stillman, J. 2014. Yet Another Reason to Watch Your Body Language: It Can Make You Happier. Accessed from: https://www.inc.com/jessica-stillman/yet-another-reason-to-watch-your-body-language-it-can-make-you-happier.html

3. Ibid.

4. 2012. The Science Behind the Smile. Accessed from: https://hbr.org/2012/01/the-science-behind-the-smile

5. Rohde, M., Troje, N. 2014. How We Walk Affects What We Remember: Gait Modifications Through Biofeedback Change Negative Affective Memory. Accessed from: https://digest.bps.org.uk/2014/10/27/doing-the-happy-walk-made-peoples-memories-more-positive/

6. Nair, S., Sollers, J., Consedine, N. 2014. Do Slumped and Upright Postures Affect Stress Responses? A Randomized Trial. Accessed from: https://www.researchgate.net/publication/265650147_Do_Slumped_and_Upright_Postures_Affect_Stress_Responses_A_Randomized_Trial#:~:text=Results%3A%20Upright%20participants%20reported%20higher,fear%2C%20compared%20to%20slumped%20participants.&text=Conclusions%3A%20Adopting%20an%20upright%20seated,compared%20to%20a%20slumped%20posture.

7. Ortiz-Ospina, E. 2019. Are We Happier When We Spend More Time with Others? Accessed from: https://ourworldindata.org/happiness-and-friends

8. 2010. Meaningful Conversation May Be Key to Happiness. Accessed from: https://source.wustl.edu/2010/03/meaningful-conversation-may-be-key-to-happiness/

Chapter 36

1. Anthony T. Hinks Quotes. 2020. Accessed from: https://www.goodreads.com/author/quotes/10093675.Anthony_T_Hincks?page=31

2. 2020. Television and Social Media Impact on Society, Children, and Adolescents. Accessed from: https://sites.psu.edu/aspsy/2015/03/25/television-and-social-media-impact-on-society-children-and-adolescents/#:~:text=Social%20anxiety%20is%20one%20among,put%20into%20such%20media%20outlets.

3. 2020. Social Media and Mental Health. Accessed from: https://www.allure.com/story/national-judgement-survey-statistics#:~:text=A%20whopping%2080%20percent%20of,judgmental%20(thanks%2C%20guys!).

4. 2020. Emotional Health: Binge Watching. Accessed from: https://www.nm.org/healthbeat/healthy-tips/emotional-health/binge-watching

5. Papadopoulos, L. 2019. Watching TV Shows Can Harm You or Make You Happy, Studies Find. Accessed from: https://interestingengineering.com/watching-tv-shows-can-affect-your-mood-greatly-studies-find

6. Hull D., Williams, G., Griffiths, M. 2013. Video Game Characteristics, Happiness and Flow as Predictors of Addiction Among Video Game Players: A Pilot Study. Accessed from: https://www.researchgate.net/publication/265606650_Video_game_characteristics_happiness_and_flow_as_predictors_of_addiction_among_video_game_players_A_pilot_study

7. Davis, L. 2015. Is It Harmful to Use Music as a Coping Mechanism? Accessed from: https://www.theatlantic.com/health/archive/2015/11/is-it-harmful-to-use-music-as-a-coping-mechanism/413236/

8. CSUN. Television and Health. 2020. Accessed from: https://www.csun.edu/science/health/docs/tv&health.html#:~:text=According%20to%20the%20A.C.%20Nielsen,years%20glued%20to%20the%20tube.

Chapter 37

1. Kenneth Wapnick Quotes. 2020. Accessed from: https://quotefancy.com/quote/1643194/Kenneth-Wapnick-Miracles-are-a-shift-in-perception

2. Colier, N. 2018. Are You Ready to Stop Feeling Like a Victim? Accessed from: https://www.psychologytoday.com/us/blog/inviting-monkey-tea/201801/are-you-ready-stop-feeling-victim

Chapter 38

1. Teal Swan Quotes. 2020. Accessed from: https://www.pinter-est.ca/pin/329677635196555585/

2. Hazen, R. 1997. What We Don't Know. Accessed from: https://www.technologyreview.com/1997/07/01/237262/what-we-dont-know/

3. Sutter, P. 2019. "I Don't Know" Is One of the Most Powerful Things You Can Say. Accessed from: https://www.forbes.com/sites/paulmsutter/2019/08/11/i-dont-know-is-one-of-the-most-powerful-things-you-can-say/?sh=511f2cce4e19

4. Huttson, M. 2020. Why You Don't Really Know What You Don't Know. Accessed from: https://www.technologyreview.com/2020/10/21/1009445/the-unbearable-vicariousness-of-knowledge/

Chapter 39

1. Vicki Harrison Quotes. 2020. Accessed from: https://www.goodreads.com/quotes/543175-grief-is-like-the-ocean-it-comes-on-waves-ebbing

2. Mendoza, M. 2019. When Grief Gets Physical. Accessed from: https://www.psychologytoday.com/us/blog/understanding-grief/201909/when-grief-gets-physical

3. Ibid.

4. Ibid.

5. Ibid.

6. Ibid.

7. Ibid.

8. Ibid.

9. Ibid.

10. Ibid.

11. Axelrod, J. 2020. The 5 Stages of Grief & Loss. Accessed from: https://psychcentral.com/lib/the-5-stages-of-loss-and-grief/

12. Ibid.

13. Ibid.

14. Ibid.

15. Ibid.

16. Ibid.

Chapter 40

1. 2018. Redefining Failure: How to Overcome Setbacks. Accessed from: https://www.heart.org/en/healthy-living/healthy-lifestyle/mental-health-and-wellbeing/overcome-setbacks.

Chapter 41

1. Winston Churchill Quotes. 2020. Accessed from: https://www.goodreads.com/quotes/6221-if-you-are-going-through-hell-keep-going

Chapter 42

1. Zig Ziglar Quotes. 2020. Accessed from: https://www.brainyquote.com/quotes/zig_ziglar_381976

2. Martin, E. 2017. How Much Money You Need to Be Happy, According to a New Analysis By Wealth Experts. Accessed from: https://www.cnbc.com/2017/11/20/how-much-money-you-need-to-be-happy-according-to-wealth-experts.html

3. Sahadi, J. 2018. Depression in the C Suite. Accessed from: https://www.cnn.com/2018/09/30/success/ceos-depression/index.html

4. Taylor, S. 2017. The Angst of the CEO: When Success Leaves You Feeling Empty. Accessed from: https://www.forbes.com/sites/forbescoachescouncil/2017/09/08/the-angst-of-the-ceo-when-success-leaves-you-feeling-empty/?sh=62fbad893c5e

5. Luther, S. 2016. The Problem with Rich Kids. Accessed from: https://www.psychologytoday.com/us/articles/201311/the-problem-rich-kids

6. Sharma, H. 2020. Top 10 Surprising Disadvantages Oof Being Rich. Accessed from: https://listverse.com/2020/07/23/top-10-surprising-disadvantages-of-being-rich/

7. Ibid.

8. Ibid.

9. Ibid.

10. Ibid.

11. Muhammed, I. 2017. 1997 "Mo Money Mo Problems" by Notorious B.I.G.

Chapter 43

1. Dieter Uchtdorf Quotes. 2020. Accessed from: https://www.goodreads.com/quotes/242808-as-we-lose-ourselves-in-the-service-of-others-we

2. Hunger Statistics. 2019. Accessed from: https://www.foodaid-foundation.org/world-hunger-statistics.html

3. Domestic Violence Statistics. 2020. Accessed from: https://www.thehotline.org/stakeholders/domestic-violence-statistics/

4. Human Trafficking Statistics and Facts. 2020. Accessed from: https://www.safehorizon.org/get-informed/human-trafficking-statistics-facts/

5. Seppala, E. 2013. Compassionate Mind, Healthy Body. Accessed from: https://greatergood.berkeley.edu/article/item/compassionate_mind_healthy_body

6. Ibid.

7. Ibid.

8. Ibid.

9. Seppala, E. 2012. The Best Kept Secret to Happiness and Health: https://www.psychologytoday.com/us/blog/feeling-it/201211/the-best-kept-secret-happiness-and-health-compassion#:~:text=Compassion%20Boosts%20Your%20Health,may%20even%20lengthen%20our%20life.

10. Raypole, C. 2020. 12 Ways to Boost Oxytocin. Accessed from: https://www.healthline.com/health/how-to-increase-oxytocin#:~:text=Oxytocin%2C%20dopamine%2C%20and%20serotonin%20are,a%20surge%20of%20positive%20emotion.

Chapter 44

1. Cornel West Quotes. 2020. Accessed from:

2. https://www.azquotes.com/quote/1558265

3. Levine, P. 2003. Ideology: Pros and Cons. Accessed from: http://www.peterlevine.ws/mt/archives/2003/06/ideology-pros-a.html

4. Ibid.

5. Zakrzewski, V. 2016. How Humility Will Make You the Greatest Person Ever. Accessed from: https://greatergood.berkeley.edu/article/item/humility_will_make_you_greatest_person_ever

Chapter 45

1. Mark Knopfler Quotes. 2020. Accessed from: https://www.goodreads.com/quotes/365234-there-s-so-many-different-worlds-so-many-different-suns-and

2. Ingraham, C. 2014. Three Quarters of Whites Don't Have Any Non-White Friends. Accessed from: https://www.washingtonpost.com/news/wonk/wp/2014/08/25/three-quarters-of-whites-dont-have-any-non-white-friends/

3. Dunsmuir, L. 2013. Many Americans Have No Friends of Another Race: Poll. Accessed from: https://www.reuters.com/article/us-usa-poll-race/many-americans-have-no-friends-of-another-race-poll-idUSBRE97704320130808

4. Ibid.

5. Foran, C. 2017. America's Political Divide Intensified During Trump's First Year as President. Accessed from: https://www.theatlantic.com/politics/archive/2017/10/trump-partisan-divide-republicans-democrats/541917/

6. Dunsmuir, L. 2013. Many Americans Have No Friends of Another Race: Poll. Accessed from: https://www.reuters.com/article/us-usa-poll-race/many-americans-have-no-friends-of-another-race-poll-idUSBRE97704320130808

7. Marder, A. 2017. 7 Studies That Prove the Value of Diversity in the Workplace. Accessed from: https://blog.capterra.com/7-studies-that-prove-the-value-of-diversity-in-the-workplace/

8. Ibid.

9. Ibid.

10. Ibid.

11. Ibid.

Chapter 46

1. Criss Jami Quotes. 2020. Accessed from: https://www.goodreads.com/quotes/588814-popular-culture-is-a-place-where-pity-is-called-compassion

2. 2016. Dopamine: Far More Than Just the 'Happy Hormone.' Accessed from: https://www.sciencedaily.com/releases/2016/08/160831085320.htm

3. Ibid.

4. Akkenon, J. 2012. The Average Person Lives 27,375 Days. Make Each of Them Count. Accessed from: https://bit.ly/32ui8ZR

Chapter 47

1. Myers, C. 2018. If You Want to Achieve Long-Term Happiness, Embrace the Growth Mindset. Accessed from: https://www.forbes.com/sites/chrismyers/2018/10/20/if-you-want-to-achieve-long-term-happiness-embrace-the-growth-mindset/?sh=2adba8e430d3

2. Bandura, A. 1989. Social Cognitive Theory. Accessed from: https://www.uky.edu/~eushe2/Bandura/Bandura1989ACD.pdf

3. Ferris, T. 2017. Tribe of Mentors. Accessed from: https://www.goodreads.com/book/show/36200111-tribe-of-mentors

Chapter 48

1. Paul Gauguin Quotes. 2020. Accessed from: https://meaningin.com/quotes/paul-gauguin/61249-i-close-my-eyes-in-order-to-see--

2. Marshall, J. 2019. Are Religious People Happier, Healthier? Our New Global Study Explores This Question. Accessed from: https://www.pewresearch.org/fact-tank/2019/01/31/are-religious-people-happier-healthier-our-new-global-study-explores-this-question/

3. Walsh, B. 2017. Does Spirituality Make You Happy? Accessed from: https://time.com/4856978/spirituality-religion-happiness/.

4. Ibid.

5. Ibid.

6. Ibid.

7. Ibid.

8. Ibid.

9. Ibid.

10. Seidensticker, B. 2016. Yeah, But Christianity Built Universities and Hospitals. Accessed from: https://www.patheos.com/blogs/crossexamined/2016/01/yeah-but-christianity-built-universities-and-hospitals/

11. Wyatt-Brown, B. 2020. American Abolitionism and Religion. Accessed from: http://nationalhumanitiescenter.org/tserve/nineteen/nkeyinfo/amabrel.htm

12. Evans, E. 2019. Faith Played a Complex Role in the Battle for Women's Right to Vote. Accessed from: https://www.ncronline.org/news/justice/faith-played-complex-role-battle-womens-right-vote

13. Religion and the Civil Rights Movement. Accessed from: https://www.pbs.org/wnet/religionandethics/for-educators/religion-and-the-civil-rights-movement-background/

14. Richardson, B. Religious People More Likely to Give to Charity, Study Shows. Accessed from: https://www.washingtontimes.com/news/2017/oct/30/religious-people-more-likely-give-charity-study/#:~:text=On%20average%2C%20religiously%20affiliated%20households,industry%20in%20the%20nonprofit%20sector.

ABOUT DR. ROB CARPENTER

Dr. Rob Carpenter—known simply as Dr. Rob—miraculously survived a tragic accident and vowed to not only rebuild his life, but to help other people rebuild their lives too. He has become a transformational author, filmmaker, and CEO who now advises professional athletes, celebrities, business titans, and everyday people so they can become the best version of themselves.

Dr. Rob has been featured in the *New York Times, Business Insider,* and *People Magazine,* has been a former professor and filmmaker at the 2x Emmy Award Winning USC Media Institute for Social Change, and is host of The Dr. Rob show. He founded The School of Happiness and has countless resources available on his website DrRob.TV to help uplift you - and to help uplift humanity.

Dr. Rob is the first in his family to graduate from college.